SEVEN ROADS *in* SUM

Voices from an Oxford S

Perilla Kinchin (b.1951) came to Oxford as a graduate student after studying Classics at Newnham College, Cambridge. She was a lecturer at Trinity and Merton Colleges before a change of direction in 1988, when she wrote a book on *Glasgow's Great Exhibitions* and established White Cockade Publishing. She has published, and also written, a number of books in the area of social and design history, and oral history. She came to Lonsdale Road in 1993.

Paul Thompson is Research Professor in Sociology at the University of Essex and a Research Fellow at the Young Foundation in London. He is a pioneer of oral history in Europe and author of the international classic *The Voice of the Past*. His other books include *The Edwardians*, *Living the Fishing*, and *The Work of William Morris*. He lived in Lonsdale Road for many years. For more on Paul see p.91.

Aerial photograph of the Seven Roads with the Banbury Road to the west and Hernes and Harpes Road to the north. By kind permission of Getmapping plc: www.getmapping.com.

SEVEN ROADS *in* SUMMERTOWN

Voices from an Oxford Suburb

Perilla Kinchin

with an introduction by Paul Thompson

Supported by
The National Lottery®
through the Heritage Lottery Fund

Heritage
Lottery Fund

Published by

White Cockade Publishing
71 Lonsdale Road
Oxford OX2 7ES
www.whitecockade.co.uk

in association with

The Seven Roads Oral History Project

British Library Cataloguing-in-Publication Data
A catalogue record for this book is available from the British Library.

ISBN 978 1873487134

Typeset in Monotype Photina
Printed and bound in Great Britain by the Alden Press Ltd, Witney

Front cover: 39 Portland Road, the home of Francis Whitlock Twining and his wife Dorothy,
c. 1908. (Margaret & Gwynneth Twining)
Back cover: Philippa Berry talking to Miss Dorothy Bridge (b.1907 in Hamilton Road) at the
Seven Roads Oral History Project display in St Michael's Church, 2004. (Perilla Kinchin)

Contents

List of Interviewees and Contributors

Name	Year	Place
Ruth Bader Gilbert	1932	Portland (2 houses) 1963–
Eric Baldwin	1920–2006	Lucerne 1980–2006
Martin Berry	1947	Lonsdale 1971–3; Hamilton 1975–
Philippa Berry	1943	Lonsdale 1971–3; Hamilton 1975–
Paloma Bevir	1942	Hamilton 1979–2000
Dorothy Bridge	1907	Hamilton 1907–1999
Sally Bromley, née Latham	1948	Victoria 1984–
Vic Brown	1919	Lucerne Road 1967–
Christine Butler	1937	Hamilton 1964–84
Maurice Cardiff	1915	Hamilton 1998–2006
Rosamund Chorley, née Jones		Lonsdale 1979–
Margaret Clarke	1926	Hamilton 1962–
Kathy Clarke	1949	Lonsdale 1975–92
Peter Clarke	1942	Lonsdale 1975–2002; Hawkswell 2002–
Sam Clarke	1948	Victoria 1986–
Joan Crow, née Hurley	1920–2002	Victoria 1980–2002
Sydney Denton	1934	Summertown trader, Banbury Rd 1970–
Sonja Drexler	1945	Lonsdale 1980–
Bill Fosdike, Rev.	1923	Rectory, Lonsdale 1964–89
Philip Gilbert	1932–2006	Portland (2 houses) 1963–2006
Celia Glyn	1945	Lonsdale 1969–
Betty Grant	1922	Hamilton 1932–
Joan Gurden, Lady	1912	Portland c.1952–
Greta Guy	1920	Victoria 1949–56; Hamilton 1964–
Peggy Hall	1916	Hamilton (2 houses) c.1970–2002
James Harle	1920–2004	Portland 1965–2004
Yvonne Hands	1930s	Portland 1956–
Kato Havas	1920	Victoria (2 houses) 1976–
John Herivel	1918	Lonsdale 1975–
Elsie Hill	1921	Portland 1965–
Helen Holland	1945	Portland 1997–
Martine Honoré	1924	Lonsdale 1953–
Jack (John) Johnston, Sir	1918–2005	Victoria 1978–2005
Elizabeth Johnston, Lady	1931–2004	Victoria 1978–2004
Catherine Jones Finer	1941	Lonsdale 1977–93
Holly Kilpatrick	1950	Lucerne 1980–
Leszek Kolakowski	1927	Hamilton 1976–
Mariele Kuhn	1909	Victoria 1938–
Bertram Mandelbrote	1923	Lonsdale 1988–
John Marsh		Hamilton 1954–89; Lonsdale 1989–
Betty Marshall, née Howes	1926	Victoria 1926–57, 1985–

Jocelyn Morris	1935	Lucerne 1975–
Peter Morris, Sir	1934	Lucerne 1975–
Donald Norwood, Rev.	1940	Victoria 1974–96
Geoffrey Paine	1933	Lucerne 1972– (river garden1947–)
Dorothea Pelham	1941–2006	Portland 1975–2006
Verity Peto	1949	Lonsdale 1978–
Beryl Phillips	1922	Lonsdale 1966–
Margaret Pickles	1928	Hamilton 1961–
Jean Robinson	1930	Lonsdale 1969–
John Rowe	1930	Victoria 1930–
David Schriger	1958	Lonsdale 2003–4
Raquel Steward	1913	Portland 1933, 1960s
Peter Thompson	1944	Lonsdale 1980–
Mary Tregear	1924	Victoria 1962–3, Portland 1963–
Gwynneth Twining	1920	Banbury/Victoria 1920–37, Hamilton 1937–99, Banbury/Victoria 1999–
Margaret Twining	1915	Lonsdale 1915–20, Banbury/Victoria 1920–37, Hamilton 1937–99, Banbury/Victoria 1999–
Nancie Villiers	1915	Lucerne 1967–
Clare Wagstaff	1927	Hamilton 1929–
MonicaWagstaff	1930	Hamilton 1930–
Dorothy White	1915–2004	Hamilton (2 houses)1915–79
Bob Williams	1926	Victoria (2 houses) 1963–
Jelly Williams	1928	Victoria (2 houses) 1963–
Margaret Willis, née Andrews, then Helsby	1921	Lonsdale (2 houses) 1954–68, 1983–

With further contributions from

Brian Aldiss
Philip and Carolyn Allen
Keith Argyle
Gillian Argyle
Cathie Ashley
Martin Biddle and Birthe Kjølbye-Biddle
Nick and Kathleen Burgess
Susan Hill
Les Holmes
Margaret Kilpatrick

Alan Knowles
John Leighfield
John Lynch
Jan Martin
Josie Patterson
Pam Robinson
Edward Shirley
Rosemary Smith
Janet Tinbergen

Foreword

It's much more varied and interesting than it looks from the outside, and there's an awful lot going on. It's amazing how much you can say about a single road!

Peter Clarke

This book has been put together from interviews for an oral history project, to give a picture of seven roads in Oxford's northern suburb, Summertown. Lonsdale, Portland, Hamilton, Victoria, Lucerne, and King's Cross Roads and Hawkswell Gardens: all were developed on two parcels of farmland bought by an Oxford businessman, Francis Twining, at the very beginning of the 20th century. The houses – built in Edwardian times, between the wars, in the 1950s and 60s, and with more recent infilling and redevelopment – are varied; and the people who live here have been varied too. It is a dense suburb, and as Peter Clarke says above, a lot more interesting than it might look at first sight.

The project arose from the Seven Roads Millennium Street Festival in June 2000, which included an oral history display: such was the interest shown that a committee applied to the Heritage Lottery Fund for help to continue the project. We were fortunate to have living in Lonsdale Road one of the pioneers of British oral history, Paul Thompson, who prompted and guided our efforts. Although he has now left the area we are most grateful for his inspiration and continued contributions: he has written the introduction on p.10.

Volunteers set out to interview a range of people who live or have lived in these roads, about their lives and how they came here and how they have found it. We also did a house-to-house survey, to collect information about people living here now. This book aims to present a representative fraction of the material we have collected. We hope that it will contribute to local history, but beyond this will build a picture of a changing middle-class community that will be of wider interest.

Many life stories we collected include rich material not immediately relevant to these roads. We cannot use it here but nothing will be wasted. The grant from the Heritage Lottery Fund has allowed for most of the tapes to be transcribed, which will make the material much more easily accessible: tapes, transcripts and other material are to be deposited in the Centre for Oxfordshire Studies.

Summertown had its exemplary historian in Ruth Fasnacht, whose book *Summertown Since 1820* was published in 1977. She looked back to the portrait of the village given by its first historian John Badcock in 1832. Badcock, the original community activist, promoted the building of Summertown's first church on what is now Middle Way, and took a great interest in the 562 inhabitants, adding to his account 'NB should any person have thought me too inquisitive in endeavouring to ascertain ages, it was merely to show the present state of the Population ... not from any rude, improper curiosity.' Historians are grateful for his persistence, especially as his lists predate the introduction of the census in 1851. Our own enquiries, reaching back to the time when Summertown ceased to be a village and developed as a suburb, have also tried to tread carefully to avoid intrusiveness.

Since the earliest houses in the roads were built in 1902 the 1901 census has been of no use to us. We await the opening of the 1911 census in 2011 with impatience. Directories and other sources have been used for background research and to check facts where possible, but in the end this is a survey drawing on people's memories. It was conducted as a community project, not an academic study. The contributors are largely self-selecting: it is people who are connected to others who are willing to be interviewed, and responses to a survey are more readily given to people who are personally known. There were in every road a handful of residents who were firmly not interested in contributing to the project, but they were vastly outnumbered by people willing to respond to questionnaires, who testified again and again to the importance of good neighbours and a general satisfaction with the neighbourhood.

We thank in the first place the remarkable people who gave us such open and interesting interviews. A number of interviewees have sadly died before the appearance of this book, which is offered in part as a tribute to their memories. We are glad to have captured something of their lives and personalities before they left the roads for good.

None of this would have been possible without the voluntary work of the committee. Philippa Berry has been outstanding as a tireless interviewer and chaser-up of contacts; and Sally Bromley, Natasha Burchardt, Margaret Clarke, Holly Kilpatrick, Betty Marshall, Verity Peto, Jackie Weaver and Elizabeth Zetter have carried out interviews, gathered information, prepared displays and attended countless meetings: warm thanks to all. Marion Haberhauer was a superb transcriber of most of the interviews we collected. We are very grateful to those who kindly lent photographs and other material. For particular assistance with images we thank the Oxfordshire County Council Photographic Archive (OPA), Martin Biddle, John Leighfield, Tim Peto and Peter Thompson. special thanks too to Bojana Kozul, who drew the map inside the cover for us. Other people too numerous to name have given invaluable help in all sorts of ways.

Following accepted practice text quoted from interviews has sometimes been condensed to remove repetitions etc.

Some further reading

Berry, Victor, *Summertown: Towards an Integrated Community*, 1971

Burnett, John, *A Social History of Housing 1915–1985*, 2nd edn 1986

Fasnacht, Ruth, *Summertown Since 1820*, 1977

Fulford, Margaret, *A Brief History of the Two Anglican Churches in Summertown*, n.d.

Kennedy, Julie, *The Changing Faces of Summertown and Cutteslowe*, 1995

Long, Helen, *The Edwardian House: The Middle Class Home in Britain, 1880–1914*, 1993

Oliver, Paul; Davis, Ian; Bentley, Ian, *Dunroamin: The Suburban Semi and its Enemies*, pb edn 1994

Introduction

Suburbs have been part of European life for centuries: indeed, the very word goes back to Roman times. Today there are probably more British households living in suburbs than any other type of location. So it is very surprising how little we know about suburbs as communities and the lives their people lead.

Suburbs were seen in the Victorian era as an ideal form of social life, combining the advantages of town and country. This way of thinking also inspired Hampstead Garden Suburb and Ebenezer Howard's Garden Cities in the early 20th century, as well as the post-1945 New Towns. But in the meantime the current of opinion among writers and thinkers swung decidedly against them, so that the very word 'suburban' became pejorative – 'narrow and unadventurous' is one meaning in Collins English Dictionary (1979). Among novelists, H.G. Wells gave a very unfavourable view of life in the villas of 'Morningside Park' in *Ann Veronica* (1909), while George Orwell in *Coming Up for Air* (1939) more trenchantly described 'Ellesmere Road' on a suburban estate as 'prison with all the cells in a row. A line of semi-detached torture chambers'. An early social critic was T.W.H. Crosland, who in *The Suburbans* (1905) argued that the commuting of so many workers out of the suburb, leaving a weekday population chiefly of women and children, must sap the nascent vitality of the local community. Perhaps most remarkably, Lewis Mumford, the great social interpreter of urban life, in his classic *The Culture of Cities* (1946 edn) asserted with unqualified confidence that the suburb 'lacked the necessary elements for extensive social co-operation, for creative intercourse'.

There was not much evidence to support this assertion then, and there has been little since. There was a series of outstanding family and community studies from the 1940s through to the 1970s, most often about rural villages, but also including ethnic minority city neighbourhoods, and some studies of very recently-built suburban public housing estates, where community had had no time to develop. As with Michael Young and Peter Willmott's classic *Family and Kinship in East London* (1957), these suburban estates were often unfavourably and unfairly contrasted with well-established inner city communities. However, in *The Evolution of a Community* (1963) Willmott later looked at the older working-class suburban Becontree estate, built from the mid-1920s, and was surprised to find that its family and community life was as rich and complex as in the old neighbourhoods. Willmott and Young were equally surprised when – alone of all the community studies researchers – they looked at a middle-class suburb, Woodford. They expected 'unfriendliness'. They concluded *Family and Class in a London Suburb* (1960): 'This has turned out not to be so. People in the suburb are on the whole friendly, neighbourly and helpful to each other. They attend clubs and churches together, they entertain friends and neighbours in their homes, they like (or at any rate they profess to like) their fellow-residents.' They suggested that while the population of Woodford was more transient than in an old working-class neighbourhood, its middle-class people had 'a certain capacity or skill at "making friends"', which enabled them to create new links as they moved, and to build up community without the bonds of nearby kin and long residence.

This is a conclusion which resonates well with the portrait of a middle-class Oxford suburb in this book. In the last 30 years there have been some excellent books on suburban architecture, but their focus has been primarily on art forms rather than people's lives.[1] Meanwhile community studies have been a waning form of social science research, and the baton has been taken up by oral historians. Once again, however, the focus of oral history projects has been overwhelmingly on working-class and ethnic minority communities. Indeed we know of scarcely any which have focussed exclusively on the lives and experiences and community of the people of a middle-class suburb, told in their own words. This alone makes this book important and unique.

You can read this book through or dip into it, and either way you will encounter moving stories and intriguing characters. The people include John Herivel, the mathematician from Northern Ireland who in 1940 played a key role in breaking the German 'Enigma' code. A more local star is Sydney Denton, who vividly brings in the other sides of Oxford, beginning by selling whelks on the family stall, working as a young man in the motor factories, and finally winning his own wealth through his chain of cycle shops. He never forgot his working-class childhood on the other side of the River Cherwell, and the trouble he got into when he once swam across.

Some of the themes here can be found in many other community oral histories: stories of the war, of the decline of local shops and rise of supermarkets, of schooling, of the much greater freedom children had to roam and play. Like working-class children, the older seven roads inhabitants remember how their parents allowed them to swim and punt unaccompanied in the river, or cycle along main roads miles into the country. There are also stories about women's work, typically teaching or clerical – and here, in contrast to most oral histories, servants are seen through the employers' rather than the workers' eyes.

There are, however, three themes which prove much more specific to a middle-class suburb. The first is the account in Chapter 1 of its development over many decades since 1900. This was made possible through a combination of oral memories with documentation which successive owners have handed down. It shows how in the earlier years the original speculative developer Francis Twining used covenants with sub-purchasers to enforce standards, ensuring that houses were built to a reasonable quality and noisome uses were kept out. In the last 30 years, by contrast, it is the residents themselves who have sought to maintain the character of the area by fighting high density infilling and commercial intrusions.

The second theme, which is explored in Chapter 2, is of the extraordinarily varied layers of the middle classes, and how their representation in the seven roads changed over time. At the beginning the population was much more local, dominated by town business people: fishmongers, butchers, market gardeners and so on. While these households 'in trade' were then seen as lower middle class, some were very cultured, such as the business-owning family who held musical evenings with their men in smoking jackets. The second significant early group were widows and spinster ladies,

1. E.g. A.A. Jackson, *Semi-Detached London*, 1973; P. Oliver, I. Davis, I. Bentley, *Dunroamin: the Suburban Semi and its Enemies*, 1981; Andrew Saint et al., *London Suburbs*, 1999.

often from better-off backgrounds but in reduced circumstances. There were also some retired missionaries and clergy. This original mix gradually changed over time. From the 1970s divorced or separated women, often with children, became as common as the spinsters. The street also became globalised rather than local, beginning with a cluster of refugees from Nazi Germany in the late 1930s, and culminating in a present-day great range of nationalities. Lastly, especially from the 1970s, more and more households were connected with university work, in Oxford and elsewhere, and with medicine. Thus the seven roads have shifted decade by decade from one middle-class mix to another, each bringing different variations of cultural expectations.

Finally, in the two last chapters we discover what kind of community this social mix produced, and how it saw its boundaries with the world beyond. There is no doubt that the seven roads made up a vibrant community. There are descriptions here of many types of organisation and activity: churches, drama groups, recycling groups, babysitting circles, street parties, and successful campaigns to win local improvements. There was also plenty of informal neighbourliness. People felt safe here, leaving the door on the latch for friends to drop in. The boundaries of the neighbourhood were clear: the main Banbury Road to the west, school grounds to the south, the river to the east, and only one narrow street connecting with the working-class Cutteslowe estate to the north. Few families in the seven roads knew these nearby manual workers, except when they employed them as domestic help.

On the other hand this acute sense of social boundaries was a handicap which had to be overcome within the shifting seven roads community. Many people maintained the convention of not speaking to others until introduced to them. Thus it has been a frequent experience to 'walk down the street here, and people who you know by sight, but you've never spoken to, will walk down the street, and they won't look you in the eye.' This behaviour is not so much 'typically English' – you don't find it in smaller towns or villages – as traditional middle-class behaviour, a survival from the formal days of presenting and leaving cards. It seems paradoxical that a such restrictive convention should be found in the midst of such lively community life. How is it overcome? You can find some of the answers here. Many people meet through their children. Others make a point of speaking to neighbours, or make contact through working at the front, in the garden, or mending a car. But there is one story of meeting a neighbour which is special because one can hardly imagine it happening outside an Oxbridge suburb:

> I was sitting in the Senior Staff Club in the University of Ibadan, having a drink with a Nigerian colleague, and this fair-haired guy walked up, and said, 'Do you mind if I join you?' And we said 'No'. After a while, I said, 'And where are you from?' He said, 'England'. I said, 'Oh, whereabouts?' He said, 'Well, in the south, in Oxford.' I said, 'Oh, whereabouts?' He said, 'Lonsdale Road'. I said, 'What number?' I said, 'Oh, well, I'm across the road from you'. That's how I met him! I met him in Africa!

This is fascinating evidence about British middle-class social relationships. This unique book is full of it. May it be known far beyond the seven roads! We have here a rare window into a community world whose significance has been too long neglected.

Paul Thompson

1 The Development of the Seven Roads

Grandfather, before 1900, had started speculating on buying property and selling it and so on, and he bought the Stone's Farm and Hawkswell Farm.

Gwynneth Twining

Francis Twining bought the two parcels of the land on which the seven roads were developed at the turn of the 20th century. Twining was a self-made Oxford grocery magnate (remotely related to the tea Twinings) who had established a small business in St Ebbe's in 1870 and gone on to build up a string of grocery shops in the city. There is more about his family on p.57ff. Around 1890, signifying his increasing prosperity and standing, Twining moved to Summertown House (still there, lurking behind a large block of flats on Banbury Road, as part of a University accommodation complex).

Summertown in the late 19th century

When Twining settled here, Summertown was a relatively new village, developed since 1820 north of Oxford, with a typical village mixture of large houses for prosperous 'carriage folk' who generally had business interests in Ox- ford, and cottages – some of them squalid – for artisans and labourers of all kinds. However in the last decade of the 19th century it was on the brink of transformation into a modest middle-class suburb. This was the great pe- riod of suburban development countrywide, but the par- ticular catalyst of growth here was the extension of the City boundary in 1889 to include Summertown, after which the City took on responsibility for maintaining roads and laying on water and sewerage. Existing resi- dents might grouse about the extra money on the rates, but the pickings for speculative developers were obvious.

By 1890 the 'ladder' of roads between Banbury and Woodstock Roads had been loosely developed up to Staverton Road with substantial upper-middle class hous- ing, much of it occupied by academics, but Summertown was still a separate outlying community. Gwynneth Twining has a vivid story about the Banbury Road at this period. When the family moved here her father, Francis junior, was still at school in Oxford, and getting home was somewhat scary.

Detail from the OS 1 inch map of 1833, showing the new village of Summertown straddling the Banbury Road north of Oxford. (John Leighfield)

There were no buses beyond St Margaret's Road, which was a horse tram. So Fa- ther always used to tell us the story of how, when they got off the bus and started walking home, they all had to get into a huddle because of the highwaymen! We think it was a bit of an exaggeration! But, apparently, there were men hiding in the bushes of the houses that were further down: the big houses by that time had been built, and they had gardens with laurel bushes and this and that – muggers, really.

A few years later, in 1896, the tram reached South Parade in Summertown, for by this time development had begun in earnest. Old Summertown had grown up mainly between the Banbury and Woodstock Roads north of South Parade, with another cluster of dwellings further south on the east side of the Banbury Road. In a significant new

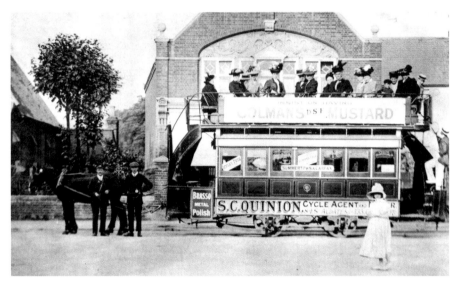

Horse-drawn tram outside Twining's new shop, 294 Banbury Road, c.1903. (Jeremy's, Oxford Stamp Centre)

development, visible on the 1900 Ordnance Survey map, three fields up against what became the new city boundary were laid out as Hernes, Harpes and Islip Roads. This was the work of Owen Grimbly, a prominent Oxford grocer who had been resident at The Lodge in George Street (Middle Way) since 1852. Not many of the planned houses, designed for skilled workers and small tradesmen, had been built by the time of his death in 1891, but the estate was sold on and developed through the 1890s. Meanwhile the Oxford Provident and Industrial Building Society had got to work south of South Parade, developing Oakthorpe, Stratfield, Beechcroft and Thorncliffe Roads from 1893–4 with slightly better lower middle-class housing. But on the 1900 map the area which would become our 'seven roads' is still untouched farmland centred on Hawkswell Farm and further farm buildings near Sunnymead. The only development is a slice off the Hawkswell property adjacent to Banbury Road, with houses on each side of a gap which would become Lonsdale Road.

The Edwardian development of the seven roads

Following his mentor Owen Grimbly's example, Francis Twining acquired two adjacent estates of approximately 25 acres each with a view to property development. On 29 September 1900 Hawkswell Farm was bought from William Emberlin, while on 29

September 1902 the two northerly fields were purchased from 'the Brethren and Sisters' of Mr Stone's Hospital (a charitable trust founded in the 17th century), and the University.

Twining set about dividing the land into plots and getting Council permission for his plans, then arranging for roads to be made and services provided. He expected to realise his investment by selling off the plots, generally to speculative builders. Lonsdale and Portland Roads were laid out on the Hawkswell Farm land, with the old farmhouse between them; Hamilton, Victoria and Lucerne on what had been the Stone's Estate.

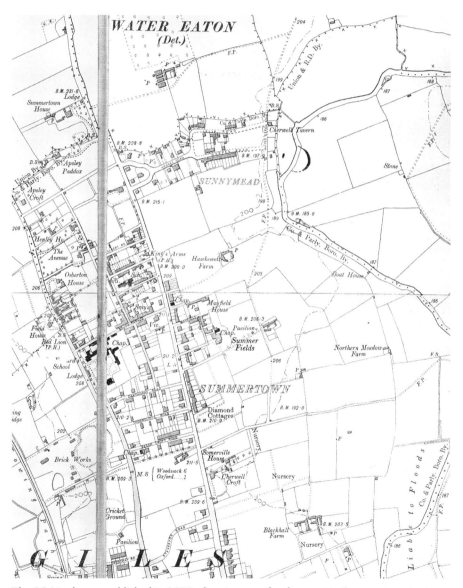

The OS 6 inch map published in 1900, showing new development in Summertown just before the seven roads were laid out. Francis Twining's home, Summertown House, is top left and Hawkswell Farm is near the middle. (John Leighfield)

Twining seems to have chosen names with a reassuring aristocratic resonance for his roads, as Gwynneth says.

Earls – Lonsdale, Portland, Hamilton. And Victoria was obviously Queen Victoria [who died in 1901]. And King's Cross was something to do with ... I don't know what!

'King's Cross' for the cross road may be a tribute to the new King Edward VII, combined with a humorous allusion to the famous London train station. 'Lucerne' was a favourite British tourist destination of the time – whether of particular significance for Twining, who did travel, is not known. Later Twining gave the slip of land for King George's Walk, the path from Portland Road to St Michael's Church, named in honour of the coronation of George V in 1910.

With his new grocery shop in place at 294 Banbury Road by 1902, Twining was anxious to see potential customers begin to populate his roads. Lonsdale Road, being closest to South Parade, was the most densely developed in these early years. The first houses were a handsome terrace in brick with stone facings and slate roofs (nos 2–10), designed by J.R. Wilkins, who had designed the Twining shop and the Co-op building and was responsible for many of the subsequent houses in the roads. The two oldest Twining sons, Ernest and Gilbert, who had been living next to each other at 23&25 Thorncliffe Road, moved into the first houses to be completed, nos 2&4, in 1902. The terrace had been for years a popular urban form, especially for modest housing (as for instance in Osberton Road) and is repeated in Lonsdale Road in nos 16–26 to the same design. It was economical to build, making full use of the width of the plot, but had the drawback of requiring rear access arrangements if coal and so on were not to be carried in through the front door.

Above: Terrace of houses on the south side of Lonsdale Road. Ernest and Gilbert Twining lived in the first two houses, nos 2&4. (P. Kinchin)

Below: Semi-detached houses, north side of Lonsdale Road. The builder Frederick Capel lived in no. 81, the left hand side of the nearest house. (P. Kinchin)

This problem was solved by the suburban semi, which became the predominant building form in the roads, more economical of ground than detached houses but offering tradesmen's access to the back of the house through narrow slots between the pairs. All the remaining houses in Lonsdale Road built at this point were semi-detached. Plots were generally sold off singly and tended to cost around £75. They mostly went to local speculating builders, who would buy plots, build a pair of houses, or maybe two or three pairs, sell them on, or sometimes rent them out, and do it again. Dominating activity in

Lonsdale and Portland Roads, as can be seen from the lists on p.222ff, was the building family of Noah Capel & Co., who had come from Temple Cowley via Bardwell Road and established themselves in 1903 at 279 Banbury Road, where Noah lived for many years. Deeds we have seen show that Frederick Capel for example built 77&79 Lonsdale Road in 1903, followed by 69&71 in 1904; he built 81&83, a spacious pair of individual design on the corner of King's Cross Road, moved into 81 himself around 1905, and continued to buy plots and build many houses. Harry Capel built the first two houses (49&51) in Portland Road in 1906 and moved himself into no.49, before building himself 44 Portland Road. No.57 Lonsdale Road was one of a pair built by Aubrey Capel on plots bought in 1906: it was sold in 1920 to its first tenant, a commercial traveller.

Francis Twining kept control over the development, with covenants over the sale of the plots, to make sure it met his standards of lower middle-class respectability. The purchaser had to agree:

that he would build a dwarf wall with iron palisading fronting the Road 4½ feet in height ... That no trade or business of any kind should be carried on ... without the written consent of the Vendors and no buildings should be used for the sale thereon or thereupon of intoxicating liquors ... That no more than one house should be erected on any one plot and the sum expended on the erection of such house should not be less than £250 and the plans thereof should be first submitted to and approved by the vendor.

The houses built at this early period in Lonsdale Road followed the standard late-Victorian L-shaped layout of a corridor hall with staircase running up the party wall, with two reception rooms one behind the other and a narrower extension at the back comprising a kitchen with a separate scullery behind it, and right at the back a coal store, larder and usually a WC for servants' use, sometimes accessible only from outside. There would be a tradesman's entrance to this part of the house. Houses on the south side of the road were larger: semi-detached pairs were usually built on three plots, leading to jumps in the numbering. Some of these larger houses had a third floor, with a room in the attic looking over the

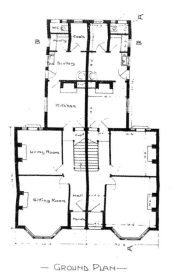 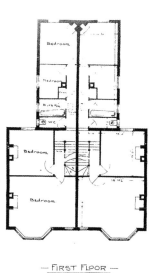

— GROUND PLAN —   — FIRST FLOOR —

Floor plans for 68&70 Lonsdale Road, submitted for Francis Twining in 1903 by the architect G.T. Gardner. There was also a large servant's room in the attic.

garden. Construction was in brick with the upper storey rough-cast and detailed with half-timbering, under a red tiled roof.

'Servant-keeping' was one definition of middle-class status at this period, and many houses in the roads were equipped for it (see p.156). Kate Jones Finer describes 48 Lonsdale Road.

Three bedrooms, lovely big bedrooms. The back one was what used to be the servant's room. It used to have a little bell: there were bell pushes in all the downstairs rooms, and then it went 'jingle, jingle, jingle' in this little room that was my study.

As we will see in the next chapter early residents of the roads ranged from prosperous businessmen and genteel spinsters, who would have live-in servants, to small tradesmen or clerical workers with little spare cash, whose families would manage with daily help.

The grandest house in Lonsdale Road at this period was built for Ernest Twining in 1908: no.76, a substantial detached house with its own coach house, just beyond the junction with King's Cross Road. Before the First World War Lonsdale Road continued no further. In 1909 the new Anglican church of St Michael and All Angels was built at the top of the road (p.185f).

The plots in Portland Road began to be developed from 1906 with a more varied assortment of generally more spacious houses – apart from an early terrace of four they

were semi-detached or detached dwellings, on wide plots. The houses here began life with names rather than numbers, a sign of their aspirations. Nos 45-51, the terrace, were 'Ivydene', 'Lucerne', 'Billericay' and 'Elmsview'. Francis Whitlock Twining, the younger brother of Ernest and Gilbert, moved in 1907 into the semi-detached 'Tintagel' (no.39, featured on the cover); the solicitor W.H. Linnell lived in the detached 'The Zayat' (no.31). Most of the later Edwardian houses show the influence of more up-to-date architectural thinking, with their rough-cast finish, greater interest in light, fashionable detailing and more generous planning. Elsie Hill lives in no.31 today.

The nice thing about them is that they have quite spacious halls.

Sandwiched awkwardly between the two new roads was Hawkswell Farm, the old stone farmhouse occupied by Twining's daughter Lottie, who had moved there on her marriage to Charles Clark, a butcher, in 1901 (see p.59). It is hard to date the house, but it is of typical Cotswold farmhouse style, with a Stonesfield slate roof, the core of it perhaps early 19th century. Dr James Harle bought it in 1965.

On the north side, there had been built a one-room, Victorian addition, with a bedroom upstairs. It's a much harder stone, and has sash windows. The earliest Deeds I've had a copy of date from 1895, and from then until the Norwoods bought it [after the

Above: 31 Portland Road, built in 1907, 2006. (P. Kinchin)

Below: Hawkswell Farmhouse, 34 Portland Road, 2006. (P. Kinchin)

Second World War], there was a succession of people – two families of Oxford butchers; and a market gardener from Cumnor. The butchers, apparently, sold sausages from the back door. They, of course, had a farmyard behind the house, which is now Kernahan's premises [a garage demolished in 2004], and that's how planning permission was obtained, with a succession of lock-up garages, a laundry, and then second-hand cars. When the Norwoods owned it they had a school for what are now called children with learning difficulties. If you could see the size of the house, it's difficult to see how they managed it!

Beryl Phillips' house, 65 Lonsdale Road, has an unusually wide drive.

It was the way through to Hawkswell Farm, at the back. There's a right of way for a horse and cart to come through the garden!

On 2 July 1903, needing perhaps to recoup capital, Twining sold on the Stone's Estate in its entirety to the Oxford Industrial and Provident Land and Building Society, and they took over the business of selling on plots in Hamilton and Victoria Roads over the following years, producing a handsome printed document to save the constant copying of the title deeds. Building activity in the country peaked just as Twining began his speculating, and the plots in these more northerly roads were slower to be developed than he might have anticipated.

A few traces of the land before it was built over survive in memory. Margaret Clarke was told of an underground stream on the north side of Hamilton Road.

No. 31 in the garden – an old lady lived there when we first came. And it bubbled up, and it flooded!

Much of the land had been planted with fruit trees, as Monica Wagstaff, also of Hamilton Road says.

It was an orchard. There's one or two very old fruit trees still left. There's one next door to us – it's a beautiful Blenheim, the fruit on it is gorgeous.

Dorothy Bridge's father had bought land at the end of Harpes Road in 1892 and built a double-fronted house (no. 78) in 1899 which is rather grander than its modest neighbours. Perhaps wanting to be nearer transport and in a 'better' road he bought land in Hamilton Road and in 1905 built another fine villa-style house, 'Hamilton House' (no. 5). As a founding director of the Building Society he presumably had the first pick of plots. Dorothy was born in the house in 1907 (see p.61f).

My father bought the two [plots] on which our house was built, and three where the next houses were built [later], and two across the road. The Turners had built their house [nos 11 & 13], and they'd also built one on the other side of the road, which is rather like it.

Hamilton House, the earliest house in Hamilton Road, built in 1905. The house to the right was built in the 1930s. (P. Kinchin)

Dorothy White, born in 13 Hamilton Road in 1915, gives a vivid picture of an empty road.

There weren't many houses in Hamilton Road. There was the double-fronted house – the Bridges' house – then a field, and a field at the corner of Hamilton Road; the Turner's, number 11, and ours, were built by Mr Jonas Carver. There were very few houses down our side of Hamilton Road, right down to Morris's [no.43] – there was two houses there, and that's about all there were then, to the corner of King's Cross.

While Lonsdale Road had been densely developed on tight plots almost wholly by speculative builders, the houses in the two more northerly roads were often built on double or multiple plots by people having a house built for themselves, and perhaps at the same time one as an investment, and the whole process stretched over a much longer period. Appendix 1 shows the much greater number of builders involved in the development of Hamilton and Victoria Roads. Margaret Clarke's house, for instance, and its pair in Hamilton Road were built in 1909, by George Money, the grandfather of Gladys Humby, who still lived in no.34 in the 1980s.

She lived in that house all her married and divorced life. And her brother, Mr Jack Money, lived in Victoria Road.

(No.36 was let out for many years and eventually sold to John Wiblin in 1930.) George Money built altogether four pairs in Hamilton Road and at least one in Victoria between 1908 and 1911.

Again the houses had names, sometimes likely to make their present owners cringe: listed in 1910 for example is 'Wilmilli' (20 Hamilton Road), next to 'Entre Nous' (no.22), which was inhabited by a teacher of French and German.

The Ordnance Survey map revised in 1919 shows the state of play before the First World War brought house-building to a halt in 1914. At this stage, there was very little on the north side of Hamilton Road, and just a few isolated houses in the main part of Victoria Road. Beyond King's Cross Road on the south side of Victoria Road, were rather more, including a neat speculative terrace, nos 88–100, closer in character and location to the dense development of Harpes and Islip Roads. These were in fact built one at a time between 1905 and 1911 by Mr G. Grant, and originally all had passageways through to the rear.

Above: 88–100 Victoria Road, 1905–11. (P. Kinchin)

Below: 1 Lucerne Road, 'The Bungalow', built in 1908. The next house was built in 1959. (P. Kinchin)

The OS map redrawn in 1919, showing the development of the roads by the time of the end of the First World War.

In Lucerne Road there was only one house, 'The Bungalow' (no.1), built in 1908 in a pleasant Arts and Crafts-influenced style, though the rest of the road was laid out as river garden plots. Nancie Villiers and her husband, who owned a river garden, and later lived in a house erected on one of the plots, describes this distinctive feature of the area.

These were all river gardens, only 25 feet wide. The people from Oxford used to drive out here in their ponies and traps. Sometimes they were more or less allotments, but more often they were just pleasure gardens, and they had boat-houses. Our own boat-house dates from early in the [20th] century. It was thatched, and it belonged to the Edwardian times when 'the river', in all its aspects, was quite fashionable.

The inter-war years

Economic recovery from the First World War took some time. Even when building started again in these roads the more northerly area felt very empty. Dorothy Bridge of Hamilton Road remembers a vanished environment.

One thing, we could always hear Old Tom – Christ Church Bell – ring a hundred and one times at nine o'clock. It still does, but you can't hear it now because of the traffic. We could always hear the trains, and hear St Edward's School clock, and Wolvercote had a peal of bells, we could always hear those. From our garden we could see to the top of Cumnor Hill.

The Gee family still ran 'Summertown Farm' at 354 Banbury Road when in 1920 Francis Whitlock Twining moved his family from 72 Lonsdale Road, an Edwardian semi, to the big house on the north corner of Victoria and Banbury Roads, 368 Banbury Road. Before this 'Park View', which was surrounded by a very large garden, had been lived in by Margaret Kilpatrick's Aunt Polly, who had made an advantageous marriage into the Beecham family. Though separated from her husband she lived in what was luxury to her poorer relations, to whom she was always very good.

It was like going into the country to go there. There were one or two servants in the house: you rang a little bell. The garden was like fairyland. It was so big, it had everything. It had been gardened well and looked after properly. I certainly remember the strawberries!

Gwynneth Twining remembers how un-built-up the Banbury Road felt in the 1920s.

When I was small, there was nothing over there. There was fields; the cottages down there; and 333 [Summerhill], which is where Ryman-Hall lived. Most of this, I think, was his land, small meadow-type fields, where I used to go across and pick flowers to take to school.

Several people recall this countrified feeling, which persisted despite new building between the wars. Raquel Steward was married in 1933 from her sister-in-law's house, 6 Portland Road: her recollection is not entirely accurate, but communicates a sense of the general openness to the north at that point.

It stopped here. I mean, Summertown finished at Portland Road, and then it was green. Orchard and allotments. A lot of allotments.

The map revised in 1937 shows the filling-in that occurred when building began again around 1923. In Lonsdale Road the new Vicarage and seven houses were built on land adjacent to the church. (The fine old Vicarage on the corner of Banbury Road and South Parade, designed by J.D. Sedding in 1878, was demolished in the 1930s for Hartwell's Garage, replaced in 1968 with Suffolk House.) Lonsdale Road was extended beyond King's Cross and several larger detached houses were built there, including Way's End, the big house which closes the vista, dated 1926 on its drainpipe. Slightly to the north and at an angle was the fine Arts and Crafts influenced house built for Gilbert Twining in 1923, Field End (no.105). Both had large gardens, with access to the river.

On the corner of Portland Road the Church Hall was built from the stones and timbers of the old Summertown church of St John the Baptist, demolished in 1924: this had been on Middle Way, which as Betty Marshall reminds us was then called George Street.

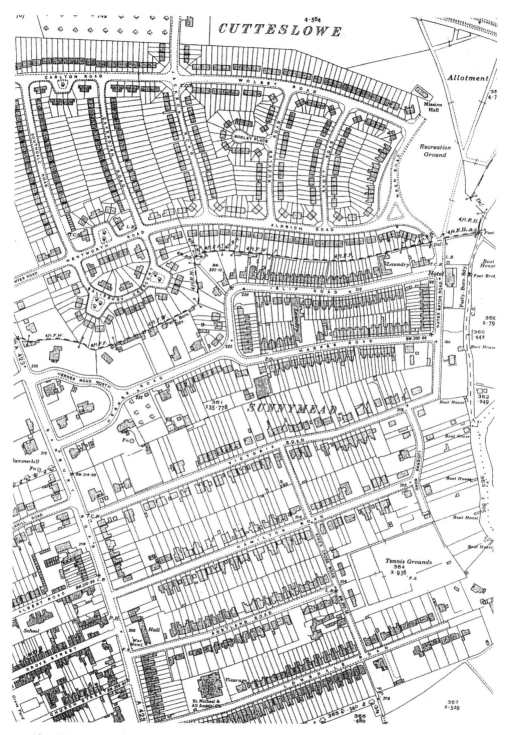

The OS map revised in 1937, showing the considerable development of the area between the wars. Note the housing estates which have appeared to the north, beyond the old city boundary.

6 Portland Road, built in 1923, to the same design as no.4, built in 1921. (P. Kinchin)

Of course, there was a great muddle, because unless you added 'Summertown', things would go to George Street in Oxford! Then they changed it to Middle Way.

The name was changed in 1956, when there was actually a suggestion that it should be called Twining Street (see Fasnacht pp.100-3). Church Street was changed to Rogers Street at the same time, and Albert Road to Hobson Road in 1961.

Behind St Michael's Church empty plots on Portland Road were filled in with pleasant houses. No.4 was built in 1922 by an architect said to have won the Domestic Architect of the Year Award, and was owned, like its mirror image no.6, by Miss Steward. It was at this period that the Hawkswell tennis courts were laid out, with access from King's Cross Road and via a path next to 103 Lonsdale Road, as Betty Marshall remembers.

Most of those houses along Lucerne Road were not built, only one or two of them. I used to play netball and tennis in Hawkswell Gardens.

A few houses were built between the wars in Lucerne Road along with more boathouses. Gwynneth Twining recalls the family river garden at this period (p.59).

It was just a garden. There was a little stream going across, with a bridge, and another bit with a summerhouse and more grass. And the stream went down one side, and over that had been built a boathouse, and there was the punt.

King's Cross Road got its first houses on the east side in the mid 1930s, including an idiosyncratic Cotswold-style stone house, no.9, beautifully built by the stonemason father of the old lady who lived on there until her recent death, and two pairs probably built by Denis Mealing, who put up a number of houses in the roads in the 1930s.

Hamilton Road and especially Victoria Road saw a lot of interwar building and thus have more architectural variety than Lonsdale and Portland Roads. Several houses in these two roads acquired garages at this period. Betty Marshall's parents, the Howes, moved in 1925 into 45 Victoria Road, one of the first of the new wave of houses.

They moved in as a brand new house. They were married in 1923, and they lived in rooms until the house was finished.

The houses looked up-to-date but were conservative in some respects: though Betty's mother never had help in the house the architect had included pre-war pretensions to middle-classness. There is a separate 'tradesman's entrance' only slightly removed from the 'front' door which is at the side of the house: both doors give into what is essentially the same hallway. And there were bell-pushes in the two ground floor rooms and the front and second bedrooms which worked a ticker board in the kitchen.

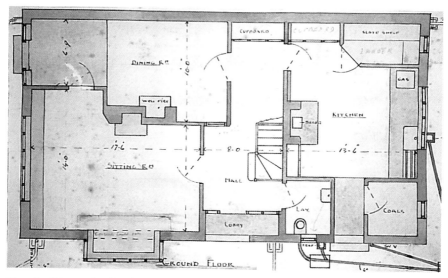

Plans for 'Nutcombe, King's Cross Road', on a corner site, now 66 Hamilton Road, built in 1924 by W.T. Coxhill of 43 Portland Road. This up-to-date floor plan does away with the Edwardian scullery and has good access to the garden from the reception rooms. (J. Wafer)

I can remember as a child pushing the bells then dashing into the kitchen and watching it tremble back and forward.

On the whole however the days of middle-class 'servant-keeping', i.e. of live-in servants, were over after the First World War and more rational designs began to be built. The footprint of interwar houses, as can be seen from the maps, is usually basically rectangular, giving a larger hall with the kitchen behind it, and better access to the garden at the back of the house than in most Edwardian houses. Houses were often stuccoed and fitted with the new metal Critall windows.

John Rowe was born in another of the mid 1920s houses in Victoria Road, with no houses opposite his home until the late 1930s.

The attractive name plate for 12 Victoria Road, built in 1926. (P. Kinchin)

There was a big hedge. [Mr Alden] had a big old country house where the flats are now in Hernes Road. It was all his garden, a meadow. On the other side of the garden was an abattoir. There was a gate where no.13 is: I used to go in there and his housekeeper used to chase me out!

All early inhabitants of Victoria Road, like Gwynneth Twining, remember the abattoir. The Aldens were another notable Oxford 'town' family.

Aldens the butchers lived in West Grove, in Hernes Road. They had a big house there, and an abattoir at the back, and we used to hear the animals.

Knowles & Co., a long-established Oxford building company, had earlier built 338& 340 Banbury Road north of the Church Hall (J.E. Knowles lived in 338 from 1910–

21) and 55&57 Hamilton Road in 1924 as a speculation. The young Guy Knowles had had an architectural training, in the office of Edwin Lutyens, and in 1932 the firm built to his design, for £2577, two pairs of houses, 35–41 Victoria Road, on the south part of Alden's land. Guy Knowles married Connie Alden in 1933 and in 1938 they moved with their small son Alan to Hernes Road.

We came to no.2, called Greengates, which belonged to the Brooks family, the estate agents, who sold it to father, plus all the ground with it which was quite extensive. The house next door was West Grove, which was where my maternal grandfather lived, that was R.T. or Reginald Alden, and my grandmother Edith.

And he was the brother of Fred Alden, who started F.T. Alden the heating company, and Alden the printers. But my grandfather remained in butchering all his life, except he did get interested in laundries – he had a laundry [in Harpes Road], the Electric Laundry, and another one in Wantage or somewhere like that. My great- uncle James East – he's the brother of Thomas Knowles – was in 94 Hamilton Road. It was called 'Bailleen'. He owned various others as well. He also had the tennis courts off King's Cross Road.

Knowles & Co. went on to develop 9–21 Victoria Road on the south edge of the Greengates garden, including the detached 'Greystones' for T.E. Knowles to live in. Mariele Kuhn arrived in 1938 and remembers the houses going up soon afterwards.

So then the building of all these houses started. No. 13 was built by this builder for his father. It is the only house that is not red brick. It is a more elegant house.

A contemporary photograph of Greystones, 13 Victoria Road, built in1939 for T.E. Knowles. (OPA)

Other owners who had invested in plots beyond their continuing needs were already beginning to sell off land for building – something which would gather pace after the war. Nos 7&9 Hamilton Road, for instance, were built in 1932 on land belonging to the Bridges, while 1&3 and 5&7 Victoria Road were built around 1930 on land originally belonging to the Twinings' big house. Elizabeth Johnston lived in no.5.

This garden was, I think, part of their orchard. When we first came here, there was a very ancient greengage tree, which had the most wonderful fruit on it. And one year, I'd had so many, we had to prop up the branches with sort of stilts, and then the next year, it just died.

The Twinings themselves left 368 Banbury Road in 1937 for a newly built house at 80 Hamilton Road.

Very obvious on the 1937 map is the massive development of housing estates to the north, beyond what had been the 1889 City boundary. Visible also is the notorious Cutteslowe Wall (p.204) dividing Carlton from Wolsey and Wentworth from Aldrich Roads. Betty Grant came to Hamilton Road before the estates were built in 1934.

> When we came up first, there was no Urban Estate, there was no Cutteslowe Estate, there was just fields. They put them up, and then they put the wall across – because they didn't like the Council people coming through the Urban Estate. So they had to all come all down and up [our] roads.

Post-war development

The Second World War brought most house building to a halt again, though one or two families, like the Kuhns, built air-raid shelters in their gardens.

> You got these blocks delivered, and they had two holes, and you filled them with sand. We never really used it. But it's very useful up to this day! We saw a lot of aircraft flying overhead, but I think Oxford was not bombed. When Coventry was bombed, the sky was red. We saw that from here.

Air-raid shelter in the garden of 25 Victoria Road, 1945. In the background are the tall chimneys of Reg Alden's house, West Grove, in Hernes Road. (Mariele Kuhn)

The blight on development persisted into the 1950s as Britain struggled through post-war austerity. The shopping area of Summertown, which was to feel the main impact of post-war development, was slow to change. On the east of Banbury Road there were still the cottages that Betty Marshall remembers from before the war.

> There were a whole lot of terraced type houses, that lay way back from the road, and they had these lovely cottage gardens as you went down towards the door, and the doors opened straight into the living room. We used to go and visit somebody there, because when I was born, you were born at home, unless there were terrific complications, and you had a nurse in, a midwife/nurse, and my parents had a nurse, and she lived in one of those little cottages, and we used to go and have tea with her.

The parade of shops still had a few of the unconverted houses in it which were recalled by Gwynneth Twining (see p.174f).

> On the west side, of course, there were all those houses which are now shops, they all had their long front gardens. I can remember, oh, half a dozen, probably, that still had their gardens, but, of course, they gradually went.

Betty Grant remembers some of the large houses further up the Banbury Road, which together with the early 19th-century cottages contributed to a villagey environment.

> It was very quiet, we had no offices up here at all. There was a beautiful house, a lovely house [Uplands, 269], and Alderman Rogers lived there. And there was another lovely house on the corner [of South Parade – Southlawn, 267].

Marston Ferry Lane ended abruptly and the ferry was still operating after the war, as John Rowe describes.

It was a made-up road as far as the bowls club then that petered out completely. The track behind the allotments used to go straight on down to the river. On the other side of the river was the Vicky Arms. There was a bell on a tree, you rang the bell and someone would come out of the pub, get in a boat, paddle across and take you across. Two old ladies used to run this pub, and their barrels of beer were in the cellar and they used to go down with jugs.

Left: Leslie Preston, an architect, surveying the river garden plot in Lucerne Road acquired in 1956, to prepare for the present house. (Mary Preston)

Right: 1a Lucerne Road, the house built by Leslie Preston, photographed in the late 1960s. (Nancie Villiers)

It was in the later 1950s that more houses began to be built on the river gardens in Lucerne Road. No.23, 'Bishop's Mill', for instance, was completed in 1957. A little later David Paine built no.17 on one of the family river garden plots in 1965, and his brother Geoffrey followed suit in 1972, recognising the attraction of living by the river.

I reckon I've got the best of all worlds here, because I'm in the middle of the town, and in the middle of the country at the same time, depending on which way you look.

Their friend Alan Knowles remembers his family's river gardens: the Knowles, like the Paines, still have one.

Mrs Villiers' river garden used to be my Grandpa Alden's river garden which we used for a long time and he actually sold to my father. When we started the development of Hawkswell Gardens we then got rid of the river garden up where Mrs Villiers is now and we had everything down at the other one – right off Hawkswell Gardens at the end.

Knowles & Co. were responsible for the most substantial post-war development in the roads, Hawkswell Gardens. Margaret Willis remembers the area in the 1950s.

There was an abandoned tennis court, with weeds coming up through it. In Hawkswell Gardens, there's a block of flats in the far corner, and behind that there used to be a flight of steps, which took you up into Lucerne. And that was the way we used to come back from school. You could bump down those steps and then get into Lonsdale Road.

As Alan Knowles explains, the firm had previously extracted gravel from this land, which belonged to his great-uncle J.E. Knowles.

You notice it's all a bit lower than everything else around about. Before the tennis courts it was a gravel pit. It was said to be a mill, and if you look at the bed of the River Cherwell it rises and goes in a hump. When we did the development we were

Hawkswell Gardens, 2006. (Jonathan Allis)

allowed to have the passage-way to Lonsdale Road closed. The footpath was originally the footpath that people used to come in from places like Islip.

Hawkswell Gardens is on the 'close' pattern popular in post-war suburban developments, with detached houses set on American-style unseparated lawns, round a curving dead-end road.

That's when I first joined the business, I'd come back from college. And we built the houses from about '58, '59 through to '63. The final bit there [1968–9] was the block of flats. [The houses] were designed by Peter Reynolds with a lot of input from my father. They were very keen at that time to have the open gardens in front of the houses so that all the drives and all the gardens in front of the houses were on a communal basis. And they hit the headlines because they suddenly appeared, in the *Sunday Times* or something in an article about property, that these people were developing these ridiculously expensive houses in Oxford. And they were selling for £5000 each!

Guy and Connie Knowles built 18 Hawkswell Gardens for themselves c.1964 and lived there until Guy's retirement from the firm, while Richard Knowles lived at no.15. After Guy Knowles died the freehold of communal areas was sold to the Residents' Association. Residents have access to their own river garden, as Peter Clarke describes.

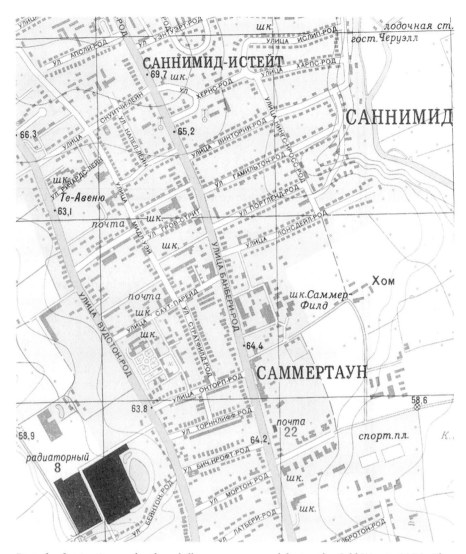

Part of a fascinating, and rather chilling, map prepared during the Cold War, in 1973. The Soviets have made certain errors in the seven roads, suggesting that they were not using a British map: they allow road access from Hawkswell Gardens to Hamilton Road, and extend King's Cross Road up to Hernes Road. The Radiator Works, bottom left, were clearly of interest. (John Leighfield)

There's a communal garden: everyone has a share in it. It's maintained by gardeners, we all pay a maintenance fee for that. We had a wedding there in July, the Indian family, their son was married and they had a massively big reception there: it was very nice – a couple of hundred people. It's just very pleasant, and people seem to use it a fair amount. It would be nice to have a kayak there, and go down the river.

Hawkswell Gardens makes a self-contained community hidden from the rest of the roads. Hilary Lloyd has lived in the close since the early 1990s.

We do feel a bit separate from everybody else. Because it is tucked away and because it's got such a different feel to it.

The development included the first block of flats to be built in the roads, Hawkswell House. Another previously very open area which has been substantially built over is Water Eaton Road. Bob Williams came to the end of Victoria Road in 1963 (p. 33f) and underlines the loss of the easy access to the river which these roads once enjoyed.

We had a view, across the garden, of a house in Water Eaton Road, which was known as 'The Pagoda', a very interesting old house where an architect lived, and he managed to persuade the City that a block of flats on his land was a good idea. Before that was built, even from downstairs, we could see the punts on the river, across his garden. We thought that that land, which borders Cromwell's Ditch, and the River Cherwell, would not be open to building. And once that had happened, Water Eaton Road has become a succession of blocks of flats.

The 1960s and early 70s was a period of much architectural destruction and poor quality building under commercial pressures. In 1962 Prama House replaced the Regency Southlawn (267 Banbury Road) with offices above, and supermarket, bank and shops below, and the same fate befell Ivy Lodge (no. 274), demolished to make way for Oxfam House (p. 178). Further three-storey office buildings with shops beneath followed on the east side, wiping out the earlier cottages. Sydney Denton remembers this change over the years that he's known Summertown.

It's been developed and developed and developed, and it's not been done very nicely, really. Summertown, originally, was two rows of little cottages on the right-hand side. And those big forecourts you get in front of those shops, of course, years ago, was the front gardens.

The Marston Ferry Road, connecting Summertown with Marston and Headington, was opened in 1971, as Lady Gurden recalls.

That was a great thing, and there was a table half way down, and people giving cups of coffee, and celebrating.

Infilling

The changing character of Summertown from the 1970s on is noticed by many, like Margaret Willis who first came in 1954.

Summertown was a village when I came to live here. It felt like a village, yes. It's become vastly urbanised now – infilling building and so on.

Isolated infilling had occurred in the roads in the 1950s and 60s: even then it seems that neighbours disliked it. Margaret Pickles and Hazel Leafe came in 1961 to 12 Hamilton Road, built in 1956 by Mr Smith, a coal merchant, on a plot where there had been two garages and two trees.

Mr Smith bought it for £1,000, the whole plot. And he had the house built specially. There was a man and a boy. The man and the boy built it, the whole thing. I think the road rather objected to another house, because it was such a little plot, and they thought it ought to have remained for a bit of green site.

Like other people in the roads who have taken advantage of generous gardens, the

Norwoods had kept part of the land fronting onto Portland Road when they sold Hawkswell Farmhouse in 1965, and built for themselves one of the few 1960s houses in the roads, something of a sore thumb with its yellow stone facing among the brick or pebbledash characteristic of its neighbours. It masks the access to the old house, of which many people in the roads were quite unaware until Kernahan's Garage in King's Cross Road was recently demolished.

Houses with large gardens were obvious targets for developers. A run of four town-houses, a new building type in the roads, was built at 78–82a Lonsdale Road on the large garden of no.84 (built for Mrs Ernest Twining when she left no.76) in 1977. The old Twining house at the secluded end of the road, no.105, also fell into the hands of a developer at the end of the 1970s. His plan to knock down the house and build a block of fourteen luxury flats was fortunately defeated by neighbourhood protest. The house survived, but now shares its plot with three new red brick properties.

The 1970s also saw the beginning of much extension activity (see p.161ff). Dr Harle of the Ashmolean Museum, who bought Hawkswell Farmhouse in 1965 and was very attached to it, made additions typical of the later 20th century's interest in light.

All I have added is an extension at the back, in 1970. And I opened up that room by putting some French windows in, because it was an extremely gloomy room, it only had a little window.

Infilling has been a feature of the last two decades particularly. Hamilton and Victoria Roads are particularly susceptible to this as their original layout was much looser, with building on a variety of plot sizes and more provision for garages. Philippa Berry describes something quite typical in Hamilton Road.

Since we've been living here, there've been a lot of houses built, filling in the spaces. In fact, we, ourselves, have built on the half plot, where the old corrugated iron garage was – we've built a garage with a room on top. The plot next door to us was a double plot, and the people, when they left, sold it as two plots, so that's now been built on.

Infilling is one of the few things that people registered in our survey as a dislike about the roads. Margaret Clarke of Hamilton Road speaks of her immediate surroundings.

The other thing that I must comment on is the amount of infilling, the new houses that have been built. If I look out of the window, there are one, two, three, four houses, and on my side, there are one, two, since we came – to say nothing of the extensions! It does feel more crowded.

The back door at 45 Hamilton Road, which bore a notice 'Tradesman's Entrance', and the old garage shortly to be replaced by an extension, 1979. (P. Berry)

Houses are certainly being slotted into very narrow spaces now. Some like Mariele Kuhn have scruples on the subject, but further building will almost inevitably occur when houses change hands.

Left: The view from 36 Hamilton Road as a new house rises on the garden of no. 33, June 2001. (M. Clarke)
Right: The refurbished 33 and new 35 Hamilton Road, with off-street parking in place of gardens. (P. Kinchin)

I asked Chancellors to give me a rough idea of the value of my house. He said, 'Well, have you thought of building on that other plot?' I said, 'No. I wouldn't do that to my neighbour, because it would come too close to her'. But, I mean, nowadays, it's land, not houses.

With pressure on the City Council to permit more and more housing to be built, and a particularly high value being placed upon living in this area, this densification is un-likely to stop until all available spaces have been used. A radical approach, effected a number of times already, is to knock down old houses and replace them with more and bigger buildings to maximise the value of the site. An example is 368 Banbury Road, the Twining sisters' old home. It was pulled down, but for its façade, and rebuilt with a substantial extension as Victoria Gate, eight new flats – to one of which Gwynneth and Margaret returned, after living for many years in Hamilton Road. Finished in 1998, this exemplifies commercial developers' recent recognition that building with deference to existing architectural style is worth the effort.

Bob Williams describes exactly how this development process happens, while ex-pressing unease at the social implications of high house prices. He and his wife moved to 115 Victoria Road in 1963.

It was called 'Apple Tree Cottage', and there was, living there at that time, a very old man, Sir Something Mott. He had been a partner in Blackwell's, and he had lived in the house for some little while. It was really a semi-bungalow, in the sense that the major rooms were downstairs. It was a strange house, in some ways, to come to, but fortunately, neither Jelly nor myself have ever looked really much at creature comforts. It had a very nice garden for the children to play in, just over a third of an acre in all. And we lived there until the end of the century, 2000. We had built an extension on the house in 1968/9, so we had an extra room and a garage.

We were stimulated, in part, by the builder, Mr Gomm, who's built quite a lot in Victoria Road, and now elsewhere in North Oxford. He had dropped us a note, suggesting that perhaps we would like to think about using our garden as a building site. When we went to estate agents, they put a price on it of £350,000. [Someone said] 'You know, I don't think you can sell that house as a family house, because the garden is so large, that a builder will bid for it, and you'll think he's a family man, and he'll get it for a song.' Now, Gomm was well aware of this, so he offered us £600,000 instead, for the whole site, and the house, which he said he would knock down. We said to him, 'Well, where do we live?' So Gomm, on his own, came back with a scheme. He would build us a house, which would be easily worth £300,000, and he would give us £350,000. So we said, 'Right. Can we plan the house?' So I had an architect, Aubrey King [who lives in Hamilton Road].

[The result] was two houses on Victoria Road, and two houses on Water Eaton Road. The house we've got is a very nice house indeed, it's far better than the one we had before. What's more, it's bigger than we intended. So if you look at the site, which the estate agents had estimated at £350,000 as a family house with a garden, it became worth £2 million. Now, I think that is absolutely disgusting. This is absolutely against all my Socialist beliefs. I cannot see how you can build a society where you have people who can't afford a house above £100,000, can't possibly, next door to a set of houses all of which

Above: 115 Victoria Road, built in 1930, c.1988. (Jelly Williams)

Below: Three of the four houses built on the site of the house above. In the background to the right is a block of flats on Water Eaton Road. (P. Kinchin)

are worth £500,000. I think the way England is now financed in property, is actually very bad news, even for our neighbourhood, because we will never be able to get on terms with the people from the estate.

Sam Clarke, who came to Victoria Road in 1986, feels that this development has led to a loss of architectural diversity, but accepts a process of change.

We had a greater variety of slightly one-off houses then, we hadn't benefitted from the development that Mr Gomm has brought us! By and large he has taken down the more interesting of the houses in the street. There are about five clusters of new houses. They've been built to a high standard, I have no objections as to how they look. What they have brought is a degree of uniformity to the street which is slightly less welcome. But the street must be ever-changing I think, and it must always have been thus.

The limited commercial premises in the roads have given way to housing under these new pressures. The 1920s dairy on the south corner of Victoria Road was one: although the front building is still a shop, 2a and 2b are new houses replacing the old dairy outbuildings. During the course of this oral history project the Toyota garage on the corner of Grove Street was demolished and rebuilt as flats, and the same thing has happened to Kernahan's garage in King's Cross Road. Erected over the original yard of Hawkswell Farm, incorporating its old barn, this unattractive building was finally demolished in 2004–5 and rebuilt as one and two bedroom units. Planning battles over this contentious site go back to the 1970s (p.197): Peter Thompson, who has lived opposite since 1980, gives an account which indicates local residents' strong feelings about the neighbourhood.

The use of that site for, if you like, industrial, and subsequently car retailing activities was historic; but by the latter part of the 20th century, was completely inappropriate to the entirely residential area that we were in. Mr Kernahan was fairly determined in trying to expand his business over many years, including buying no.83 Lonsdale Road, converting it into two flats, and basically extending all of his car retailing operations into and over the old garden. Over the years, ever since we've lived here, there was a whole series of running battles with Mr Kernahan. On

Above: Kernahan's garage in King's Cross Road standing empty, c. 2003.

Below: The new development on the site by Thomas & Co., 2006. Most of the units were bought by one person for letting. (Peter Thompson)

at least one occasion, we fought a Planning Application, very vociferously, which was to create a complete showroom frontage along King's Cross Road. There was a lot of rebellion about that, and I did quite a lot of work in drumming up opposition to it. I'm pleased to say that it was comprehensively rejected.

He closed his business himself [in the late 1990s], and subsequently leased the premises to another car dealership, who never really used it seriously for sales, and, in fact, abandoned it altogether after about a year, and the premises then stood empty, looking increasingly dilapidated, and suffering a certain amount of vandalism. So it was actually quite a relief when the Planning Application was made, by Kernahan, to develop residential accommodation on the site. The objection that we all had was that the architectural merits of the designs that were submitted were absolutely non-existent. There was no attempt to provide anything that was complementary, in any way, to the existing developments in the area, and the effect on the King's Cross street scene, I think, would have been horrendous. So, again, together with Verity Peto, I worked fairly hard at preparing a very detailed series of objections to the Planning Application, and that got firmly rejected. Mr Kernahan then did what he should have done to start with, which was start consulting some of the locals about what sort of development would be acceptable and considered appropriate, and we ended up with quite a reasonable compromise.

The flats are disguised as a large Edwardian-style pair of semi-detached houses.

In some ways it was a bit of a cop out, because it was a kind of a pastiche, and it might have been nice if they'd engaged some real architectural talent to come up with something that was actually, you know, innovative, and looked like the 21st century, rather than merely blending reasonably well with the existing stuff. But, there you go!

Just such a house in a more modernist idiom, one of a few oddities in the roads, has in fact recently been built further up King's Cross Road. There are a couple of older 'architect-built' houses in Victoria Road. But most new building now is in 'traditional' vaguely Edwardian style, which people generally seem to prefer as less intrusive.

Some of the units in the 'Courtyard', as the garage site was tastefully marketed, do not have a car space or the right to a parking permit. This, as Peter comments, reflects an attempt to tackle the increasing number of cars which has accompanied the growing residential density of these roads (see p.164ff).

'King's House', 2 King's Cross Road, built in 2003. (P. Kinchin)

The City Council [is] trying to encourage more of a car-free environment within the City boundary. It's actually perfectly feasible to live very comfortably here, without owning a car. The public transport facilities are very good, the proximity of the shops is such that it's possible to walk or use a bicycle, and for many people, the numbers of occasions on which they do need to use a car could be very well served by car rental, or membership of what is effectively a car rental scheme. And, indeed, there are plenty of people resident in Lonsdale Road who don't run cars. But it's interesting that a commercial property developer considers that the most profitable development solution for this particular site involves putting as many very small properties [as possible] on the site.

Around a century since construction began the seven roads might seem to be finally more or less fully developed, but it is safe to assume that skips will continue to be a regular feature of the street scene. There is more on houses and what people have done to them in chapter 8.

2 A Changing Middle-Class Community

You think of all of us who had these houses that we bought, and what they now fetch when they change hands – of course, the sort of person occupying them has changed.

Margaret Willis

This chapter gives a survey of the sort of people who have lived in these roads over the course of a century, in what has always been a mixed middle-class community. The people highlighted in the next chapter, who have lived here for a long time, are good examples of the largely 'town' population of the area in the first half of the 20th century, which was slowly changed in the second half by the arrival of more diverse academic and professional people, some of whom are represented in chapter 4.

'Town not gown'

Gwynneth Twining speaks of a time when shops were locally owned, mentioning some well-known names now lost from Oxford's city centre.

In those days, most of the shops, or many of the shops, were owned by local people. You didn't have a Marks and Spencer's or a Sainsbury's, they were mostly local people, and, of course, Grandfather knew all these people – Babcock, Webber, Elliston, the Taphouses – they were all local families. There was a great community amongst the traders.

Summertown was a 'tradesmen's village' from the start, and as it developed more housing for the middle classes many people with business in Oxford chose to live here. Gilbert Twining built himself a large house at the far end of Lonsdale Road in 1923 and soon had fellow 'merchants' as neighbours – notably William Oliver of Oliver & Gurden who moved from 47 Portland Road to a new house, 103, in 1925. Margaret Willis, who now lives in the old Twining house, 105, recalls some of the prosperous 'town' people later living in this part of the road.

On the whole, these houses were owned by people who'd made their living in the shops. That house at the end [Way's End] was owned by a Mrs Pearson, who was a daughter of the Boswells – she'd been a Miss Boswell. And there was another former Miss Boswell further down the road. And this house was Mr Hanks, who was from Cowley, the principal engineer at Morris Motor Works, I believe. The Geddeses, the carpet people, were at 103. And the Paynes, the silversmiths on the High Street, they were towards King's Cross Road [no.89].

Mr Bridge, who built the first house in Hamilton Road, owned a printing business in town, and his family was typical of the better-off residents of the road (p.61f). Monica Wagstaff gives a snapshot of other neighbours from before the Second World War.

Banks, shops, civil servants. One or two who had their own businesses. We had

Joseph Shirley of 74 Hamilton Road, who worked as a milkman for the local Edmonds dairies, outside the now vanished Cherwell Arms in Water Eaton Road, c.1937. (E. Shirley)

the Hunts and the Broadhursts. It used to be down Botley, Hunt & Broadhurst, they were paper makers – it was quite a big factory. Down at the Broadhursts they used to have musical evenings, soirées. They had a woman who used to come, and she sang 'Cherry Ripe'. My little sister used to imitate it in a wobbly soprano voice – and if you opened the windows ...! The Hunts up the road, they used to have musical evenings too, but they were playing violins It was lovely to see them, because they were wearing smoking jackets, and little hats.

Also in Hamilton Road were the Coopers, who 'had a lovely fruit and vegetable shop in the market', as recalled by Betty Grant. The Kuhns, coming to Victoria Road in 1938 as refugees, one of the few academic families in the roads at this stage, were surrounded by 'town' people, including Mr Lindsey of the long-established Oxford butchering family on one side, and Mr Thornton of Thornton's bookshop in Broad Street at no. 34.

Opposite lived somebody, he and his family was called Salter. He had something to do with the boats. On the other side of the Lindseys, was Mr Walker and his family. He had a plumbing business. Then next to us there was a plot [which] belonged to Mr Alden. Alden was the butcher in the market.

These connections could be useful, as indicated by Mariele's story of wartime.

The potatoes next door were fed by the butcher's blood from the slaughterhouse, so his potatoes were bigger than ours! When we had chickens – I kept twelve Rhode Island Reds, I hated them! – when one of the chickens was ailing, or stopped laying, Mr Lindsey, next door, took it to his butcher's shop. Apparently, among the people in the market, there was a certain amount of black market. Sometimes he would bring us a banana or something.

Victoria Road filled up in the interwar period, when many houses accessible to the lower tiers of the middle class were built, with a particularly high concentration of 'town' business people, many of whom were still there after the war. In addition to those mentioned already, Betty Marshall and John Rowe between them recall the Gees, of the established market gardening business at 63 Banbury Road (now Gee's restaurant); Mr Parker, with a fishmonger's shop in the market (he became mayor of Oxford); Mr Bing, co-owner of Dobson & Bing's furniture shop in St Giles; Mr King of Zacharias, a clothes shop in Ship Street; Miss Woodward, who had a tea and cake shop in Oakthorpe Road; and the Horns, with long-established South Parade business activities; as well as a tailor, two jeweller/watchmakers, a barber, an optician, a chiropodist, a piano-tuner, three bank employees, an insurance company employee, two sales reps, employees of Pressed Steel and Morris Motors, an architect, two teachers and two civil servants.

Yvonne Hands remembers some similar neighbours when she came as a young academic wife to 43 Portland Road in 1956.

There was Argyle, the fish people, lived at the very top of the road. We paid £2,000 for our house, and we bought it from Parker, the fishmonger in the market. So there was a mix, on the whole.

Mary Tregear arrived in the 1960s when more academics were beginning to move in.

There was much more a feeling of a village. There were quite a number of people whose families had always lived here, and who were sort of residents of this area, and didn't have anything to do with the University, didn't have anything to do with anything but their own shops or their business in town.

Spinsters and widows

From the early days of the roads there were a large number of women listed as householders. They might be widows, perhaps letting out rooms, or spinsters living on a small private income. Some were unmarried daughters who inherited the houses they had grown up in, like those mentioned in the next chapter, who worked for a living. 25 Portland Road, for instance, first owned by Mrs Goodman (the wife of the owner of no.27), was lived in from 1918 to 1951 by Miss Hilda Bellairs with her maid, and from 1951 until 1967 by a widow, Mrs Mellanby. Miss George of 10 Lonsdale Road, whose father had worked at Elliston's department store, is remembered by Margaret Willis.

She was born, brought up and died in that house. She taught domestic science at Milham Ford and played strenuous tennis. She kept the house beautifully and she had a real gift for plants.

Old ladies are recurrently remembered as neighbours or previous owners of houses. The Thompsons in Lonsdale Road bought their house in 1980 from a Miss Arnold.

A little old, rather fragile lady. She had lived in the house, with her parents, from quite an early age – possibly all her life. And our neighbours in the other half of the house bought their house about a year after us, from a Miss Walker, who told us that she had actually moved into the house when it was brand new, in 1908, as a young girl.

Lonsdale and Portland Roads seem perhaps to have had a higher gentility quotient than the more northerly roads. Martine Honoré, moving into the far end of Lonsdale Road, beyond King's Cross Road, with her husband and two small children in 1953 found herself surrounded by people from another era.

They were mostly elderly – in fact I think the only noise in Lonsdale Road was due to us. There was a number of ladies, widows, retired from India, who used to cross the road at four o'clock with gloves and hats, to have tea with each other, and talk of the time when their boys used to prepare the tea trays and so on. It was another world, the Raj and so on.

Two elderly spinsters lived together across the road, and there were two unmarried sisters living next door to their widower brother in another pair of houses.

[They were] absolutely delightful, just out of a Jane Austen book, and liked children, were very friendly.

A generation later the Berrys found themselves youngsters in the road after they bought their house in Hamilton Road in 1975 from Mrs Loring, an elderly widow.

Poppy Day in Portland Road, 1961, a photo from the album of Delia Hill, who lived at no.43 for many years. (D. Hill)

In those days, the neighbourhood was very different, because there were many elderly ladies, including Mrs Maynard, who had a lot of connections among the clergy. So there were lots of old ladies to admire the babies in the pram and all that kind of thing.

Elizabeth Johnston, who lived opposite, remembered Kay and Margaret Wood-ward at 2 Victoria Road, widely known as 'the Red Cross Ladies' (p.198f).

They sat behind lace curtains, so you couldn't really see them, but they saw everything that went on, and we used to wave to the lace curtains, even though you couldn't see, when we went out, and the curtains would part, and a hand would appear, and they would wave back. They were very good, because they could tell you who had called while you were out, or anything like that. They were both in the Red Cross, and had marvellous uniforms, and when they collected for the Red Cross, they appeared in all their glory. And Margaret, the younger one, had been a cook, a chef, and she had had a cake shop during the war, and Kay had looked after children, and they were both very much sought after as baby-sitters.

Many of these single women worked or took in lodgers. Miss Eugenie Knight, for instance, who had been a teacher, also took student lodgers in 91 Victoria Road while she devoted herself to running an animal hospice in the garage and garden until the early

1970s. Margaret Willis mentions two neighbours from when she first lived in Lonsdale Road in 1954–67.

> There was a little lady in blue, Miss Thornton, who lived a few doors from us. And then there was Cicely Davies. She'd certainly taught at the High School, and I think she had taught at Headington School, and she gave up both those jobs when her elderly mother came to live with her. [Her mother] had died a little while before we came and she then taught for Beechlawn Tutorial College, and had the pupils coming to her house. She was a very very nice woman, a great friend of ours till the end of her life.

It was very much assumed that single women would take on a carer's role when necessary. Peter Clarke remembers Mary Harrison, who lived with her brother (see p.76f).

> Her last years, last nine or ten years of her life, Tom became very introverted, and wouldn't go out and she had to take care of him, and she was very active and that really took away a lot of the pleasure in life, I think. She was glad when Tom went eventually. He got on her nerves eventually, very badly. And she was so patient, it was unbelievable! There weren't so many Old People's Homes, I don't think, in those days.

Sylvia Steward (p.77) lived in 6 Portland Road, having returned from missionary work in Canada to good works here. She let rooms, as Dorothea Pelham remembers.

> There were three old ladies upstairs, it was like an Old People's Home in a way! And they just sat there, they didn't do anything. I mean, she just made sure that they got their food and things, and their relatives came and helped them.

Sylvia was the daughter of an Indian civil servant: the British Empire and service overseas echo through the life stories of many residents, and there have been several retired missionaries in the roads. Margaret Clarke for instance remembers Miss Bridge's companion-lodger in Hamilton Road.

> A Miss or Mrs Fox – who had, I think, been a missionary. She was terribly evangelically minded. I mean, she was always very friendly, but I can't say I knew her, except that in her side garden, she let Canon Burrough grow tobacco for his pipe!

Refugees and other incomers

The Second World War precipitated a mixing in of new kinds of people. In the late 1930s the roads became home to a notable number of refugees from Hitler's Germany, as intellectuals found a shelter at the University: see p.77ff for more on these distinguished people. The houses here were cheaper than in the North Oxford area favoured by mainstream academics at the time, and more importantly many were available to rent. Perhaps the first to arrive were Frank and Arne Burchardt – not Jewish, but politically outspoken – who came to   The Burchardt family, c.1947. (Elsie Hill)

Günther Hill after he joined the British army in 1940. (Elsie Hill)

41 Portland Road, which they rented from Miss Strange at no. 51. Next door at no. 39 (rented from the Geekies at no. 37) were their friends the Walzers. Elsie Hill, the second wife of Günther Hill, tells his family's story. Günther was married to Agnes, daughter of the well-known publisher, art collector and trotting horse enthusiast Bruno Cassirer. The family escaped to live with the Cassirers' other daughter Sofie, who was married to the scholar Richard Walzer.

The two old people, Richard and Sofie, Günther when he was there, and Agnes, and Thomas and Dorothea (their two children) all lived at no. 39 Portland Road, which had only three bedrooms, and there they housed a lot of remarkable pictures which belonged to Bruno, and Günther's grand piano. He said he would sleep on it, or he would sleep under it, but he wouldn't sell it! Now, as they had come from a huge house in Berlin, it's difficult to imagine how they all managed, but they did. But then

Bruno never reconciled himself to having been pushed out of his beloved Fatherland, for which he had fought in 1914–18, and he died, rather suddenly, in 1941. Meantime, Agnes – Günther 's wife – had obtained the tenancy of no. 31, and she moved here with her mother, who died a year later, probably of a broken heart, because she couldn't bear life without her husband.

Richard Walzer (left), Günther Hill (right), with Günther's children Thomas and Dorothy and son-in-law Michael Kauffmann, taken from outside 31 Portland Road, c.1956. (Martin Kauffmann)

Yvonne Hands' neighbour, Mary Callear, remembered the Cassirers and gave a poignant picture of them, so out of place in these cramped suburban surroundings.

Bruno Cassirer was a great chap, apparently, very dashing, very clever, very much part of the Berlin scene of the 20s and 30s. And Mary said he and his wife used to walk up and down Portland Road, desolate, this man who'd been a very big name in the publishing world. I always think of them walking up and down Portland Road, really not knowing what to do with themselves.

Elsie Hill thinks there were no problems with acceptance of these incomers, although several suffered internment early in the war. Her husband did change his name.

His birth name was Günther Hell, and he changed his second name, because people suggested it would be a difficult name for his children at school in England. And because he was in the British Army, he was asked to change his first name, and so he Anglicised it to George, but, in fact, we never ever called him anything except Günther. Certainly the people immediately around were perfectly relaxed and friendly – but then I think that's North Oxford for you, probably. Well, Richard [Walzer] was interned on the Isle of Man, for a period, and so was Frank Burchardt, very briefly – I think his wife managed to get him released very quickly, with the help of the Warden of All Souls.

However Mariele Kuhn recalls an incident concerning the Guttmanns in Lonsdale Road which reflects a jumpiness about enemy aliens.

Their son was interested in watching birds, and he had a little mirror out of the window to see the nest. But people pounced on him, they were so afraid he was giving signals to the Germans. People were paranoid.

Heinrich Kuhn, who had arrived in Oxford in 1933, was not interned. The Kuhns settled easily into Victoria Road in 1938.

We had no money to buy, we rented it. Yes, it was something like £100 a year. But finally, we could buy it. We had very nice neighbours [the Lindseys], very charming family. They were Congregationalists, really good Christians, and made us very welcome. In Germany, nearly all the higher schools learnt French and English. That was just accepted. When war broke out, we never spoke German, it was difficult enough to have a foreign name, and so we didn't want any complications for our children. There was no prejudice, in fact. Well, it was the Cutteslowe boys who somehow heard, 'You are the Nazi boy'. Somebody must have told them that we'd come from Germany. They wanted to strip [my son] of his pants, and he cried. So we had a certain amount of fight with the Cutteslowe boys! We had an apple tree, so they tried to pick our apples, so I asked the head leader in. I said, 'How would you like it if we went into your mother's garden, and took her apples?' He departed with a biscuit or chocolate! So that was all right. I made friends in Victoria Road, it was easy.

Above: Mariele Kuhn and her sons in the garden of 25 Victoria Road, 1939.

Below: The Kuhns' house, 25 Victoria Road, c.1939. (Mariele Kuhn)

People were friendly. I mean, one knew each other. They were fire-watching together, the husbands, and we were exchanging vegetables.

The Kuhns were hospitable to other refugees who were in need.

We had a lot of people from London, just knocking at the door, could we take them in for a night, just to sleep. So they slept on the couch or something. One was Laura Bierwald, she came from a good family, a young girl of about 19, and so she helped me with the children.

Summertown was clearly considered sufficiently countrified to have plenty of evacuees billeted in the roads during the war (p.97f). Afterwards Margaret Willis remembers a family of orphans living in 58 Lonsdale Road.

They were not related to each other, but I think they had been evacuees, and they'd all been, as it were, unclaimed at the end of the war. There were about a dozen of them. And a Trust had bought the house and put them in, in the care of a Miss Doris Sayer, who I think must have been a teacher or something, who looked after them. And she ran this household of several boys and girls, mostly from the kitchen on the ground floor. That was their family. And I believe that they still meet and regard one another as brothers and sisters.

After the war more people from varied backgrounds began to find homes here. John Marsh recalls the Fodors in Hamilton Road.

I think they were Hungarian, came over at the time of the Rising. He worked in a hospital, as a technician in the operating theatres. We never discovered where she came from, but she was somewhere in Middle Europe. We often wondered whether she'd had a bad time, perhaps been in some concentration camp or what, because she was a restless creature.

Adolph Kurtz, a Lutheran pastor, came to 24 Hamilton Road in the mid 1950s, and Yvonne Hands remembers the Peetzs, German Quakers, in Portland Road.

They were an elderly couple, they'd both been missionaries in Madagascar, with no children.

Beryl Phillips of Lonsdale Road was part of an extended family which came here from Wales before and after the Second World War.

My Aunty Mary, her husband was a railway man and he came to Oxford to work, and so I came to Oxford then [in 1940] and lived here. I always wanted to leave Wales really. Village life is lovely of course, but everybody knows everything about everybody. It can be a bit overpowering. I don't know whether that was the real reason, but anyhow I wanted to spread my wings.

They lived first in Hobson Road (then Albert Road) and then in Hamilton Road, where they later built another house too. After returning home for a few years Beryl came back after the war and married her husband, who had followed her from Wales, in 1948. Her sister and her husband decided to come here too, followed by her parents.

Of course my mother said if my sister was coming, and I was here, and my aunt and uncle were here, she wasn't going to stay in Wales! So my mother and father came up as well.

They were followed by another aunt and her husband, and an orphaned cousin. Until recently Beryl had cousins in both Lonsdale Road and Hamilton Road.

Everybody was very happy up here, they loved it. Being together. They wouldn't have come to Oxford, moved away from Wales, without each other.

Mary Tregear on the other hand was born in 1924 in China where her parents worked for the Methodist Missionary Society. She went back there as a young adult.

I was teaching art in a girls' school in China, for a while. And then, gradually, taught English in the University where my father was teaching. And got stuck by the revolution there. This is the Mao revolution. It was difficult to get a visa to leave, and so I had three years instead of two. It was very interesting!

She came here to work at the Ashmolean Museum, living in Victoria Road, and was joined by her parents in 1963, when they bought a house together in Portland Road.

So Summertown was sort of my place, really, from then on. I think most people who've been abroad in a somewhat unsettled country, do find a sort of fragmentation. Then when you come here, and there's absolutely nothing in the way of upsets going on – it just seemed extraordinarily settled and rather intriguing.

Class issues

Beryl Phillips lived for some time in Headington, but she used to visit relations in Summertown regularly.

I used to notice if I came on the bus from Headington, when people got out in the city centre, in Cornmarket another lot of people came in and they were entirely different. The accent changed, the way of speaking. I always found that North Oxford people spoke very loudly. This plummy accent 'Oh ectually, oh my dear, ectually ...' It was just like a different race of people!

While the 'North Oxford' element was well diluted in these roads, the houses were still more expensive than they would be in other parts of Oxford. The Phillips sold their house in a more working-class area in Headington for around £2500 and bought 67 Lonsdale Road in 1968 for a good price (£5000) because it had been let to students and was in poor condition. Coming here with two teenage boys she found lots of spinster ladies and few children, but encountered no snobbishness.

Sydney Denton gives a perspective from his working-class background on these recognisably middle-class roads after the war.

The women of Summertown – even in those days, it was a bit prim and proper. It was North Oxford still. You were middle-class if you made Victoria or Hamilton Road, not very many working chaps could afford a mortgage of that size. Let's take an average semi-detached house on an estate in and around Oxford, in '58, '59, '60. 1960, an average semi-detached house, £3,000, right? If you were talking Victoria Road, you would say £4,500. Well, you couldn't find the difference on a mortgage, a working-class man couldn't, impossible. So they would be management people, they might be a lesser employee of the University. So Summertown, I thought it was really posh.

Kate Jones Finer bought 48 Lonsdale Road in 1977 from the kind of person Sydney Denton may have meant, an old lady who had lived there all her life.

Very upright sort of lady. Very respectable. A sort of person who would have been on some Church Committee, or voluntary work.

Helen Holland's relations in 22 Portland Road were perhaps typical of the upper end of residents in the roads. Her grandmother Frances Stewart lived there with her unmarried daughter Elizabeth, and a maid (p.160), from 1954.

She was rather a fierce old lady, and I have very few memories of her, because there was a rift in the family. She objected strongly to my father – her younger son – having married my mother [Helen's mother was Jamaican, Roman Catholic, older than her father *and* divorced]. My Aunt Elizabeth, who carried on, as it were, the

Above: Frances Stewart (with dog), and her daughter Elizabeth on her left, at a tea party in the early 1950s. The summer house sat in the garden at 22 Portland Road for more than 40 years. (Helen Holland)

Right: Elizabeth Stewart at the same occasion. (Helen Holland)

struggle, really refused to countenance my parents' marriage, up until the very end, although they would come and visit her. She'd put them in separate bedrooms!

When [my grandmother] died, Elizabeth took the opportunity to leave her job as a domestic science teacher, here in Oxford, and go out to visit her brother, James, who was working as a Schools Inspector in Tanganyika, and loved it so much, she actually stayed for several years, and was much loved and appreciated for her work there in the various Missions and schools. She was, at heart, a very kind woman, and much appreciated by many of the neighbours, who remember her baking cakes and being very neighbourly, and she, like her mother, was also very devout, both of them regular churchgoers.

James, a much loved uncle, later retired from Africa to live with his sister in Portland Road (p.107). Now Helen lives in the house – she is a counsellor and communication skills trainer, married to a publisher specialising in digitising archives, with five children – exemplifying within one family a characteristic change in the roads.

At the lower end of the class spectrum in the roads were small shopkeepers or skilled workers who would have seen their families as emerging from the working class, like Betty Marshall's parents (her father was earning only 25 shillings a week as a jeweller and watchmaker when they married). They had another couple as lodgers when they moved into 45 Hamilton Road, and took student lodgers from the late 1920s.

My parents let to undergraduates – one at a time, I mean, because, in those days they had to have a separate sitting room and bedroom. They were not allowed to have a bed-sitter, that was absolutely verboten! You charged for the room, and then other things were 'as required'. Mum would always provide a breakfast. She would not provide an evening meal, because we had a midday meal. But I don't know many people that let at all, not these days.

Ted Shirley's parents at 74 Hamilton Road (Joseph was a milkman, his mother had been in service before marriage) also relied on lodgers, who themselves contributed to the social diversity of the roads – Ted remembers Hungarian refugees called Fuchs during the war, and students and others afterwards: one of them was visited by Crown Prince Hussain of Jordan; another was the concert pianist Marion Stein, later the Countess of Harewood. Similarly John and Doris Marsh took lodgers in Hamilton Road from 1954.

We had planned, of course, to have a couple of students, because we couldn't afford on what I was earning then [as a telephone engineer for the Post Office].

The Marshes' immediate neighbours in the 1950s included a postman, a bishop's daughter, a boilerman at the Radiators, the owner of a greengrocery in the market, and a University lecturer in Spanish, well exemplifying the social mix in the roads at the time. And Ted Shirley remembers:

Everyone was very courteous: they greeted each other, doffing caps and so on.

Change from the 1960s

A change in the roads began to be felt as more young professionals and people connected with the University started to move in. There had earlier been only isolated academics here. One of the first seems interestingly to have been 'el-Ghamrawi Sheikh Mohammed Hasanien', a lecturer in Arabic at the University, who appears in the directory at 20 Lonsdale Road for a few years from 1909. Some of the larger houses attracted academics, like the historian David Ogg, a fellow of New College, who moved into 76 Lonsdale Road before the war. Otherwise it was those in some way on the margins and with less money, like the refugee intellectuals mentioned above, or young University researchers or demonstrators who moved here in the 1940s. Mariele Kuhn mentions the Forteses in Victoria Road in the later 1940s (p.86).

All sorts of interesting people came, there was Meyer Fortes, they were Jewish anthropologists.

Yvonne Hands came in 1956 when her husband was still doing a doctorate and moved on when he got a fellowship.

Anthony got a fellowship, so we moved to Shotover, to quite a big house then, two acres of garden. But, in a way, I was quite sad there, because I missed this community. I'd rather live in a little house surrounded, than in grandeur!

The availablity of houses and rooms to rent continued to diversify the population after the war. Hawkswell Farmhouse was let out at this period, as Dr Harle recalled.

> After World War II, it was rented, I believe [to] a man called Elliott Smith, who was a surgeon here, apparently a very well-known, and, I think, a much loved one. It was known as Elliott Smith's house. Some American once came back here, who had rented it at some point, and the lady had had a child up in the bedroom.

Margaret Willis, then Margaret Helsby, married to a dentist, remembers a lot of renting in Lonsdale Road when she first lived there in 1954–67.

> There were quite a number of people who came as lodgers, renting some of these houses. For a long time, the house next to us, no. 53, was let on an annual basis, to visiting academics. We met a great many delightful people who were here for a year. Very interestingly, since I've been married to Terry, we've met numerous people that he knows, who, at some point, had a room in Lonsdale Road, because there was space there. Lots of people were here for brief periods.

When Mary Tregear came in 1962 the area still felt quite remote from the University.

> There was still a lot of German people, who'd come over at the beginning of the war, they're intellectuals, and settled in Oxford, and had been an enormous addition to Oxford life, and to University work. And they were very much a part of social life when I came, and that was quite interesting. They were people who gave parties and

Lewis, son of Leslie Preston, an architect, in the Lucerne Road river garden on which his father built a house, 1956. Lewis later became an architect himself. (M.Preston)

> soirées and things in the evenings, and I get the impression that that wouldn't have happened because there was a lot of town and gown feeling, I think, still, then.

When Peter Clarke was a student at the University in the mid 1960s Summertown frankly seemed the back of beyond.

> When I was in Oxford, I never thought of coming anywhere near Summertown: that was a sort of way out distant place, dreary little suburb, with nothing in it!

Christine Butler, married to a university mineralogist, felt similarly when she moved into Hamilton Road in 1964.

> I associated it with landlady land, because when we'd first come to Oxford [in 1959] it was very much landlady land. It was heavy, it seemed gloomy. There weren't many young people around. One said 'Good morning' and one made polite conversation but one didn't know their names unless they were married people with children. A slightly forbidding place to live, with these little children, who made a noise. It was very sedate.

Many academics were accommodated in college property closer to the city centre and only came to these roads when they were evicted for some reason, perhaps on retire-

ment, or if college accommodation was not on offer. Family life was still not altogether countenanced by the University: when Bob Williams married his Dutch wife Jelly Büchli in 1952 he was breaking the rules.

My marriage had to remain secret while I was a Junior Research Fellow at first, because you were not supposed to marry when you were a Junior Research Fellow, and so I didn't tell anybody in College for some time.

They eventually moved into an unfurnished Merton College house in Holywell Street. It was after returning from the USA in 1963 that they came to 115 Victoria Road to establish a family home (p. 33f). The roads were by this stage rather run down, as Jelly Williams says.

When my Dutch parents came to visit in 1963 they thought it was the most scruffy road we could possibly live in. And it was, all those falling fences, and nothing uniform, and not properly tended front gardens. Whereas Mrs Kuhn says the front gardens used to be quite well tended.

The scruffiness of the roads continued through the 1970s, when a lot of rented properties and a more transient population had an adverse effect on the general environment. John Herivel remembers Lonsdale Road when he retired here in 1975.

I think almost all these houses seemed to be split up into flats, or a lot of them. There were a lot of people always chopping and changing. In the house [opposite] there was a man who was evidently a motor engineer. He spent a lot of time fixing various cars. He looked as if he was running a small business.

John Marsh says the same thing of Hamilton Road.

Hamilton Road began to rapidly fill up with students. [The house opposite] had a mixed, sort of chequered history of coming and going, and being sold, or divided into flats. That was full of students, because it's got about eight rooms.

Dorothea Pelham recalls Miss Steward's problems with letting out the second house she owned in Portland Road.

There was always hassle, because she could never get a good person to stay there. And it did get very grubby from people not looking after it.

Peter Clarke found squatters in his house, 69 Lonsdale Road, when he and his wife returned from Africa in 1978.

The original people we'd rented it to just ran away, and left it with this group, and so we had about six people in there. Stamping cigarettes out on the carpet, the lot. Couldn't get them out. I went to the Local Authority, and they said, 'Oh well, they've got to have somewhere to live, you know.' And I said, 'Yes, but my son's only one, and he's got nowhere to live. And I've had no rent since January.' I can remember the lady I was talking to, she was very kind of insistent that they had rights and I didn't, because they were there. That's what it was like in those days. And the dining room was painted black! It was really bad.

John Marsh, who had problems himself with student neighbours in Hamilton Road (p.215) explains how a change in the law in favour of tenants actually improved the neighbourhood, together with a general move back to living in town.

A law was passed, guaranteeing people the same rights [in unfurnished accommodation] as those in furnished rented accommodation. This led to a panic selling by landlords who were wondering whether they'd get drop-outs in, students and so on. So things then sort of rapidly improved again. And then there was a spell where the petrol went up very dramatically. Before that, a lot of people had been moving out into the country, and they all started coming back in again. And then the road became extremely popular again.

Sam Clarke's story of how they came to Victoria Road in 1986 after his wife Ali became pregnant with twins is typical. Sam was working at Oxfam in Summertown.

We were living in South Leigh and I cycled into work every morning – a 9 mile ride. It was quite an isolated little village with really no facilities at all. Ali decided there was no way that while she was nursing the babies did she want to be stuck out there and particularly she did not want me to be away from home any more than was strictly necessary. At the drop of a hat we abandoned this little rural idyll and moved to Southdale Road to the first house we could find. It was a house that neither of us liked at all and we stayed there 18months/ two years until we found something much nicer and even closer to Oxfam, which was this house. And we've been very delighted with that decision.

Academics and professionals: mobility and diversity

The number of academics and professionals in the roads grew as the University and hospitals and so on expanded and it became harder for those on such salaries to afford houses in the more sought-after areas of Oxford, or to live outside the city. Jean Robinson and her husband were part of a wave of young academics who started to move in in the late 1960s.

When we first came, it was young academics, not even older academics, and there weren't, so far as I knew, any doctors or lawyers.

A surprising number of the people who came to live in these roads, even if not academics, made their first connections with Oxford as students at the University (p.124ff) and have stayed or returned as a result. Since then the number of residents in some way connected with the University has increased steadily – until Geoffrey Paine, a 'native' of the roads, can say:

It's always been a funny neighbourhood. There are an awful lot of people live here that aren't in the real world! Lots of University people, for one thing!

Peter Thompson's comment rather supports this. He had a busy life as a civil engineer.

If I was asked, at a party, what I did for a living, and I said, 'I'm an engineer', people would immediately assume what I meant was that I worked in the Engineering Department of the University, because it seemed to be inconceivable to anybody around Summertown that anybody actually worked in the real world as an engineer.

In the 1970s there was considerable mobility alongside a settling in: some families passed through on their way to better things; others decided it suited them and began to improve their houses as they became more prosperous; some older residents just stayed as they were. Peter Clarke describes Lonsdale Road at the time.

People like the Flemmings went on to Park Town. It was considered a stepping stone for Park Town, I suppose, for the upwardly mobile and ambitious. And then there were those who thought, 'Well, this is my final resting place', you know. So it was mixed. It had this smattering of different kinds of people, mostly professional people. Quite a lot of economists. Not many from overseas.

In the decades after the war obviously 'different' people were indeed rare in the roads, and racist attitudes were still embedded in some quarters. Helen Holland (b.1945) only occasionally visited her grandmother Frances Stewart in Portland Road, because of her grandmother's disapproval of her Jamaican mother (p.46).

According to our nanny, who brought us down to visit, she came into the bathroom when we were being washed, and looked at us in the bath – my little sister and me – and said, 'How sad to think I shall never have little pink grandchildren', because we were sort of a dusky colour. But that was the way it was in those days. The same nanny can remember taking Robin and me into Sloane Square Gardens, where we were perfectly allowed to be – my parents had a key to the gardens – and somebody saying, 'Coloured children are not allowed in these gardens. Take those children out of here.'

Christine Butler reports an instance of absurd racism from an old-fashioned neighbour in Hamilton Road in the late 1970s.

She was very formal and I remember her saying to me one day, I suppose after the Esiris had come and Salma was living here as well, 'Awful lot of blacks in the road, aren't there'! And the only two families that were non-white were the most upper-crust sort of people you could imagine! There was Esiri who was regal, he came of a very distinguished Nigerian family. Salma had been an undergraduate when I was an undergraduate at Cambridge – after Partition her father became the High Comissioner for Pakistan. Salma's sister was married to the then Crown Prince of Jordan, and went to Princess Anne's wedding, and we watched her on the television! I can remember one night this cavalcade of cars came with this aristocratic sister to visit Salma. We had our few moments of excitement and regality!

Greta Guy speaks warmly of the Esiris who lived next door in Hamilton Road. Dr Margaret (now Professor) Esiri had met her husband, the Nigerian surgeon Prince Esiri, when they were both studying medicine at Oxford. He was a memorable figure in the roads, always immaculately dressed.

They were very nice people. As a matter of fact, it would be difficult to get anyone as good as them, really. Dr Esiri was really good, because she saved my life, because I was ill, and I didn't know – I'd ulcer. Prince Esiri he worked at Stoke Mandeville. He used to go around with the buttonhole. I was seeing [a friend] out, and Dr Esiri stopped and said something to me, and she said, 'Oh, you've been to a wedding!' I tried to shut her up! And then he went. 'Look', I said, 'he had these delivered every day'.

With the influx of young academics came more children. Kate Jones, who taught at Birmingham University, came with her older husband Sam Finer, Professor of Politics, to 48 Lonsdale Road in 1977 and comments on this.

It was just beginning to be families who either had small children, or were about to. Next door, he was a professor in the Open University – Government – and they had three or four, and just as they more or less grew up, got to sort of mid-teens, they moved out, and the Bacons moved in. Sam said to me, in despair – not really in despair, they were nice neighbours – he said, 'It's all going to happen again, isn't it!' And, sure enough, they had four! And then they moved out when the youngest was 15.

At the same time the roads also became popular with academics nearing retirement. Joan Crow, for instance, a fellow of Lady Margaret Hall, moved to Victoria Road in 1980 after her husband's retirement from Oriel College, and they spent the rest of their lives here.

Verity and Tim Peto, a solicitor and a doctor, with their young family, 1986. They moved to their Lonsdale Road house in 1978. (V. Peto)

While a few people, like those featured in the next chapter, are still living in the houses they grew up in and inherited from their parents, this kind of permanency has become uncommon. Holly Kilpatrick (then Peebles), came to Lucerne Road in 1980 with her solicitor husband Alex.

This is not an area where you meet many people who were born and bred here, who have lived here for generations. Since I moved here, I've only made three friends who are Oxford girls. Maybe because I moved here at a time when we were late twenties/early thirties, and that's the time when people are still going up a career ladder. Maybe I was more unusual, staying. But certainly there's very few people I'm friendly with now who I met when I first came.

Joan Crow, a fellow of Lady Margaret Hall, who moved to Victoria Road in 1980. (J. Cunningham)

Verity Peto, a solicitor married to a doctor, who came in 1978, seconds this.

This is our children's experience with school friends, too. Quite a lot, especially at primary school age, are the children of academics who come for only a year, and move away again. It's certainly the case that not many people live here because they had parents who lived in Oxford. It's quite a shifting population here, I do think that. I'm rather surprised to find that I'm one of the people who has lived longest in this neighbourhood, out of all my acquaintance.

Other social changes have led to less stability in general. Whereas people were once left single by the death of a partner, the cause is commonly now the breakdown of relationships. Given the size of the houses, a surprisingly large number of people in the roads are living by themselves. This began to be more common in the 1970s and 80s, as Jean Robinson remarks.

The thing that did change around us, both immediately and in the larger circle, was marriages going down like ninepins, one after the other. It wasn't just them, it was something that happened all round, in respectable sort of families that seemed to have, as far as one could see, everything, and reasonable relationships, although one never knows what goes on inside. But it really affected one's perceptions of society and solidity, and what was stable, what was reliable, what could be depended on, what mattered and so on.

Peter Clarke reports a question from his son.

Andrew once said to me, 'I'm about the only one in my class whose parents haven't split up yet. When are you going to split up?'

He and his wife did later separate. Peter opted to stay in the house and then took lodgers.

I had lots of students – Japanese, Chinese, all sorts – because my mortgage increased massively when I was separated, and I had all that space, and I thought I might as well use it. I didn't find it so convenient, because you lose the use of your own house somewhat, but I did it for about ten years.

With this increased mobility the roads have certainly become more mixed in ethnic background. Professor Leszek Kolakowski and his wife, expelled from Poland in 1968, exemplify this general change. They came to Hamilton Road in 1976: they now have a Serbian married to an Englishman next door in a house where a retired policeman used to live.

On the other side, there was an elderly couple, very pleasant people – she was an anthropologist. They died in short distance from one another. And then the house was bought by a couple who are Iranians, but he's working at the University.

The roots of such diversity have been there for some time, even if it has recently become more obvious, as Martin Biddle and his Danish wife Birthe Kjølbe discovered when they gave a neighbourhood party in Hamilton Road in 1982.

It was very cosmopolitan: Martin was not the only English person there, but he was in a very small minority. and this has continued to be a characteristic of the road, and people have told us it was always so, at least back into the 1940s.

Peter Clarke recently moved to Hawkswell Gardens from Lonsdale Road, and comments on the diversity of the area now.

[Hawkswell Gardens] looks a very unexciting and uneventful place, but, in fact, there are quite a lot of people here that are doing all sorts of different things, from all sorts of backgrounds and countries and cultures: so you've got a Lebanese, you've got Indian – at least two Indian families. And then you've got some indigenous British people around, and you've got a Belgian lady – she was the first one, I think, to live in this close, Bertha Hills – she married an English chap. Lonsdale Road seems to me to be much more ethnically diverse now. You kind of lift the cover off, and you'll find a lot of diversity, whereas somebody just walking through for the first time, would assume, 'Oh, it's suburban British, white, Caucasian ... people all doing the same thing, professional.' But it's not like that, it's much more diverse and varied now. Chinese, Asian, Middle Eastern, just walking down the road, you hear much more in the way of foreign languages spoken.

Rising house prices and gentrification

Steeply rising house prices over the last decade or so reflect a changing demography as Summertown has become a particularly desirable suburb. Peter Clarke has seen this happening, noticing a large number of doctors in Lonsdale Road now.

A lot of the people who were there, people who had retired, people whose parents had handed on the house to them, who were not necessarily professional people, a lot of that's gone now, and I think most people in there are professional people now. I think it's become, in that sense, more gentrified. It's very solidly professional. And the professions are some of the high professions.

Donald Norwood, Minister at the United Reformed Church, who lived at 100 Victoria Road from 1974 to 1995, describes three sorts of people in the road then: academics, architects, and people working in a variety of town jobs – banks, motor works and so on. He liked the friendly blend. Jelly Williams looks back over 40 years in Victoria Road and laments the recent shift in social mix.

What was nice about Victoria Road, and is less so now, is there was a better social mixture. There was the fireman who has just died, Mr Faulkner, and a few houses away – well he had a good job actually – it was the head butcher of Sainsbury's, and we became friendly with them. It was a very very happy place in that way. The road is less mixed than it was. It has mixed more upwards. We have commuters to London who have bought the newly built houses which academic people can't afford, let alone people who don't have good salaries, and I think it's a loss. I think Victoria Road looks a little better, less scruffy.

Peter Clarke himself chose to live here years ago despite having an academic job in London. His wife and small son were established here.

The price of houses in London was much higher than in Oxford at the time, so to give up the house on Lonsdale Road and move to London, to live in a suburb, say an hour on the Underground from King's, didn't make any sense. For an hour extra, in terms of time commuting, I had the quality of life here.

Commuters now are associated with high-salaried city jobs, perhaps with two earners in a household, bringing in a level of income not earlier seen in these roads. Philippa Berry comments on this different wealth profile.

In our day, there were lots of young families coming in, lots of pram pushing and buggies and all that. Nowadays it is quite different, because we're getting a lot of more London commuter-type people moving in, because these roads are now extremely expensive to buy into.

Overall the social change has been quite marked over the last quarter century, as Verity Peto sums up.

The area seems to have become gentrified since 1978, when we moved here. The population of these roads, when we moved here – well, certainly Lonsdale Road – was multiple occupancy student flats, and quite a lot of little old ladies who lived in large houses all by themselves. There were very few families. In fact, there was only one other family with children of our children's age, when we first moved here. There were probably some mid-teenage children, who I didn't, at that time, count as children, because they seemed so grown up compared to ours! But there weren't many families, and now it's become a desirable place for people with families to live, where one parent or the other, or both, work in London. People seem to gravitate to Oxford from London, because of the schools and so house prices have really soared through the roof. It's become an inaccessible place unless you happened to have bought a house here, as we did, when it was inexpensive.

A changing mix

The mix of people in these roads is changing, but the notion of a mix remains fundamental to the nature of the community in these roads, and to what many people value about it. A balance between younger and older seems to be maintained in a natural cycle. Betty Marshall, who had grown up with a lot of other children in Victoria Road in the 1920s and 30s, returned to live here in 1985.

When we came back, there seemed to be fewer families. But recently, over the last three or four years, we seem to have had more families move in, so there's a greater age range of children now.

Sir Jack and Elizabeth Johnston in the garden of 5 Victoria Road, 1990. They came in 1978 after a diplomatic career, so that their son could go to the Dragon School, and lived here happily until their recent deaths. (John Johnston)

Families grow and people age: in some roads there is a preponderance now of the middle-aged, as Martin Berry comments of Hamilton Road.

When we moved into the street [in 1975], most of the houses were occupied either by elderly widows or spinsters, or by young couples with young children, and obviously there were other people in the road, but there seemed to be a very high proportion of those two categories of family here. Mrs Loring had lived here, I think, for about 20 years, and we've now been here even longer.

While some older people may be forced out by practicality and economics, finding houses too big and council tax high, those who are financially secure see this as an excellent place for retirement: Margaret Willis's response to the question of whether she will stay is clear.

Oh yes, until the end. Certainly. As long as I can walk up the road to the shops!

Peter Thompson points out its attractions.

It is just such a convenient place to live. I guess the prospects of moving to attractive little country cottages are kind of diminishing. If we were ever to do anything like that, pretty obviously it would only be for a temporary period, because as one gets older, one can't sensibly live in isolated locations.

Maurice Cardiff (1915–2006) represents someone from an upper-middle-class background (p.124f) who chose to downsize to suburban Hamilton Road for exactly this reason. He and his wife of more than 50 years had lived in a beautiful old farmhouse at Little Haseley, friends of the great gardener and decorator Nancy Lancaster at Haseley Court. After Nancy's death, and then the death of his wife, a sense of isolation in a changed village and the problem of car dependence brought Maurice into Oxford in 1998.

So although the roads are becoming more prosperous overall, at the beginning of the 21st century they still accommodate a wide range of people in what seems a notably tolerant mixed middle-class community. University connections have certainly brought increased variety, and have perhaps contributed to a generally unmaterialistic ethos, appreciated by many who live here. Jean Robinson noticed this when she moved here in the later 1960s.

> What I liked was it wasn't like the stockbroker belt, where people dressed up, or cared about how the house looked, or possessions, or having a posh car, or any of the things I didn't like. I'd noticed, when we'd lived in Sheffield, there was great emphasis on looking right, and things of appearance, which just didn't fit in with my way of seeing the world. [Here] people, you eventually realised, actually had a lot of money, but didn't flaunt wealth. I think the world's changed a bit and moved on since then, but certainly in academic society, that was the ethos, and it was egalitarian in that sense. And although there were, and are, lots of things about the Oxford life which irritate me, there were, nevertheless, values which I came to appreciate.

Peter Clarke agrees that there is little competitive awareness of status.

> I think we're sufficiently distant, in our minds, from the University, not to over-rate its importance. There is a steadiness about what people think, and a kind of informed view of the world, that's fairly unusual I would have thought. There's very little striving after so-called status. I think there'd be many other roads and suburbs in which people would be beavering away as if it were the first time ever that this opportunity had come for them, to move on, to move up, to acquire, to achieve status, whereas [in these roads], there's a lot of taken-for-grantedness about all of that. No one's kind of competing with their neighbours, as far as I'm aware. Money doesn't dictate very much about behaviour, I don't think.

Jean Robinson, who is of working-class background, is honest about the appeal of the middle-class environment she finds here.

> When I was working at the Women's Refuge, and having the daily impact of the absolute messiness of people's lives, and the feeling that this was almost expanding and taking over society, as this kind of breakdown and so on became more common, I used to walk home, get off the bus, turn into Lonsdale Road, and say, 'Thank God I live in a middle-class area', you know, to be somewhere quiet, where you were surrounded by people with civilised values, and even if they hated your guts, there would be a fairly civilised dialogue!

3   Born and Bred

We are town, rather than gown, as you gather!

Gwynneth Twining

In this chapter we focus on the lives of several people who have had a particularly long connection with this area, and who typify in many ways the pattern of life of those who lived here in the earlier part of the 20th century. Some of these narratives touch on wartime in Oxford.

Margaret and Gwynneth Twining (b.1915, 1920)

The family memories of the Twining sisters, Margaret and Gwynneth, carry us back to the earliest times of these roads. Francis Twining (1848–1929) 'born in a yard off St Aldate's', was the son of a stonemason who was killed by a train in 1858. In the census of 1861 Francis, the youngest of four children, was already out of school at 13 and working as a 'grocer's boy'. He was apprenticed to the quality grocer Grimbly Hughes in the Cornmarket, a shop fondly remembered by many (demolished in 1961). Owen Grimbly seems to have spotted the young man's ability: he probably helped Twining set up on his own in 1870, after his marriage to Elizabeth Ann Smith. Their family grew along with the business. Gwynneth gives a picture of her grandfather.

Grimbly was very good to him, I think. He had a very good business brain, did grandfather. He made a real go of the shop, and in no time at all he seemed to have a branch here and a branch there. He ended up with branches all over the place, and had a main shop in Cornmarket. He lived in St Ebbe's, above the shop. And they had eight children: two of them died in infancy, and the others all survived and flourished. He did all sorts of wheeling and dealing. He would buy property and then sell it the next day at a great profit, and things like this.

The move to Summertown House around 1890 was a confirmation of Twining's hard-earned status.

Francis Twining's shop at 53 Cornmarket, 1906. (M. & G. Twining)

Grandfather was on the Council, and he was a Councillor and then an Alderman. He was Sheriff in 1885, and then he became Mayor in 1905. He lived in style up in that house, I imagine, with gardeners and pony and cart and everything else. Then a motor car, fairly early on.

Though their grandparents lived nearby, the children did not have a close relationship with them, at least in the case of Gwynneth, the youngest.

I never remember going there for a meal. I don't even remember having tea or anything there. My eldest sister, Betty, and my brother John, they both used to go. They were older, of course, and they used to go to parties there. We used to go and visit Grandfather, and he used to say to me, 'And who's the best little girl in Oxford, then?' If I said, 'Yes', he gave me sixpence. Riches to me in those days! Very distant. I think he was a nice enough man. We never had presents from them. Never.

Francis and Elizabeth Twining at Summertown House on the occasion of their golden wedding anniversary in 1920. (M. & G. Twining)

Francis Twining's wife Elizabeth (1841–1927) was some years older than him. She had clearly been important in the establishment of the business, but Gwynneth remembers her only as an invalid.

Grandmother Twining was rather a poor thing. She apparently had an accident in Wales, at some time, and hurt her leg badly, probably broke it and it didn't heal. Kicked by a horse, was the family story. She was a very dim figure, I never really knew her. I was only four when she died. Margaret remembers Grandmother always had to have the newspapers taken to her in the morning room, and there she would sit and sew them all up the middle, so that they didn't get scattered!

Francis Twining remained fit and active, and liked travelling.

He had a housekeeper who looked after Grandmother a good deal. But then he used to go off on quite adventurous holidays: he took Father a couple of times. They went to Italy in 1907. And then in 1911, Father went to Russia with his father and mother, and the housekeeper. They went to St Petersburg.

Margaret's and Gwynneth's father Francis (b.1879), known as Francis Whitlock Twining to differentiate him, was the youngest son to go into the family business, becoming a partner of what was then Twining Bros in 1907, along with his older brothers Ernest (b.1871) and Gilbert (b.1876), who had become partners on their marriages. Francis Junior managed the Twining's shop at 294 Banbury Road, adjacent to the Congregational Church, and opened in 1902 as the fifth branch of the business.

> [It was] a class family grocer's you don't see the like of these days. He had this shop in Summertown, purpose-built. It was built by the same firm that built the Congregational Church, Kingerlee's. And Grandfather had the design put on the top, with the fruit, and his initials are in the centre – FT.

In 1899 and 1900 respectively Ernest and Gilbert had married two sisters, Ellen and Julia Clark, daughters of a prosperous butcher who lived in the big house 'West Grove' in Hernes Road. The couples lived next door to each other at 23&25 Thorncliffe Road, before moving into the first two houses to be finished in Lonsdale Road, nos 2&4, in 1902. Meanwhile the Twinings' only daughter Lottie married her sister-in-laws' brother Charles in 1901, and moved into the old Hawkswell Farmhouse, which Francis Twining had newly acquired. Gwynneth has a vivid child's memory of a rather oppressive house.

> She was a very poor old thing. She married Clark, who was a butcher. He made sausages which were quite famous in the market. She had some illness which we have never really come to know what it was, and she couldn't walk very much. She was a funny old lady. And that house was very dark, and rather sort of stuffy and we used to have to go down and visit her, which we didn't like very much! Had to play halma with her.

Members of the Twining family at their Lucerne Road river garden, c.1912. Gilbert and Julie Twining are on the left and Nell and Ernest on the right. (M. & G. Twining)

In 1907 Francis Whitlock Twining married Dorothy Diddams, the daughter of an ex-butler who became a Keble college servant.

> After [her father] became too old to do too much, he used to go back to the College to carve the joints, because he was a very good carver. They were not very well-off.

This was a good marriage for Dorothy, who had met Francis when he was running the North Parade branch of Twining's. They lived first at 39 Portland Road, then in a bigger semi-detached house, 72 Lonsdale Road. Also living in Lonsdale Road, at no.30 from 1910, was the youngest Twining brother, Sidney, and his wife.

Grandfather set him up in a wine shop in Cornmarket. He went off in the war and he had a scorpion bite and died.

Margaret's and Gwynneth's father was not physically strong but had also been sent abroad later in the First World War.

By 1916 they were a bit pushed for men, so he was sent in, and he was sent to Mesopotamia, and he was only just there a few months and he got heatstroke, and was very ill. When he started to get better, the Army sent him to India, up in the hills, to recuperate. I suppose it was easier than sending him home. He was there until after the end of the war, when he came back. Mother was told he had six months to live. And he lived another 50 years! My early memories of him, he was a poorly man. But he was well looked after, so there you are!

Around 1920 the family moved to a large house on the corner of Victoria Road, as Gwynneth relates.

The story goes that Mother was expecting her youngest child, which was me, Grandfather arrived at the house in Lonsdale Road, and plonked some keys down on the table, and said, 'There you are, there's the keys of your new house', which he had bought for £500, and that was 368 Banbury Road. That's just hearsay. It may not be absolutely true, that.

Although many relatives lived in these roads Gwynneth describes a disconnected family.

I don't ever remember seeing any of Father's family at Christmas, either to go to, or came to us. They all kept to themselves, I suppose! Father had two brothers and a sister, all living within a stone's throw of each other. They were a very funny family, things going on always. We were never invited for tea or anything.

The Twining's house 368 Banbury Road, decked with flags for the coronation of George VI, 1937. (M.&G. Twining)

Margaret thinks there were 'feelings about things', hidden family feuds that they never understood, 'things that weren't discussed' – although their own mother was hospitable. They did see other cousins, the youngest daughters of Owen, the second Twining brother, who had made a hash of a separate grocery business.

Owen was a very poor fish. I don't think he was very bright. Grandfather set him up in the end in Lower Valley Farm in Noke. He died in 1930. His wife ran the farm and brought up seven children. Mother used to have [Joan and Barbara] to stay in the holidays and the four of us in the summer used to go off and play.

'Park View', 368 Banbury Road, was large but chilly.

It was cold. Very cold, draughty place. Great cavernous hall. And then at the back of the hall, going up three storeys, a staircase going round. Very cold it was!

For the children the glory of the house was the garden, which has now been built over.

From the mid 1920s the next house was 25 Victoria Road: before that it was no. 37.

> There was a chicken run and an orchard, and a vegetable garden, and a great big lawn going nearly up to the next old house up there. We had a gardener who came every day, I think, to begin with. Except Sundays. His name was Mr White. Mother was rather fond of gardening. We had visitors once, and I can remember saying to them, 'Well, of course, it's only Mother's garden on a Sunday. It's Mr White's the rest of the time!'

With the family leaving home, Francis decided to build a smaller, modern house and they moved to 80 Hamilton Road in 1937. The Twinings' parents thus lived in all four main roads covered by this project.

Margaret Twining trained as a teacher in Bedford.

> Basically it was very good, but we were treated like schoolgirls! If you had boyfriends you had to have parents' permission to go out with them.

Margaret and Gwynneth with older siblings John and Betty in the large garden of 368 Banbury Road. (M.& G. Twining)

She went abroad, to South Africa, after the war.

> I just wanted to get out of the country and I wanted to go where there were mountains. South Africa was lovely for outdoor life but there wasn't anything old and I missed all the culture here.

She came back in the early 1950s and taught near London before returning to Oxford after her mother had a stroke. She then taught for 20 years at Greycotes. Gwynneth trained as a nurse in Luton and worked for a time at the Slade Hospital for infectious diseases in Headington. Their mother died after many years of immobility in 1966, and their father at the ripe age of 90 in 1970. The sisters stayed on in Hamilton Road until 1998, when they moved into a new flat in the very house they had grown up in (p. 33).

Dorothy Bridge (b.1907)

Our oldest interviewee was Miss Dorothy Bridge, who was born in 1907 in the house her father built in Hamilton Road. She lived there for more than 93 years until a fall forced her to move into a residential home. Her father was another Oxford businessman.

> He came from Bedfordshire. He decided to come to the University Press and take up printing, and he went in partnership with a man in George Street, called Mr Reid, and then bought him out. My mother went for some memorial cards to be printed, that was how they met. I think they should never have married really, they were not suited. My mother was devoted to my brother, but not to me. I think she wanted a boy to start with, and she had a girl!

'Hamilton House' (no. 5) was the first house in Hamilton Road. Mr Bridge had bought several plots, and Dorothy evokes a spacious self-sufficient home (p. 19).

> It was my father's hobby, gardening. We had two huge greenhouses – one for the

plants, the other for tomatoes. And we had an allotment across the road, and the three plots next door, that was a field in my young days, and my brother and I used to play cricket on there. We never bought a vegetable! I thought it was terrible when the days came when we had to buy a potato! As soon as my father died, we had all the orchard cut down. We couldn't cope with the fruit, we were paying to have the plums picked, and giving them all away, so we had them all cut down and all made into a lawn.

Dorothy's memories reach back before the First World War. Before the roads were properly metalled dust was a problem.

They used to come down the road with a dustcart, and pick up the dust. Then another day they'd come down with a water cart, and all the water would come out the back. I think the dustcart came about twice a week. I remember when trams started, because we used to have horse trams. Then they had a thing connected to a wire. Didn't go past South Parade. ... I used to hate seeing the soldiers march along Banbury Road. I used to think it was horrible. I remember we couldn't get marmalade. We had a huge orchard, masses of plum trees, and my mother and father, one evening, had made plum jam, and my father was counting it, and he said to my mother, 'That's 108 pounds'. So I've hated plum jam all my life!

Deliveries would break up the day at home: Dorothy recalls an outstanding service from the postman, as well as a memorable milkman.

The postman used to wear a uniform – a three-cornered hat and a cape. He came at eight o'clock in the morning, and eleven o'clock, and three o'clock, every day. His name was Mr Worth. [The milkman] had a long beard, which went down to his waist! And he had a big can of milk, and used to dip a thing in. I was afraid that his beard would go in the milk! His name was Mr Pharoah.

After leaving school Dorothy went to work at 17 for Morrell, Peel & Gamlen, a firm of solicitors at 1 St Giles, at £1 a week. The understanding was that if she kept the job for six months she would have a man's salary: she never got it, nor a pension, though she took over a crucial role in handling the firm's invoicing and worked there, highly respected, into the 1970s. She was clear that she never wanted to marry.

I worked there all my life. I loved being a secretary. I loved shorthand. I mean, they didn't have computers in those days, you had to take down everything by shorthand. I'd hate housework, I'd hate cooking! I'd be no good. I liked my work.

Dorothy White (1915–2004)

Dorothy White was born in the next oldest house in Hamilton Road, no.13. Her father, who was a carpet-buyer at the department store Elliston & Cavell (now Debenham's), died during the First World War when Dorothy was two. The family was typical of those left in difficult circumstances at this period by the death of a breadwinner.

Our father died in 1917. Pneumonia. He caught trench fever from somebody who came back from the war, and never got over it. And then for six years Mother let the house, because she didn't feel she could stay there, and we wandered about from different places. Lodging, and staying with friends. We came back to 13 Hamilton Road in 1923.

Dorothy left Milham Ford School just before she was 16. Her uncle Fred, who lived at 44 Portland Road, had taken over her father's job at Elliston & Cavell and she went to work there too, earning 'Five bob!' – five shillings a week (25p in new money).

Things were a bit hard for Mother, and I started at Elliston & Cavell's. I got a ground training in the business, and then went into our own business, and helped her.

Although Dorothy thought of her mother as 'just sort of ordinary', she was a woman of considerable enterprise: she had set up one of the earliest businesses to be operated in these roads.

She started up a hand-knitting business, and that developed into a bigger enterprise altogether. We had big knitting machines, and she had the original 'Made in Oxford' knitwear. We used to supply Adamson's and Faulds and Sackville Street in London. We actually supplied the pullover for King George VI to go to his boys' camp. [In 1939] Mother died of cancer. I carried on the business for three years, but I then packed it up, because it was no life, and you didn't meet anybody or anything, you're just stuck in there. I took up typing.

Like other spinsters in the roads, Dorothy White found a female companion to share the house when she was left on her own – her immediate next-door neighbour in fact.

There was a friend from next door, Beryl Turner, she came to live with me in '42, because she didn't get on with her mother, and her marriage had gone bust. Then in 1947, her mother and father decided to go abroad and live with their daughter in Nairobi, so their house was going for sale. It was the west house, whereas mine was the east, so we decided to change over – I bought theirs and sold mine.

Dorothy learned to drive at 17 – there was no test. And she was clearly one of the first to create off-street parking.

Someone who'd driven us up to London, said, 'Well, why don't you drive home?' So I did! After we moved to no.11, I knocked the pillar down in the front and made a wide gateway, and laid down slabs of stone, that we could drive a car in there.

She worked at Hartwell's, the garage business established in the 1930s on the south corner of South Parade, up to 1964, when the firm moved to Botley; and then in the accounts department of Blackwell's until she retired in 1977. Dorothy was always independent and like Dorothy Bridge said she had no wish to marry.

I'd got my own home, so I didn't see why I should take on anybody else! I'd rather drive my own caravan!

She and Beryl left in 1979 for a smaller house in Wentworth Road; later Dorothy moved into a residential home in Cassington.

Betty Marshall, née Howes (b.1926)

Betty Marshall still lives in 45 Victoria Road, bought by her parents new in in 1925 (p.24). Here she was born in the front bedroom, into an Oxford family.

My great-uncle George kept the Post Office in South Parade from when I was little to after the war. He sold bits of ironmongery, and rough vinegar, from the barrel, I remember. Another great-uncle had a milk business in Gloucester Street. My grandfather lived round the corner on Banbury Road.

She tells how her father, Walter, met her mother.

He worked for his father, who was a jeweller in St Aldate's, and he used to see this young girl going up and down the road – she worked in a shop which no longer exists, called Webber's. He asked somebody, who worked in Webber's, who she was, and finally got an invitation to a whist drive.

Betty was an only child, probably because her parents felt they could not afford a larger family. There were still horse-drawn deliveries in the road.

There was a rag and bone man who had a horse, and all the housewives used to hear him coming and they'd all go out with their buckets in the hope that the horse would do what horses do, and they could put it round their roses! Something that I've always remembered was, in the winter, my mother would stand me on a stool [at the window], and say to me, 'Watch out for Boffins' – the bread people, anyway – and they used to come round with their horse-drawn vehicle. They'd come along King's Cross Road, turn into Victoria Road, and you could see the lights on the side of the vehicle, and I would be watching for it to turn in, and then Mum would buy bread and usually some cakes.

The Second World War broke out when Betty was a teenager. She remembers rationing.

My aunt ran a café down on Salisbury Plain, and she'd send us a little bit of butter, or a bit of tea, to help us out. We didn't have bread rationing until after the war was over.

Betty left school when she was not quite 17 and went to the Oxford and County secretarial college. However her mother died of breast cancer in 1944 and she had a breakdown. She remembers with warmth the care she had from her family doctor.

He was the one who brought me into the world – he was absolutely wonderful, John Wood. He had somewhere that he would see patients in his own house, in Canterbury Road, and I used to go there, and we'd sit and talk. He kept an eye on me. If he was visiting a patient up this end of Oxford, on a winter evening, when he'd finished, he'd pop in here just to make sure we were all right, and sit and have a cup of tea. A real family doctor.

She used to go regularly to plays at the New Theatre and Rep as well as joining in amateur dramatics.

The weekly Rep was absolutely incredible. It was wonderful. Oh, I loved it. I still love the theatre, anything and everything!

Betty worked for Wood's Booksellers in Broad Street (Mr Wood lived at 71 Lonsdale Road for many years) then did a Social Sciences diploma, after which she worked as a welfare officer up north and as a secretary in London. Then she decided to go to Kenya – just for a couple of years, she thought.

Mrs Howes and Betty in the garden of 45 Victoria Road, c.1937. (B. Marshall)

I had an itchy foot, and I wanted to go somewhere warm, and I knew more about Kenya than I knew about anywhere else, through somebody I met, actually, through the Dramatic Society, and he just became a family friend. Promised my father that he would make quite sure that I was all right! You can imagine my father, with his only child, and that child being a daughter – he was panic-stricken – going to foreign parts! The Suez Crisis was on, so we trailed all the way down the West Coast. But that was fun, because we pulled in to Ascension Island. When I moved to Mombasa, I met my husband – through a Dramatic Club again! We had a lovely little theatre. The first thing I would do, normally, wherever I went, was to join a Drama Club.

She settled in Kenya, had a son, and lived through independence for the country. But eventually her husband's ill health made return to England inevitable.

There you have no State Pension, you have no State anything. If you're out of work, you don't have a dole, you pay for all your hospital treatment, all your dental treatment, all your schooling. We didn't have insurance, we couldn't afford it. And so we could never have afforded to have stayed there.

Betty was away for over 28 years altogether. After living 13 miles outside Nairobi, coming home to Victoria Road in 1985 (the house had been let after her father's death in 1971) was a culture shock, and gave her an interesting perspective.

I felt terribly crowded and cramped. There were houses either side, and houses in front, and masses of traffic, and [you] couldn't seem to get away from anything. I found it rather unfriendly. It took me a long time, but I wasn't to be put off. I still went around chatting to people, because that's what we did in Kenya. I found this sort of isolation here, everybody behind their closed doors and closed windows, rather off-putting.

Fortunately Betty finds Victoria Road now a very friendly community.

John Rowe (b.1930)

John Rowe was also born in one of the interwar houses in Victoria Road, built around 1926, and though both his parents came from large families John was, like Betty, an only child: families in general became much smaller at this period. His mother was from an Oxford family, and was a machinist: this is how she met John's father, a tailor, who had come from Suffolk seeking work – he and six brothers were all in tailoring with their father, but had to disperse in the hard times after the First World War. John's parents bought the house in 1928, moving from Stratfield Road.

My father was attracted by the garage since he'd got a car – the houses at the top end were built with garages. He bicycled to work. But on Sunday afternoon you had a drive round. It was purely for an afternoon out, go kite-flying and this sort of thing. But during the war the car was in the garage for about five or six years – you couldn't use a car. He was also attracted by the beautiful garden: it had been laid out by the Gee family, market gardeners, who had a shop selling fruit and veg at North Parade. They had the house next door [no.4 – there are now two houses in between]. Old Mr Gee used to talk to me when I was about 10. He would have been in his 80s. In his youth he used to go pheasant shooting down this road. He said the little cottages at the top of Banbury Road on the other side were all agricultural labourers. The Gees had a large garden – they were well off.

John inherited his father's green fingers and has always gardened himself (p.194). He left the Oxford High School in 1947 and went into Lloyd's Bank in Summertown as a trainee (his uncle, who also lived in Victoria Road, was in banking), but was called up for National Service in 1948. Coming out towards the end of 1950 he went back to the bank but found it hard to settle.

My uncle used to be manager of a bank on the High Street. So my mother was keen I should go in. The banks were staid and old-fashioned. Having been with young chaps I thought 'I can't stand this'. So I left the bank. There were big arguments about that! I painted the house outside as a kind of sop.

One day he called into the Pressed Steel Works at Cowley.

I cycled in there and went to the employment office and asked if they had any jobs in the accounts section, the clerical section. And this old man Mr Howes said 'Crikey, you're just the man we're looking for'. And I started the next week. My mother was disgusted with me working in a place like that. I said 'It will be temporary probably'. And I was up there for 40 years! The funny thing was they put me in the cashier's office and there were two young chaps in there, one had been at the National Provincial Bank, one at Barclay's. National Service upset things: it broke up the equilibrium of your life really. I was happy up there. I used to look forward to going to work. I started on a bike. Then I went up on my motorbike. I enjoyed the motorbike. I used to go down to Bournemouth to see [relatives] on a Sunday.

John's father died in 1962, but his mother, though an invalid, lived to be 83, dying in 1980. He has stayed on in the house, though he realises that down-sizing might be more practical and financially sensible. He is happy in the road without wanting to be active in community groups.

I know a lot of people, it's a friendly road. But the rates are hard if you're on a pension. I don't get involved; I'm not a joiner. It's a loose community.

Clare and Monica Wagstaff (b.1927, 1930)

The Wagstaff sisters have lived in Hamilton Road all their lives. Their father worked for the Inland Revenue and the family moved to Oxford from Kettering in 1929 with Clare; Monica was born in 1930, in the North Oxford Nursing Home at 181 Banbury Road. They had a younger sister too, Dorothy. The family was typical in having home help from women living in less well-off circumstances nearby.

May lived in the cottages where [the Co-op] is now. She was lovely. She came when she was 14. She stayed till she got married when she was 22. It was a very happy set-up altogether. She took us out, she got the tea. She did everything exactly the same as mother or father did, she was another offshoot of the family. She was one of eight children, and they were living in a little cottage, two up, two down, and they were all clean [and] beautifully behaved.

The sisters have clear memories of wartime in these roads.

Because it was a war people used to put up with things, it was all for the common cause. Oliver & Gurden's was a cake factory, and you could get about half a crown's worth of cakes, and you didn't have to use your BUs – your rations – at all. So there were massive queues there, right the way down to the Rec. And there would be queues as well at places like greengrocers, when they had things like oranges. Children were allowed oranges. No bananas, of course.

Many in the roads grew vegetables and kept chickens to supplement the ration.

Most people began to grow veg. We had a big allotment we used to help my father with, down where the High School is now. That was marvellous soil. We dug up quite a bit of the garden at the back – that wasn't such good soil. Quite a few people kept chickens, because you were allowed chicken feed: people kept them at the very bottom of their gardens. Our aunt had got a very big garden in Kidlington, and she used to keep a pig at the bottom.

Mr and Mrs Wagstaff with Clare, Dorothy and Monica in Hamilton Road, 1942. (C. & M. Wagstaff)

Oxford itself was busy during the war.

There were the dances in the evenings. It's amazing what did still happen. There was a big American club in Cornmarket – there used to be a big hotel there. They had geraniums outside, in window boxes. One or two odd bombs dropped, but nothing to worry us at all. There were a lot of servicemen around, and in St Hugh's, that was a military hospital and they were all in bright blue with red ties. They used to push them out into the Parks. And all the colleges were ministries.

The sisters' careers were typical of those of many single women in the roads who worked all their lives. Clare did a secretarial course and began work for the British Council when it was based in Oriel during the war. Later she worked at the Clarendon Laboratory for 23 years. Monica was a teacher and worked at various Oxford schools. Their younger sister Dorothy, like other young people who emigrated after the war, went to South Africa, then Canada, and was the only one of the three to marry. This passage from the Wagstaffs' joint interview expresses a contentment with the life they have achieved, a modest sufficiency gained through working.

We've always lived in a very pleasant place. We've always been able to get work, as well. We're financially comfortably off. You become more and more grateful for what you've got. You don't think about what you didn't have. Sometimes when I was working, when my mother wasn't well, I would like to have travelled, but I've been able to do it since I retired. So, if you wait, very often, things work out.

Geoffrey Paine (b.1933)

Geoffrey Paine was born into a well-known local bakery business. He has a twin.

> I was the third child. My eldest brother, who I never knew, was born about two years before me, fell into some hot water, and because of medicine in those days, he basically died of shock. I wasn't even expected. I was born eight weeks premature. My brother arrived, then the midwife said, 'I think there's another one here!'

His parents had lived at 77 Victoria Road, then two flats, after they were married in 1926, and then moved to 2 South Parade, the family business of G.W. Paine & Sons. Geoffrey's mother Florence, daughter of a lady's maid who married a coachman, became one of Summertown's best-known personalities (p.75f). His father died in 1962, which Geoffrey attributes to his having started smoking during the First World War.

> He smoked because if you smoked, you didn't feel hungry, because people actually went hungry during the First World War, which is why rationing was brought in in the Second World War. He was born in 1899, so he must have put his age on: he was a pilot in the Royal Flying Corps.

Geoffrey was a child during the war.

> I was six when the war broke out – or, technically, I suppose I was five, at least, my birthday was ten days later! The thing I remember more than anything else is, I knew something was wrong, but I didn't really know what it was. Children can sense atmospheres very quickly.

Like many families they became blasé about air raid warnings.

> At the beginning of the war, we used to traipse down to the cellar when the air raid siren went. We gave this up after a time, and thought we might as well be killed by the bombs. I can remember an aircraft crashing in Linton Road, where Wolfson College is now, an Allied aircraft. It was a very peculiar time, because there was practically no traffic – there was no petrol for pleasure motoring whatsoever. The buses used to have little containers at the back, making reducer gas, which were little fires. They had them on the number 4 route, which was Woodstock Road. They didn't have them on the number 2s because the buses couldn't get up Headington Hill.

There were advantages to being a business family.

> Being in the bakery trade, and having an uncle who was a butcher, we were probably a little more fortunate than some others. I don't think people did go hungry during the Second World War, because, interestingly enough, there wasn't any bread rationing until after the war. Sweets were the last thing to come off ration. After a time, people ate less sweets than they did when they were rationed! If they were rationed, you were jolly well going to have your ration and eat them!

A river garden plot in Lucerne Road was bought in 1947 and added to.

> We used to have wonderful fun. The river garden was bought as somewhere for us to come and play, actually, and then the one next door came up for sale, so Father bought that one, and then the other person said, 'There's not much point in me having that, you'd better have it'.

The bakery business was sold in 1958, before Geoffrey could join it, so he worked all his life for Wenn Townsend, an Oxford accountancy firm. Both he and his brother David, who later left Oxford, built houses on the family river garden plots.

Sydney Denton (b.1934)

Sydney Denton's colourful background is a foil to the middle-class lives we have been looking at. His energy and natural gifts are apparent from these extracts from his fascinating interviews. Sydney's paternal grandfather was an important influence on him and he spent much of his childhood in St Ebbe's, where his grandparents lived.

My grandmother was a daughter of a German-Jewish surgeon, who was working in London at the beginning of the First World War. He was threatened with being interned, and he committed suicide. My grandmother, Jessica, was thrown out onto the streets, with nowhere to go, and my grandfather, fortunately, was a local barrow boy who came along, picked her up, dusted her down, and eventually married the girl!

He used to sell hot chestnuts in the winter, ice creams in the summer, and would put his hand to all sorts of manual things. He decided that they would move down to Oxford and set up a similar business, in 76 Blackfriars Road, St Ebbe's, which was right next door to the gasworks. My grandfather was somebody quite special. He was a real character, my grandfather. I loved him, because he smelt of tobacco, beer, and newsprint, and the gasworks. Everybody had a smell of the gasworks down there. We sold cockles and whelks at all the fairs in and around Oxford. He had a concession to sell the race cards at Eights Week. And he also did all the point-to-point races. His nickname was 'Milord', because he doffed his hat and cap so many times to all and sundry! He was a prizefighter. Not very tall, about five foot five, but he was so well-built, and he was so muscular, and he could take on anybody. Him and my Uncle Bill would go and do the theatre, they would go along the people queuing up to get in. Or the cinemas. They'd go along singing, if they were short of a bob or two for a pint or two. And they were always short of money, because they drank. The whole family drank.

Sydney has vivid memories of St Ebbe's and Oxpens before their redevelopment.

All the women would be out in the street. They used to wear long skirts and big aprons to keep them clean, and everybody, but everybody, polished their brass front doorstep. They looked worn. Most of them were middle-aged by their late thirties, because of the very hard life, and so many children they had. It was a pretty hard-knock life. The Ox Pens was still very much alive. That was a brilliant place! To be a young boy, going round on your granddad's shoulders! Cattle used to come in big livestock lorries, or they would come in on the rail. They'd have drovers who would run them up from the railway station. Then it was all the market stalls, and a lot of banter which goes on with markets.

The family moved to one of the new council estates in Marston when Sydney was two.

The house that we were allocated, 22 Croft Road, Marston, was a modern house, built in 1934. There were numerous estates built to the same pattern around Oxford. We had a bath! They used to come down on Boxing Day, my Auntie Win, which was my father's sister, and my grandmother. And they used to have a bath on Boxing Day!

He was a nice soft chap, my father. But he was a sentimentalist. On a Saturday, he would come down the street drunk, and under his left arm, he'd have a huge parcel of sprats. I didn't have any regard for him when I was younger, because I just could see him wasting money. And he earnt good money at different times. My mother was a slight cut above the rest. Not that she had airs of grandeur or anything like this. But she was a very smart woman, intelligent. She used to wear very simple blouses, and she was quite a beautiful woman. They did have their rows from time to time. Who wouldn't, living in those conditions? Always under pressure. My mother – she used to dish it out, I tell you! She used to rule with a rod of iron. Mind you, we weren't easy kids. We were streetwise, and we were rough. That was our environment. If you weren't up to it, you were ploughed under. We would never dream of stealing from anybody – no such thing as a mugging. Never knew the word. But we would scrump apples, we would play knockers.

Sydney had scarlet fever when he was about six.

They took me into an isolation hospital. They carried me down on the stretcher, down the stairs. Either side of the path was all the neighbours, because they'd all come to see you off, and wishing you good luck.

The family – Sydney had three brothers – was poorer than those living in the seven roads, and mothers had to be skilled at making do.

My father was in the RAF, and he brought home RAF trousers. And mother would undo them all. We all went to school in RAF uniforms, virtually. And she could put a whole heel into a sock. And any old garments we could get, they were unpicked, and we used to have sort of paisley coloured jumpers. We used to have the packman come. We used to call him 'The glad and sorry' – glad you got it, and sorry you had to pay for it! You could buy anything from him. My brothers and I, we used to share a gobstopper. My brothers had never seen bananas: I remember taking one of my brothers round to the local shop, to show them what a banana looked like on an advertising sign.

I never went on a holiday with my family, ever. Didn't know what a holiday was! As a child at school, we were all co-opted into going potato picking, and, my God, that's a back-aching job! There were no other people here to do it, so they took us out of school to gather the harvest in. I joined the Scouts, purposely, so I could go on a camping holiday.

Sydney was adept at supplementing the family diet and his income from an early age. As well as keeping chickens and pigs, he had prize pigeons, and went poaching for rabbits.

I had my own pigeon cote. It was like a Noah's Ark, all made out of all bits of rubbish. We lived pigeons. I had quite a reputation for having good pigeons. Well, of course I did, I knew what I was doing; and I enjoyed them. Ferrets was the next thing. Well, there was a bob to be earnt! I used to go poaching over at Blenheim Palace. I could carry, maximum, eight rabbits. I used to go there at least once a week, and I used to get a shilling for good rabbits, and I could get threepence for the skin down at Warburton's, down St Ebbe's. And then we used to bring ducks home. Ever so easy to collect, ducks, especially the ones round University Parks, because they were all tame. And this went on for some time, until my mother learnt where I got them from! So we used to really feed off the land. We got rabbits, ducks, eggs. We'd get plover's eggs, moorhens. We used to get mushrooms, crabapples, blackberries. And then flowers for Mother. You've got to remember that Marston is all water meadows. I was always interested in wildlife. I used to love the country. You could read it. I used to watch dormice in the hawthorn trees, I would sit for hours and watch things. I could always take you to find a big pike laying up some- where.

Running was a great joy to me. I would run for the pure pleasure of running. I would run out of my house, and I'd jump over the gate. I used to run along the main Marston Road to St Clements, and then chase a bus up Headington Hill. We were so fleet of foot! You'd get a sort of ecstasy.

He gives a different perspective on wartime from the interviewees above.

A lot of my friends acquired 'uncles' during the war. I was quite envious of the ones who had American, GI uncles. The men were away in the war. And there was dances going on. Fathers returned. There was all hell let loose. When they had very young children when they left, when they came back, the children didn't recog- nise them. Some mothers had additions to the families, and it couldn't possibly be the husband's. Well, there were terrible rows.

Courting happened in the town centre.

There was what is known as 'The Bunny Run'. What us boys did, we would get ourselves into one of the shop doorways, and we would stay there. And the girls who were on the Bunny Run, would go round in a circle. They would go down George Street, up New Inn Hall Street, along Queen's Street, along Cornmarket, back down New Inn Hall Street. And if we were successful, then we'd arrange to see them in the cinema. And we usually went to the Electra Cinema, which is now the site of Marks and Spencers.

In those days, I was a Teddy Boy. Oh, my goodness me! You should have seen me! I had the drapes, as they were called, and the brothel creepers. And I went home one day with a DA haircut, duck's abdomen, or in our words, duck's arse! That was all the fashion of the day. We used to go rocking and rolling, and we used to chase after all the big bands.

Sydney's first real connection with Summertown was through his five-year apprentice- ship at Paine's in South Parade in the early 1950s.

I became apprenticed as a baker/confectioner. I was indentured. It meant I had to go off to night school, and do a lot of studying.

National Service in 1955 took him to Kenya and made him an ace shot.

I'd been deferred, so I was 21 before I went in. The training was pretty hard and ruthless. They took boys and made them into men. But they broke a few on route, believe you me. There was a little lad who was sleeping in the bed next to me, and you could hear him crying in the night, and I used to try and help him as much as I could. But he was a soft little lad. He wasn't streetwise, he was just a pleasant young lad who, at 18 was more like a 15-year-old.

We went out to Kenya. We were fighting Mau Mau. That's why we were there. Some of the things I did over there, I'm not proud of. But I was in the Army, I was told when to jump and how high. I used to love night patrols, between the villages and the forest. There was curfew, so anybody out there was fair game, right? You had to get away from the camp, and then just sit around for half an hour, and just let everything adjust to the darkness. All the animals are talking. They're all going about their business. There's rustles here and rustles there. It's when they don't rustle, you want to be more alert.

I used to absolutely love shooting. I was the best light machine gun shot in the battalion. Shooting is about being quiet, and it's about breathing, and it's a soft activity, it's poetry. You must lower your breathing, and you must lower it and stop breathing and let nothing interfere with you at all. You must never pull the trigger, it's a squeezing.

Sydney Denton preparing for night patrol in Kenya, 1956. (S. Denton)

A year after his return he married and got a job at Morris Motors in Cowley. He eventually bought a house at Wheatley.

I'd been courting a girl, Lilian Roberts, who's now my wife. We got married and we moved into a caravan. I didn't want to live in a Council house, I wanted to earn money, and I wanted my own house. I was ambitious. I always was ... still am! And so I got my father-in-law to get me a job at the car factory. I could only afford a semi-detached house. I wanted a detached house. Unbeknown to me, it was one of those inflationary periods where houses rocketed away. So I had to settle for a semi-detached house. Funny that! I still live in one now!

Sydney Denton in his Grove Street office, 2005. (S. Denton)

There is more on Sydney's energetic development of the bicycle business for which he became well known in Summertown on p.143f. He also became a substantial property owner, and a collector and patron of contemporary design. He now lives on the Banbury Road in an Edwardian house next but one to 294 Banbury Road, the original Twining's shop, which he still owns.

Sally Bromley, née Latham (b.1948)

Sally Bromley, the only one of the 'natives' in this chapter born after the war, was brought up on the 'Urban' estate, just to the north of these roads. Her mother worked at Grimbly Hughes in town before marriage, while her father had come from the North East as an orphan with his guardian, a cousin of William Morris. He eventually got a job at the Morris Motors car factory in Cowley, later transferring to 'The Radiators' in Woodstock Road, an important local employer for people on the estates. Her parents were married at St Michael and All Angels in Lonsdale Road in 1943.

> Canon Burrough wouldn't marry them without proof that my father had been baptised. So my father was baptised and my mother was his godmother!

They lived with Sally's grandmother in Cavendish Road, before moving to Carlton Road, where Sally was born. Her father was diagnosed with TB, which was still ravaging poorer communities, but was saved by treatment under the new NHS.

> When I was about a year old, there was a screening at Morris's, with a mobile X-ray unit, and they discovered that my father had got a shadow on his lung. So my father was really very very ill. I can remember him holding me. He wasn't supposed to have any contact with anybody, but my mother said, 'I'm sorry, but I can't keep this man from his children.' We had to have a phone because of his illness. We were allocated the only phone in, I think, the whole of Carlton Road. And the nurse used to come every week and wash it! My father eventually ended up at the Slade Hospital, and he was on what my mother referred to as 'Death Row', with the rubber sheets, to sweep the snow off, because they had to be out in the fresh air all the time. But streptomycin came in, and, well – he eventually lived to be nearly 80.

Sally and her brother became guinea pigs for the new inoculation programme.

> There was a new inoculation coming in, called a BCG. My mother put us forward for a programme of research, so I was inoculated when I was about two-and-a-half. This was a new drug from Norway, and it came to the Churchill Hospital because it's a big teaching hospital, and my brother was scared of the needle, so I was done first. The story goes that I'm the first person in England to have a BCG! But we cursed my mother for allowing this, because we used to go tanking off up to the Churchill which was several bus rides away, when we were children, and it was always in August when it was really hot, and we'd go and have to have all of this stuff done to us, then this injection, and we used to come back grumbling, and in two days' time we'd be scratching it and scratching it! And then we had to go up two weeks later, through all these convoluted bus routes, all the way up there again.

Sally went to grammar school and then to train as a teacher.

> I went on to a College of Education to train to be a teacher. My brother had gone to university before me. There was one girl down the road who went to do a catering course at the Tech, as it was – now Brookes. But I don't have any recollections of anybody I grew up with actually going on for higher education, which is a big change to today.

She married and taught in London before returning to Oxford with two small children, and buying her parents' house in Carlton Road.

My husband and I decided we'd come to Oxford, because we'd always promised ourselves that we'd educate the children in Oxford. My husband left me very soon afterwards, which is a big trauma for any mother.

However she was supported by her parents and the community in which she grew up.

I knew a lot of the older people there, because, of course, I'd grown up with them, and they were very kind to me, and my parents were just amazingly generous. My mother walked down to me one evening, and she put my hand in hers, and she said, 'Sally, I'm going to offer you a year of my life. I will do anything you ask me to do, for a year. And I want you, by then, to be settled'. She did all the childcare, which was quite immense, because Libby was too young even to go to nursery school. Of course, at the end of the year, she didn't want to give up that year of her life! She went on doing the care, my parents were the childcarers while I went out to work.

Sally was well known locally as a teacher (p.121). She met her husband Jonathan at the Summertown Choral Society, and they married in 1984 from Victoria Road.

Everybody, by this time, was teasing me, trying to sort of locate some man for me. I have to say I wasn't actually searching for a man! I felt that I could cope on my own. But anyway, people were pushing and shoving me, and eventually they got the two of us together. We couldn't actually get married at St Michael's Church. We are talking, now, about just months before the changes with divorced people, who could get married in church. So Jonathan and I got married, 'above Sainsbury's', because that's where the Registry Office was, on August 31st, but we regard our wedding day as September 1st, when Jonathan and I, and the two children, walked out together, from this house, and went to St Michael's Church, and went down the aisle, as a complete

Jonathan and Sally Bromley with Sally's daughters Katie and Libby outside St Michael's Church, at the blessing of their marriage in 1984. (Sally Bromley)

family, to be married. Jonathan, particularly, wanted to make promises to the children, because, of course he felt he was marrying three people, not marrying just me!

4 'Local Celebrities'

There are quite a number of very interesting people live round here, and quietly, because you don't know who they are. And that's very nice – local celebrities!

Mary Tregear

Here we tell something of the many colourful and distinguished people who have lived and live still in these unassuming roads. We do not pretend to include everyone of note, particularly among those living here at present, but these glimpses will add to a sense of the wide range of interesting people who have lived here over the years.

People who left an impression

We begin with some examples of 'ordinary' people who stand out for the strong impression they made on those who knew them. Many remember Florence Paine (1902–91), a gifted business woman who with her husband and brother-in-law ran the family bakery at 2 South Parade, and lived on there after it closed. Her son Geoffrey describes her.

She knew everything that was going on. She always had people calling in. She was one of these people who was always cheerful, and people liked meeting her. If you're unhappy, if you're miserable, people steer clear of you. But she was the opposite, so she greatly enjoyed life. She knew a lot of people.

Florence Paine, aged 88, in her well known Morris Minor, Lucerne Road. (G. Paine)

Sally Bromley also remembers her.

She was a very petite lady, and she had sort of Titiany-coloured hair, and she was always very warm. A very very capable lady, she was very efficient. There was no small talk, there was no hanging about. She was very active, very energetic, and she had a very very quick mind. She knew everybody.

Sydney Denton had once worked at Paine's (p.173f) and it was Florence who tipped him off about the premises at 294 Banbury Road which became his bicycle shop.

My best friend. I was number one boyfriend. Well, I thought I was the only one, but evidently there was another one. She knew I had a sweet tooth, she would ring me up and say, 'I'm making pancakes, Sydney, come on over.' It was a drop-in centre.

Several people, like Josie Patterson, testified to the achievements of Mrs Corden of Lonsdale Road, who ran the Children's Pantomime Society for many years (see p.191f).

> She was just a quiet woman, very composed. I don't ever remember her getting cross with the children, flummoxed or fazed in any way.

Joan Crow also paid tribute to her skills.

> Mrs Corden marshalled; and you can imagine the organization required because there would be a cast of about 40 children. She was a wonderful woman: she took the whole thing very seriously and so did the children, and they loved it. She had very high standards: some parents used to grumble a bit as they thought the standards were too high and they were taking it too seriously.

Arthur Manders of Lonsdale Road was well remembered by his neighbour John Herivel.

> He was a true born Englishman. His father had been the chef at Lincoln College, and as a boy, he had the run of the kitchen. He didn't receive any higher education, but he'd got into a solicitor's practice, I suppose an errand boy to begin with. He ended up by doing the conveyancing for the City of Oxford. So he was a very able person. He had one son. And this son went to Magdalen College School. He was really smart.

Peter Clarke speaks of Arthur too (see p.216f).

> Arthur was a character. He was very proper, very correct, very formal, always took his hat off when he passed a lady. I think he was from an old Oxford family. He was a good musician, played the piano quite well. Very good at chess. Didn't like being beaten at all! And we had him in a lot, for tea. And he doted on his son.

At 67 Lonsdale Road, living with her brother, was Mary Harrison (p.41). Her neighbour Beryl Phillips, gives a vivid picture of Tom, who was assistant vicar at St Giles for many years and also wrote thrillers.

> He was something like out of Mary Poppins. He was very short, and round, and I expected to see his umbrella taking off, and flying in the air!

Kathy Clarke remembers Mary with great affection.

> Mary Harrison was really a wonderful person and someone that I'll remember all my life. She was totally selfless.

Like many other women of this time and background Mary surrendered her own life to others. An Oxford graduate, she went out to work as a missionary in South Africa.

> She was only out there for about a year or so and absolutely loving it, when she was called home because I think her mother died, and her mother was nursing her aunt, and she was called home to nurse her aunt, and once her aunt died she then had to be a housekeeper for her brother, Tom. He was quite a cranky old chap, and wouldn't allow any animals in the house or anything, and Mary looked after him without ever a complaint, really sacrificing her life. As soon as Tom died she got a little kitten, Debbie, whom she loved.

Mary was devoted to the church, attending St Margaret's in Polstead Road.

> She became a deaconess by the time she died, and if she could have been ordained … But she wasn't a holier than thou person, she was a very down to earth, practi-

cal, sensible, lovely lady. She was one of those remarkable people. She was a lovely dear old soul.

Peter Clarke remembers her equally warmly.

Mary had this little car that she couldn't drive, and it was always getting bashed, and it was parked in the middle of the road, more or less, because she couldn't park. She was a Liberal, and the only nasty word I ever heard her say was that had she the opportunity, she'd do something very sort of destructive to Mrs Thatcher! She was a brilliant person.

Sylvia Steward of Portland Road was another typical spinster, who devoted her life to others. Dorothea Pelham met her in the 1960s.

She was a person of tremendous willpower. She was actually a missionary, or had worked at the Mission in Canada, for many years, and she was very devoted to the Church here. There was two garages all full of the most amazing rubbish, which she used to periodically trundle out into the front and have a garage sale! She had her old friend called Mrs Smith. And Mrs Smith used to always turn up, and it was quite a neighbourhood event! Very touching. And she'd say, 'I made £30 for the Church'. Everything would go back into the garage, and then a couple of months later it would all come out again!

Her niece Ursula Steward recalls her affectionately.

Aunt Sylvia was surprisingly relaxed, considering she was the classic old Oxford aunt. There was a real feeling of freedom. She was always very kind to us, and I used to come and stay here when I was at the University, before and after term. It wasn't the last word in comfort, but I always did feel this ... support. She was very classic, had a sit up and beg bicycle. And she was very adamant that we should never disturb her during 'Woman's Hour'.

Representative of the numerous eccentrics who have enlivened the roads is the 'great character' who lived next door to the Wagstaff sisters in Hamilton Road.

We called him Nibby. He collected everything, even to tins of sardines – he washed the tin, just in case it might be useful. All our childhood he had sheds out the back and they were all full of junk. And his own room, there was a sort of alleyway to his bed and his chair, and then piles of stuff. He kept all the newspapers, everything. He was a fascinating old man. He had a big white beard and a bicycle. He was very clever, but he never got going at anything.

Yvonne Hands tells a story about a neighbour in Portland Road.

Next door was this chap who thought he was Jesus Christ. And this was fine until he'd got a friend who also then felt he was Jesus Christ, and apparently there was a big row, and almost a fight!

Refugee intellectuals

The University connection has been responsible for many distinguished residents over the years, but something that has emerged as a a special feature of the roads is the number of notable academics who arrived as refugees from Hitler in the late 1930s, and brought a new cultural sophistication to the neighbourhood (see also p.41ff).

Mariele Kuhn (b.1909) still lives in Victoria Road (p.43f). She came from an eminent intellectual family – her father was a professor of philosophy at Göttingen, while her mother, from Vienna, was a cousin of Ludwig Wittgenstein. Mariele went to the famous school run by Kurt Hahn, who later founded Gordonstoun. She was not Jewish, but her husband Heinrich Kuhn (1904–94), a physicist who worked on molecular spectroscopy, was 'only half Aryan'.

His professor was a Nobel Prize Winner – Gert Franck – who was fully Jewish. When I was a schoolgirl, Franck's daughter, Dagmar, was my best friend, and her mother was Swedish Jewish – she was a great pianist, so one day Einstein was at the Francks' house, and we schoolchildren listened to Einstein playing the fiddle! Ja! It wasn't very good, but it was very nice.

Like other scientists Kuhn was helped by Lord Cherwell, who was trying to promote physics at Oxford.

Lord Cherwell, who was called Lindemann, visited Franck and said, 'Are there are any people who will fall under Hitler, and have to lose their job?' He said, 'Well, one of them is my colleague and assistant, Heinrich Kuhn', so Lord Cherwell asked my husband, would he care to come to Oxford?

They left from Hamburg in 1933 after some string-pulling by the Warburgs.

We stayed for a couple of days with the Warburgs. My husband contacted the British Consul in Hamburg, and he says, 'No way. You can't get to England'. So Mr Warburg, who knew him, spoke to him, so everything was all right. We were on a lovely ship. In fact, it was a Jewish ship, apparently. Then we made our way, by train, to Oxford, and we took lodging in the King's Arms. This was a rather shabby little place. We hadn't much money, so it was cheap,

The Kuhns at the seaside, shortly after their arrival in Britain in 1933. (M. Kuhn)

and we were in the middle of all the lovely colleges and buildings. We thought it was wonderful.

Heini Kuhn came to work with the flamboyant Derek Jackson at the new Clarendon Laboratory.

He and Jackson worked together for six years, until the war broke out. Well, Derek Jackson's just a chapter by himself. He was married six times!

During the war Kuhn was working on the nuclear bomb, as well as teaching at University College.

He was on the atom bomb project. So that was terribly secret. I had no idea what he was doing. And he made contact, of course, with other physicists. Then Balliol was looking for a physicist. Balliol College had chemists, but no physicists, so he was the first real physicist of Balliol College.

The family lived in Headington to begin with, before moving to Victoria Road in 1938. During the war Mariele volunteered as an interpreter at St Hugh's where brain and spinal injuries were being treated.

They had some German prisoners-of-war alongside the English boys. Some of these prisoners were flown directly from the Normandy battlefields, and they didn't know anything, they were just too badly injured. It was a very distressing time, to see young men from many nations, badly injured, lying bed by bed. I had to write a kind of diary, I was so depressed. So when I came back, I jotted down in which ward they lay, what their names were, and what happened.

A copy of this diary is now with the Imperial War Museum. After the war Mariele was on a committee for Hungarian refugees.

I would go up to the Youth Hostel in Headington. There I saw a young girl, very pretty, very small, her name was Julie … it was a Jewish name, Rosenberg or something. I said, 'Well, look, I think we take you home.' She said, 'Tommy must come too.' Tommy was her friend. It was an innocent friendship based on music, because she was a lovely pianist. So Tommy came too! And they were very sweet and very polite.

Heinrich Kuhn was elected to a fellowship at Balliol in 1951, and to the Royal Society in 1954. Despite offers and honours he never thought of leaving Oxford for Germany.

Also living quietly in Victoria Road, at no. 36, from just before the war to the late 1950s were Frederick Heinemann and his wife. He had been professor of philosophy at Frankfurt until 1933, author of Existentialism and the Modern Predicament. *Erwin Schrödinger (1887–1961) was a Nobel Prize winner for Physics in 1933 who was another to leave Germany for Oxford, though subsequently returning to Austria, from which he had to escape again in 1938. He scandalised Oxford by openly maintaining two households: he lived with his mistress Hilde March and her husband in 86 Victoria Road from early in 1934.*

At 41 Portland Road Frank Burchardt (1902–58) was a German economist whose career was blocked by the regime's dislike of his outspoken politics after Hitler came to power, though he was not Jewish (p.41). In 1935 he was offered a research post by All Souls College and came to Britain. Elsie Hill knew the family.

He was very charming, everybody loved him, he was the ultimate workaholic. He died of a heart attack, of overwork. He was [from 1948] a fellow of Magdalen, and the Director of the Oxford University Institute of Statistics.

Friends and immediate neighbours at 39 Portland Road were the family of the eminent Jewish publisher and art collector Bruno Cassirer (1872–1941) (see p.42). Cassirer's daughter, Sofie, herself a connoisseur of impressionist painting, had married Richard Walzer (1900–75), a scholar of Greek and Arabic, who was warned not to return home from Italy after being dismissed from his job in Berlin in 1933. When Jews began to be persecuted under Mussolini they left for England and came to Portland Road. The rest of the family left their escape to the last minute, as Elsie Hill relates.

Günther, Agnes, their two children, and Bruno and Else came in 1938, with only five days left in their passports, and I think they were quite mad! But neither Günther nor his father-in-law believed that their Germany was going to be smashed up forever, until Kristallnacht, so they didn't start preparing to come until then. [Cassirer] did have quite a remarkable collection of pictures which he, very sensibly, had sent on loan to a Swiss museum, and managed to get them here, and they were, quite a number of them, hanging in no. 39 Portland Road. So that place was quite an art gallery in its time. In fact it's a good example of how much the country benefitted from this family: Sofie when she died left a Monet [*Bathers at La Grenouillère*] and a Cézanne [*Landscape with Poplars*] to the National Gallery, and to the Ashmolean the Cézanne which was stolen on Millennium Night, plus two Manet oil sketches and a very early Monet painting.

Günther Hill continued to run the notable Cassirer publishing business from 31 Portland Road, later with Elsie's help (p. 146). Richard Walzer became a member of Oriel College and held a lectureship in medieval philosophy during the war. In 1950 a post was created for him in the faculty of Oriental Studies, and he later became a professorial fellow at St Catherine's. Living with the Walzers was another distinguished Arabist, Samuel Stern.

He was a sort of adopted son of the Walzers. He was a very accomplished scholar in some aspects of Arabic, a fellow of All Souls. Very sadly he died when he was only 48, died of asthma.

Richard Walzer, c.1970: 'he was a sweet-tempered man but he had a great brain'. (Elsie Hill)

Yvonne Hands, a neighbour in Portland Road, remembers them all.

Dr Walzer was a very famous Arabic scholar, and Samuel Stern was a very brilliant man. They would all sit in the garden, in the summer, talking together, in English, very slowly. I suppose they talked in English because Samuel was Hungarian. They were all Jewish. But they used to argue and fight all the time, in very slow English!

Staying briefly in Hamilton Road, apparently, was Bruno Cassirer's cousin, the philosopher Ernst Cassirer (1874–1945). He left Germany in 1933 to lecture in Oxford for a couple of years, before moving on, as Leszek Kolakowski mentions.

He went to America, and died there shortly thereafter. But he's a very important figure in the history of 20th-century philosophy.

Another extremely important Jewish refugee who lived during and after the war at 63 Lonsdale Road was the neurosurgeon Ludwig Guttmann (1899–1980). After Jewish doctors were forced from 'Aryan' hospitals in 1933 he worked in the Jewish Hospital in

Breslau and witnessed Kristallnacht in 1938. In 1939 the family came to England where A.D. Lindsay, master of Balliol, was instrumental in finding a house for him. In 1944 he opened a centre for the treatment of paraplegics at Stoke Mandeville, and his work there revolutionised the treatment of this kind of injury. Natasha Burchardt knew him.

He was a great man. His patients absolutely adored him. He had this extraordinary active programme of things that had never been tried before: he was really into self-help. The Paralympics were his idea [beginning as the Stoke Mandeville Games in 1948].

Leszek Kolakowski, a distinguished philosopher, was a later refugee, expelled from Warsaw University in March 1968.

It was a kind of purge, and five professors from Warsaw University were expelled then. We were accused of being responsible for the Democratic Movement of Students – and there were some riots and so on. We came to Oxford, because I was elected to a Fellowship of All Souls College. We could stay in America, but we preferred to be here, in a country where it's closer to Europe. It was interdicted for me to publish anything in Poland. I was on the black list in the Communist country, and so there would be no point to go. So after some time we applied for British Citizenship. So now we have double citizenship, because after the political change in Poland in '89, the passports were given back to us.

Leszek Kolakowski at All Souls, a college which took in many refugee intellectuals, in the mid 1970s. (L. Kolakowski)

Wartime heroes

Many people with remarkable life stories have retired to live quietly in these roads. A tale of extraordinary wartime experiences was narrated to Peter Thompson by an old man, Josef Jaske (1913–2001), who lived in Hawkswell Gardens.

Whilst [I was] tinkering with one of my old cars, out by the garage, this little old man came up behind me, tapped me on the shoulder, and asked me to help him with his garage, because he couldn't get the door open. To cut a long story short, I ended up solving his problem, then having a cup of coffee with him, and asking him – because he had a strong foreign accent – about his background. His name was Josef Jaske, he was Czech in origin, and he recounted this unbelievable tale about his experiences joining the Czech Air Force, subsequently escaping via France – via Poland, France and North Africa – and arriving in Cardiff, joining the

RAF in England, at the very beginning of 1940, being trained to fly Spitfires, flying in the Battle of Britain, being shot down five times, and surviving every one of those. In 1942, in a light two-seater plane, he was flying from Northolt to St Athan in South Wales, in very bad weather, and at an altitude of 3,000 feet, they flew into the tethering cable on a barrage balloon, which split the fuselage of the aircraft in two. His colleague was killed straightaway, and Josef Jaske fell out of this aeroplane, with no parachute, at 3,000 feet, and landed in the Bristol Channel, where he spent an hour and a half in the water before he was picked up. I think he said he had five fractured vertebrae, and most of the rest of his bones were broken, but 18 months later, he was back flying. He stayed in the RAF till the end of the war.

He went back to Prague immediately after the war. In 1948, when the Communists took over, he and his wife – he'd married by that stage – decided they didn't want to stay there, so he had some hair-raising experiences escaping by swimming across the Danube from near Bratislava, into Austria, whilst being shot at. They then made their way back to England. He rejoined the RAF. Initially he was doing flying training, and subsequently he had an administrative job, before finally retiring [in 1968]. Latterly, he was based at Benson, so when they retired, they moved into a flat in Hawkswell Gardens. It's quite an incredible tale, that seemed quite unbelievable, until he dropped in my letterbox a photocopy of the RAF Accident Report – which I still have – and if you look up his name on the internet, it confirms all the details as I've described!

Another to survive the terrible experience of falling from his aircraft, in an accident while training for the Battle of Britain, was Gerald Hall (1914–99), as his wife Peggy relates.

It was a 'death spin'. The cockpit was open and he was forced out, but he couldn't find his parachute, his arm was broken. He fell to earth and his parachute opened about 1000 ft above the ground and he blacked out. He was hurt very badly.

Transferred to hospital in Oxford he took up studying philosophy and was offered a place in New College by the Warden. This was where Peggy, who was working for the Ministry of Food, met him in the garden in 1945. They married in 1949 and while Gerry remained to a great extent ill and shattered he found relief in promoting the philosophy of Rudolf Steiner, coaching maladjusted children and doing practical work which calmed his nerves. He did up an old house, 84 St Bernard's Road, where he and Peggy later ran a school, which became Temple College. They bought 65 Hamilton Road in the 1960s and later 75 Hamilton Road, a house in bad condition which Gerry converted to five bedsits after 1975. They wanted to take as lodgers students who were interested in their philosophy. Peggy stayed living in a bedsit in no.75 and seeing people occasionally to talk about 'things that really matter' until her death in 2004.

John Herivel's outstanding achievement was as a code-breaker at Bletchley Park during the war. Born in Belfast in 1918, he studied at Queen's University Belfast then went to Cambridge as a bright young mathematician.

Towards the end of January, in 1940, there was a knock on the door, and Welchman, who had disappeared to go to Bletchley, he was my supervisor at

Cambridge, he came in one evening and asked me if I'd like to come and join him at Bletchley.

At Bletchley John soon came up with the insight christenend by Welchman the 'Herivel Tip', which enabled the breaking of the German Air Force Enigma Code. This is a complicated story, on which John is writing a book. The Herivel Tip involved patiently looking for clusters in the opening letters of the message that transmitted the key for the day, indicating the setting of the wheels that the receiving Enigma machine needed to use. A cluster might result from laziness in rescrambling the wheels.

John Herivel, 1939. (J. Herivel)

The Enigma was a machine for scrambling the original German text, and producing something which was gibberish. The scrambling was done by these wheels. It was a wonderful scrambling operation. And it would have been, I suppose, impossible to do anything about it, except that we actually had copies, or replicas, of the machines the Germans used. The insight was that if there was a cluster, then the cluster could give you a very good idea of what was called 'The Ringstellung', which was a vital part of the key of the day. It was changed every day. The idea never worked from the middle of February [1940] until the middle of May. And then, of course, once the Blitzkrieg started, there were many more messages, and they were working under enormous pressure. So, presumably, that's why, suddenly, it worked when it hadn't worked before. On the day the 'Herivel Tip' worked, I came into the room and discovered these people working at the machine, and getting German out, you see, they'd decoded! And once we started it, it's amazing, we just did it every day. It changed from being nothing to everything, overnight almost.

The Germans continued confident that the Enigma could not be broken. The information gained in 1940 later enabled the Bombe, an early computer, to break the codes.

In the period of about three months, when we were breaking it every day, you got an enormous amount of information about the sort of message the Germans sent. In other words, cribs. Once you had the Bombe, then it was really inevitable it would be broken every day.

I felt rather embarrassed, really, in a way. You don't stand up and say, 'Oh, what a marvellous idea I've had'. That must have been obvious to everyone! And so, for quite a few months, I felt queer, rather self-conscious, that would be it. Rather self-conscious.

A memorable experience was Churchill's visit in 1941.

News went round that the great man had come to Bletchley to have a look at us. So Welchman showed him round. We all stood at attention [facing our machines] as he went round, and eventually Welchman stopped behind my back, with Churchill, and then he introduced me to Churchill and I turned round and I found this person glowering at me, rather! Later the same day, we were told that he would like to have a talk with us. Behind Hut 6 there was a little pile of builders' waste. And he walked up on top of that and we all gathered round. I do have a very vivid recollection of being surprised to find this person whom I'd thought would be very imposing and bluff-looking, he was a rather frail figure really. And he told us how grateful he was, and the Cabinet, for all the good work that we were doing at Bletchley Park. And I could see a tear almost in his eye, because he was a very emotional person. He really did mean it. That was something one doesn't forget.

Later Welchman gave John a reference for a job at Queen's University Belfast, where he taught for many years.

That memorable day, when I came in and discovered that the Luftwaffe key had been broken, he drew me aside, and said, 'Herivel, this will not be forgotten.' So that was one of the occasions where he didn't forget it!

John later moved from mathematics to the history of science, publishing a book on Newton in 1964.

Newton had a beautifully legible hand, both as regards letters and symbols. You could see his thoughts just flowing gently, like a lovely tune, a bit of music. There were never any mistakes.

The academic life in those days was a pleasant and unpressurised one.

As I often said to people, in those days, 'We're the last of the gentlemen!' Such a wonderful life. As long as you did some research, nobody bothered what you were doing in the summer. Most of the time you could do what you wanted.

John and his wife Elizabeth, an Oxford graduate whom he had met at Bletchley, decided to retire to Oxford, partly to escape the troubles in Belfast, and bought a house in Lonsdale Road in 1975.

Scientists of all kinds

Lonsdale Road seems to have had more than its fair share of distinguished scientists of various kinds, including two Nobel Prize winners. The Dutch Nikolaas (Niko) Tinbergen (1907–88), an authority on animal behaviour, had spent part of the war in a German camp as a hostage after protesting at the removal of Jewish professors from Leiden University where he taught. In 1949 he resigned and moved to a less prestigious lectureship in Oxford, where he built up an influential research group in ethology. As his daughter Janet explains:

My father wanted to bring his science to the English-speaking world: it was a new science, ethology, which was a new development of biology.

Tinbergen developed ethology in a different direction from that of the other key figure in the field, Konrad Lorenz. From 1966 he was professor of animal behaviour at Oxford and shared the Nobel Prize for Medicine with Karl von Frisch and Lorenz in 1973. He was always an energetic populariser of the subject through books and films. He and his wife Elisabeth, who worked with him, lived for many years at 88 Lonsdale Road. They are remembered by their neighbour, the artist Ros Chorley.

They were very interesting neighbours. His thing was animal behaviour, and it was very amusing because he would imitate the sounds of all these birds that he'd studied. He spent a lot of time in Iceland, studying colonies of sea birds, and he tried hard to learn Icelandic. When he'd been over about five years, he asked a friend how he was doing. 'Very good', said the friend, 'You speak it like a three-year old!' He did some television programmes, which we saw. They were very friendly – hospitable to their neighbours; but they didn't go for the usual University status-conscious thing. Mrs Tinbergen did the garden, and it was always beautiful. One time, my sister's dog got through the hedge and barked at Mrs Tinbergen. And she thought this was an outrage – (a) getting into the garden, and (b) barking! But Niko thought it was ever so amusing and confirmed his theories, because the dog was just establishing new territory!

Niko Tinbergen, c.1970. (Janet Tinbergen)

Round the corner in Hawkswell Gardens lived in the early 1990s an ex-student and protégé of Niko Tinbergen who has become another famous populariser of science, the evolutionary biologist Richard Dawkins (b.1941), best known as author of The Selfish Gene. *An undergraduate at Oxford, he did his doctorate here under Tinbergen and later became a Fellow of New College.*

Lonsdale Road's second Nobel Prize winner was Abdus Salam (1926–96), who was born in Pakistan. Professor of Theoretical Physics at Imperial College from 1957, he is best known for his long directorship of the International Centre for Theoretical Physics in Trieste, which he founded in 1964 to promote opportunities for scientists from the developing world. He was a Nobel Laureate for Physics in 1979. From the mid 1980s he lived next door to Margaret Willis at the far end of Lonsdale Road, where she continues to have distinguished neighbours.

Next door is Louise Johnson, who is a Professor of Molecular Biophysics. She's immensely busy, very distinguished. And so is Peter Hirsch [a metallurgist], he's also very distinguished. He's knighted, she's a Dame!

The Willises bought their house from the Silvers: Josh Silver, 'a tremendous inventor', was a fellow of New College, a physicist who has generated all sorts of practical ideas, most notably self-adjusting glasses which can be cheaply produced, of great application in the Third World. His wife Cindy was a well-known jeweller. From her earlier time in Londale Road Margaret Willis also remembers the Argyles who lived at no.30 from 1954 to 1964: Michael (1925–2002) was an inspirational social psychologist, Sonia a formidable classicist who worked on the Greek Lexicon.

They used to give terrifying parties, really, with these awful brain-teasing games! They were a wonderful pair! Lovely!

Michael's second wife and widow Gillian now lives in Portland Road.

Michael was really the founder of Social Psychology as an academic subject – he actually coined the term 'social skills' – and he pursued it with tremendous energy, and to great international acclaim. He had the first lectureship in social psychology here from 1952, but the subject was not perceived to have sufficient gravitas for him to get a Fellowship, or a Professorship – it was Oxford Brookes that made him professor later on. So he got together with other similarly rejected-because-of-subject academics, who like him had chosen to stay on in Oxford despite being offered tempting international Professorships, and, with money from Lord Wolfson and Isaiah Berlin as President, they founded the first mixed, international, family-orientated, egalitarian graduate college – Wolfson.

Philip Morsberger, who was then Head of The Ruskin School of Drawing & Fine Art, was living with Mary Anne in a rented house on the other side of Lonsdale Road. He remembers one Sunday morning being woken up by jazz being played very loudly out of the window by Michael. He rushed out in his pyjamas and the two of them waltzed down the road past sober citizens walking to church. Incidentally, Michael was a devout Anglican and Philip is a devout Roman Catholic.

Sam Finer (1915–93) was the son of pre-1914 Jewish immigrants from Romania who became an important political scientist. He was an undergraduate at Trinity College, Oxford and went on to teach at Keele and Manchester, before returning here in 1974 to the Gladstone Chair and a fellowship at All Souls. An exuberant character, he lived at 48 Lonsdale Road after his second marriage to Kate Jones, also an academic. At this time there were several economists in the road, including John Flemming, chief economist to the Bank of England, and later Warden of Wadham.

Among earlier academics living in Victoria Road was Meyer Fortes (1906–83), an innovator in the field of social anthropology with his work on African social organisation, who lived at no. 57 after the war before taking up the chair in Cambridge in 1950–73. A more recent scientific resident of Victoria Road worthy of note is Professor Bob Williams (b. 1926), a pioneer of 'biological inorganic chemistry', who describes his uneasy start as a student in Oxford on p. 126f. Professor Williams has been an important local figure as a tireless campaigner for the less privileged roads of Cutteslowe (p. 196f).

Medics

Numerous members of the medical profession now live in these roads. One of the most distinguished is Professor Sir Peter Morris (b. 1934) of Lucerne Road, the eminent transplant surgeon. He and his wife Jocelyn, also a doctor, had spent time working in England in the early 1960s before returning to Australia via Boston. In 1974 they came to Oxford, where they have been ever since.

I had a call from Richard Doll. 'Would I be interested in the Chair of Surgery?' So we came. I thought I would probably go back to Australia after about ten years, but nothing seemed better in terms of research, so I stayed.

He retired as Nuffield Professor of Surgery in 2001, after which he became President of the Royal College of Surgeons. His career here was marked by unwelcome attention from the animal rights campaigners whose activities are still very prominent in Oxford.

It began in the late 70s; for example we had obscene calls during the night for months on end, the fence painted 'Animal Murderer', the footpath outside painted 'Animal murderer lives here'. Pamphlets were handed out at school with all about me and the work I was doing, accusing me of being an animal murderer, so our kids got that and obviously didn't like it much. Some of my staff had their cars stripped with paint-stripper. It went right through to about the mid 1980s and then Colin Blakemore came to Oxford and his work took all the heat off me, because it was more attackable, if you like. My work was trying to develop cures, more successful transplants, cures for diabetes – the public could understand. But we always still have a police guard – our own policeman, as he calls himself.

Sir Peter Morris, painted by Jon Friedman for the Royal College of Surgeons, of which Peter was president from 2001–4. (Sir Peter Morris)

Though three of their five children and six of their eight grandchildren are back in Australia, the Morrises think they will stay now.

It's been very good to me, I've enjoyed it thoroughly. The only thing I don't like are English winters. Every winter I keep thinking of Australia.

Outstanding in the field of mental health is Bertram Mandelbrote of Lonsdale Road, who came to Merton College from South Africa as a Rhodes scholar in 1946 to pursue his medical studies (p.128). He became interested in psychiatry and worked from the 1950s in this fast developing field. He came to Littlemore as Physician Superintendent in 1959, a post he held until retirement in 1988. Here he developed his pioneering work, unlocking wards to create 'open' hospitals, and establishing therapeutic communities and group homes.

There were meetings in which patients were encouraged to talk and to discuss things and it was really a way of bringing people with mental illness out and treating them with respect. It resulted in a marked reduction of the number of people in hospital.

He also made important innovations in the treatment of drug and alcohol dependence.

In those days the Minister of Health would visit, and Enoch Powell was Minister of Health in the early 60s and came down to Littlemore. I took him round and discussed various ideas that I had, including the fact that people with drug dependence and alcohol dependence problems were not catered for adequately and it

Bertram Mandelbrote in 1961, photographed for a lecture tour in the USA. (Bertram Mandelbrote)

wasn't appropriate for them just to be admitted to the psychiatric hospital, which was what was happening, with a lot of disruption.

His ideas led eventually to the establishment of the Ley Clinic in 1970, followed by the Ley Community in 1971, which continues as a successful treatment centre for drug dependency. Another pioneering initiative was the establishment of the Isis Centre in Little Clarendon Street in 1976, staffed mainly by volunteeers, where people could just drop in for treatment 'and not have to be labelled as people with psychiatric problems'. Bertram's work load was enormous, but sustained by his enthusiasm for his work.

I enjoyed what I was doing and it was a great pleasure to see the changes that took place. It meant that people who were mentally ill and who had these problems were seen as individuals rather than stigmatised as people who were 'bad'.

Campaigners

Looking at health care from the other side, from the point of view of the consumer, was a woman who has had an enormous impact through her high level voluntary work (see p.141f). Jean Robinson, living in Lonsdale Road since the late 1960s, gave a long interview in 2000. Her roots were London East End working class.

To my mother's disgust, I had gone off and joined the Labour League of Youth – she was a working-class Tory. From the earliest age, I was interested in people being less privileged and that life wasn't fair, and that something should be done about it. I don't know how that came about.

She eventually came to Ruskin College in Oxford, as a mature student in 1953 (p.128). Having married Derek Robinson, a miner's son from Yorkshire, who became an economist at Oxford, and a Fellow of Magdalen College, Jean began to do voluntary work of various kinds, 'to keep my brain engaged', in the mid 1960s.

I got involved with the local Consumers' Group, which was just starting up. What I was interested in was a better society, and I wanted it yesterday. I haven't mellowed as I've got older, one iota. I still want that. But I realised that doing practical things for people, in fact, could improve the quality of life.

From 1966 to 1973 she served as 'the token housewife' on the Regional Health Board, becoming a formidable asker-of-difficult-questions.

I was put on the Regional Hospital Board, and that was where my career, as it were, began, which has become a self-taught course, looking at health care from the point of view of the people who receive it. I think I was the only person under 40, I was one of only two women, and apart from the Trade Unionist, the only one who thought of herself as working-class, as it were, coming from the people. I'd been on the Board, I think, about six months, and I turned up for the meeting, for the ritual glass of sherry, and Dame Isobel took me on one side, and she said, 'Mrs Robinson, are you really happy with us? Is this really the kind of thing you want to do?' It became obvious they didn't want me, but, you know, my initial drive was simply to understand what was being done, so that I could make an effective contribution.

She was later summoned to see Richard Crossman, who was then the Minister.

'I've never, in all my public life, seen so much pressure to get rid of someone', he said. 'They absolutely hate you.' Crossman was very indiscreet! I went on to tell him what was really going on, about the fudging of statistics and going round hospitals and so on. We had a Labour Government, and I was a Labour Party member, and apart from the Trade Unionist, I swear to God I was the only Labour Party member on that Board. And I was supporting what was government policy and government circulars, and being opposed at every turn.

Jean subsequently became Chair of the Patients Association, advising on complaints against the medical profession, at a time when the culture of the Health Service made criticism very difficult.

What I had learned at the Regional Board was, never assume that because these people are the officials, that they know it all, that they're the ones who know best. It was much assumed, in society, that the people at the top know best. It's not necessarily that they're wrong, but it sure ain't true that they're necessarily right. I quickly discovered that patients who had a complaint were quickly labelled as 'awkward' and 'difficult': it must have been because *they* were difficult, not because anybody did anything wrong.

At the same time Jean was increasingly involved with the Association for Improvement in Maternity Services, as an honorary research officer, often challenging received opinion on subjects such as induced labour.

I wrote a letter to *The Lancet*, pointing out the faults in this study, whereupon another doctor wrote and said, 'Well, who really wrote that letter?' Obviously the Chairman of the Patients' Association didn't write it, there must have been an obstetrician in the background. So I replied, 'All you need is a Bodleian Reader's Card, and letters from 400 women who have had induced labour', which I had analysed, and which were horrifying. And the great thing about being back in Oxford, which was a disadvantage careerwise, is I'm surrounded by good libraries, and I can get anything. And it's bliss! I get my fix, like people get chocolate, I get my fix from libraries!

She brought her self-acquired knowledge and voracious reading of medical literature to her position as a lay member on the General Medical Council, on which she served for 14 years until 1991. Again she often found the establishment closing ranks against her attempts to show up problems. Her husband has been an uncompromising support.

He said to me, 'You don't resign. If it's a major issue which is so important you can't stay, you do it, but remember, you can do it only once. You've played your only card.' He's a sort of Yorkshire grit man. The road may be tough, but you plough on if you think you're right. Truth is truth, and honesty is honesty, and you go for what's right.

Jean also helped found Consumers for Ethics in Research and became involved with the Prevention of Professional Abuse Network.

I was profoundly affected by the effects of sexual abuse, and got emotional burn-out. The burn-out was not the problem itself, but my reaction to what I saw had been done to these people. I could not bear it. In the end, I was in a state of grief.

She is now interested in social work, though feeling too old to become actively involved.

I guess I always like pioneering. When I started doing consumer work, it was a pioneering thing. And then when I moved on to consumer work in health care, at that time, it was an almost untrodden pathway. And now I think, 'Gosh, I wish I had my life again, to start looking at social work'. I think I am always concerned about people who think they can make decisions for other people's lives. I need another three lifetimes to read all I want to read, and do all I want to do!

Someone who is taking a lead in environmental campaigning against global warming, the most crtical issue of our time, is Sam Clarke of Victoria Road. Since leaving Oxfam in 1988 (p.145f) he has worked with various organisations, but is now focusing on his roles as Chair of Friends of the Earth in the UK and in Ireland, and, importantly, as co-founder and chair of the Stop Climate Chaos coalition.

We've got to try and make it fulfil its potential, which is about putting pressure on politicians, mobilising lots of people to do stuff a bit differently, so that politicians

realise they have permission, if not positive pressure on them, to do the right thing. The science is now clear and understood and is not disputed. What is disputed is what do you do about it, and how much can you afford to do about it. There are a hundred things the government could do and it's rather reluctantly and rather slowly doing a few of them. It's the issue of the next decade. It's very frightening, and it's particularly frightening for people who don't have the resources to do anything about it. In this country we can afford to adapt. But third world people will not only lose their livelihoods they will lose their lives.

Sam Clarke compering at Tim Peto's birthday party in 2000. (V. Peto)

Historians and writers

A lot of writing goes on in these roads, partly because so many academics live here. For some time, for instance, 59 Victoria Road was owned by Balliol. Through it passed two now well-known academic writers: Christopher Ricks (b.1933), author of many works of literary criticism, who has been since 2004 Professor of Poetry at Oxford; and the colourful historian of France Richard Cobb (1917–96), a fellow of Balliol from 1962 and Professor of Modern History from 1973, who made a name by the accessibility of his writing and interest in the history of ordinary people. An earlier historian of Stuart England and author of standard general works on 17th-century Europe, David Ogg (1887–1965), lived at 76 Lonsdale Road for many years.

Paul Thompson (b.1935), the founding father of British oral history – and chief instigator of the Seven Roads project – lived in Lonsdale Road from 1977 until 2001. He got his degree in history and his doctorate at Oxford. His pioneering interest in oral history began around 1969 with research for his big book The Edwardians, *first published in 1975, which was based on around 500 interviews. He started the* Oral History Journal *and then founded the Oral History Society in 1973. His classic book* The Voice of the Past, *came out in 1978, and explored the methodology of this new and widely appealing kind of history. A little later Paul was the founder and first director of the National Life Story Collection at the British Library.*

Paul Thompson in 1981. (P. Thompson)

Living in Lucerne Road for many years was the famous sailor and author of around fifty books on the sea and sailing, Commander Alan Villiers (1903–82), who sailed a replica of the Mayflower across the Atlantic in 1957. He was a Trustee of the National Maritime Museum and a contributor to National Geographic. We were able to interview his widow Nancie (b.1915), who herself arrived from Australia just in time for the war and got a job at John Murray's.

I came to England in 1939, just to see the world. This was before the great influx of Australians, rather! I got this job through a man who is now forgotten, but was quite famous in his day, called Axel Munthe, [who] wrote a book called *The Story of San Michele*, which was a great best-seller in those days. He was on the ship when we were coming over, and he insisted that I couldn't go to Germany as I intended, in 1939. He said, 'You must get a job in England. Come along to John Murray's.' They were his publishers.

She married Alan Villiers, who was already well-known, during the war.

I'd met him in Melbourne, because I was very interested, through an uncle, in sailing ships. He was there with the *Joseph Conrad*, but he was just being divorced at that time, with the sea as co-respondent! It was through hearing him on the radio – that's how I knew he was back from Arabia. Through mutual friends I met him, and then we got married. Myself in uniform! We were married in Fort William, where he was stationed then. It was a horrible wedding! It was Christmas Eve in Fort William, and we were staying at Corpach across the loch, and Alan met me,

Nancie and Alan Villiers in the garden of their house in Lucerne Road, c.1970. (N. Villiers)

and he said, 'Dear, today is your wedding day. I've organised it!' And I said, 'Well, I'm going back to put on a clean shirt, and clean my buttons!' I was an Aircraft Woman at that time. I think the Registrar was very cross at being called out! When I said that my name was Nancie, he said, 'Agnes?' I said, 'No, Nancie'. 'We'll have to put you down as Agnes. It's the rightful thing in Scotland' or something! Anyway, I nearly got put down as Agnes!

The impending birth of her daughter brought Nancie down to Oxford. While the Villiers lived in Davenant Road they acquired a river garden in Lucerne Road. They later moved into a house which had been built on one of the river garden plots in the 1950s.

Brian Aldiss, commonly held to be England's greatest living science fiction writer, remembers slightly ironically the pleasure of moving to a middle-class road from Kidlington when he and his wife came to 69 Victoria Road in the late 1950s.

I made a couple of good friends nearby with children the same age, as you do, one in Lonsdale Road and another in Portland. Otherwise I hated every minute of it, especially as we had a really bad winter our first one there and all I remember is pushing a push-chair along pavements rutted with frozen snow! I was so happy to move out to the country.

My father had bought us a Taylor Woodrow house in Kidlington as a wedding present – I hated it. Victoria Road was like an oasis after the desert! I sat in the back bedroom and wrote *Non-Stop*, my first science fiction novel, which was a great success and is still in print.

Others were less enamoured of their suburban surroundings. The novelist Susan Hill lived in 105 Victoria Road in 1978–80 as a temporary expedient while she and her husband looked for the village house they wanted.

Most famously Iris Murdoch lived with her husband John Bayley at 68 Hamilton Road. Perhaps because he is rather rude about it Bayley changed the address to '54 Hartley Road' in his published account Iris. *The couple had lived for 30 years in the village of Steeple Aston, in an old house. An instinct for something more manageable brought John Bayley into Oxford: on p.220 he describes driving to the first house on his list up 'a long straight street in Summertown, a leafy suburb of North Oxford. There it was on the corner, a pleasant little brick house. My heart warmed to it at once.' Knowing that the houses in this area were extremely sought after he rushed back to the estate agent. Iris was not impressed but they went ahead, though both realising that they were making a mistake. The house was 'a predictable disaster' – the neighbourhood children screaming all day, and the burglars visiting at night. They 'stuck it for three years, longing to go' until in August 1989 they moved to more upmarket surroundings in Charlbury Road.*

The celebrity is well remembered though few had direct contact with her. Greta Guy's husband Jack often used to fix things for the couple, or help with the shopping.

> She was very nice. But she was very eccentric. I mean, you could see that she dressed with two different socks, and things, and big hats. And she was far away. He was as well. They lived a life on their own.

Philippa Berry once went with her son to retrieve an aeroplane.

> Thomas was playing with the boy next door throwing toy aircraft up into the air, and Thomas's landed on Iris Murdoch's flat roof. So we had to go round and ring the doorbell. She was very welcoming. We went into this dark house, upstairs to a dark room, which was full of stuff. She said to Thomas, 'Now, I'll open the window, and then you can hop out'. So that was our little encounter with the great Iris Murdoch. I don't know what it was about Hamilton Road that she didn't like. Very strange!

Donald Norwood, living in Victoria Road, met the author through his dog.

> We got invited to a party there once. If you've got a dog it opens up conversation. She liked dogs.

William Horwood, author of the Duncton Chronicles, *and more recently a memoir about his unhappy childhood, lived in the roads twice, so perhaps was less averse to them – he lived in Hamilton Road, moved away, and returned to Portland Road to a house backing onto his old garden. He now lives elsewhere in Oxford, not far from where he was born.*

> *Finally, a brief visitor here at the end of the 1970s was the American feminist writer Marilyn French. Having advertised in* Spare Rib, *she came and lodged with a couple in Lonsdale Road for a week, gathering material for her novel* The Bleeding Heart, *published in 1980!*

Artists, musicians and media people

There are several artists and designers living and working in the roads – like Rosamund Chorley and Peter Lawrence in Lonsdale Road, and Ruth Bader Gilbert in Portland Road – whose work has often been seen during Art Weeks and at other exhibitions. There are many residents too who have worked or work in the arts and broadcasting. Among these we might pick out Dr Cormac Rigby. He was a student at Oxford, then for 20 years a familiar voice on BBC Radio Three, where he was Presentation Editor. In 1985 he left to train as a Catholic priest, becoming parish priest at Stanmore in 1999. He is the only original owner still to be living in the flats in Hawkswell Gardens.

> *Musicians who have lived in the roads include several teachers: Janet Tinbergen, herself a cello teacher, mentions Elizabeth Brazell of Victoria Road.*

> She was a music teacher, who was very good, she was an enthusiast, and she founded the Oxford Music Festival in the early 70s, which has become one of the major festivals in the country. It's a competitive music festival, a platform for amateur musicians of all ages and stages, and emerging professionals. I was involved peripherally then and am still involved now.

We close with extracts from our interview with a world-renowned violinist and teacher, Kato Havas (b.1920), who has lived in Victoria Road since the late 1970s (p.154).

I was born in the part of Hungary which was Transylvania, where Dracula comes from! And just when I was born, that part of Hungary was given over to the Romanians after the First World War.

She was a child prodigy whose family moved to Budapest so that she could attend the outstanding Academy there.

By the time I was 18, I went to America to give a concert in Carnegie Hall, and the war broke out. And Hungary declared war on America. I mean, talking of little countries! And I have to go to Montreal, Canada, because I went on a Visitor's Visa, to come in as a refugee.

She married an American and started a family – but found difficulties with playing.

This is when I discover that all the stresses and strains ... I began to lose the pleasure in playing, which I had so much pleasure before. So I realised that, while I was bringing up the children, I stop concerts. I wanted to be a mother.

Later she moved to England, and lived near Corfe Castle, in Dorset. The memory of Hungarian gypsy players stayed with her, deeply influencing her thoughts about playing. Her inspirational teaching was 'discovered' and she wrote a book.

Kato Havas, c.1927. (K. Havas)

The Hungarian gypsies played completely from inside out. They never had a lesson. They did it all instinctively. It went from generation to generation. They are the gypsy aristocrats. One of these gypsies, in my summer holidays, became a very good friend. He was about 60 and I was about 12. And I remember his dark face in the bushes, when I practised in the garden. I knew he was listening, so I pretended I didn't see him, and pulled myself up and played Paganini for him. In the evening, when we went for a meal, he pretended he didn't see me, and he played – oh, my God, didn't he play! They knew how to move people, they knew how to give pleasure, and that's what music is all about.

And suddenly I realised what help it was, how wonderful it was, and I was very excited about it. By accident, somebody came to look for horses – our cottage was on a farm – and he watched me teach, and he turned out to be the Music Advisor of Reading, of all places! He couldn't believe what I was doing! I thought it was the most natural thing in the world. He said he would like to write some articles for *The Strad* magazine, the English string magazine. I never played here, nobody knew who I was, and I was just living in the country. By that time, I was by myself with the children. And the articles took such terrific furore, I was so surprised, because I thought everybody would be so glad there is an answer to all the stresses and strains. Not at all! 'Who is this newcomer?'

I believed very passionately. I began to teach here and there and everywhere. Then I got a letter from the music publishers – could I write a book? I said, 'No, no, no, I can't write, I can't spell'. They said, 'Just write the way you talk'. So I wrote *A*

New Approach to Violin Playing, with the help of my children; they corrected my English, and they said, 'I don't understand what you mean here', and so they were my best editors, because I wanted everybody to understand what I was talking about. That was the beginning of everything. Afterwards came the American tours, other publications. I got the American Teachers' Association highest honour [in 1992].

Kato founded an international association – KHANA, the Kata Havas Association – with representatives in countries around the world, and ran summer schools, including two informal workshops which still take place each year at the Church Hall.

I had a Summer School at Teddy Hall. And in connection with it, at University Church, we had a recital every week, and it was for Oxfam, and we collected thousands of pounds. Conductors from America, from Belgium, from all over they came to conduct. They didn't get any fee. They knew my work. And all they needed was hospitality, and friends put them up.

I never give an audition, by the way. I don't believe in taking only those who can play. I believe that anybody who wants to play, ought to have a chance. So I took anybody to the Summer School. If somebody came to me and said, 'I want to be a concert violinist', I wouldn't take him. If he says, 'I have a problem, I can't play the way I would like to play', I'd do my best to help in every way. That would be a whole new book of mine, about the history of my pupils.

She remains passionate about her work.

I put everything in balances, in interrelated balances inside the body. A lot of attention to the rhythmic pulse, and to internalise the music. We sing a lot, and there are exercises. It is a very exact – I don't like to call it a 'method', because that's such a stiff word, but it's a discipline – mind, body and spirit together. The gift is something to give through. Yes, I'm very gifted, and I'm very grateful for it; but it's not mine. It doesn't belong to you. Music is the greatest thing. It's one of the most basic things in our whole life, whether you are a musician or not.

Kato is a British citizen, and her achievements were honoured with an OBE in 2002.

When the letter arrived from the Home Office, I thought 'Home Office? My God! What did I do?' I was so impressed with Prince Charles. We were about a hundred people getting this, and he made everybody, certainly he made me, as we were the only one. He knew what I was doing, he loved Hungary – I can't tell you how impressed I was! As a foreigner, what I found fascinating are these very formal parties, what ease they handled it – the combination of the informality and the formality, which is so British.

Well into her 80s, though alone again after the death of her English husband of 30 years, Kato still teaches busily and appreciates very much living in Victoria Road.

I used to go to America four or five, six times a year. That's why I'm not part of the community here. I have wonderful neighbours, and I'm very lucky with that. And I think Banbury Road, for shopping, is wonderful! I feel lovely belonging here, because I get notices of what goes on, and I think it's wonderful. And maybe, when I really slow down, I can do a bit more!

5   Children's Lives

Really we had a freer time as children; we didn't have much in the way of toys, etc. of course. We used to chase each other on bikes up and down the road. You couldn't do that now.

Monica Wagstaff

The interviewees we met in chapter 3 all gave a lively picture of a child's life in this area in the first half of the 20th century, and there is ample opportunity for comparison with more recent years.

Childhood in the early days

Dorothy Bridge's memories take us back to the years before the First World War, to an ordered domestic life punctuated by some vividly recalled happenings.

> We used to spin our tops on the pavement outside our back gate, and one day, [the old man opposite] came over and sat on our back step, and said he wouldn't let me go in unless I let him kiss me. And I thought, 'You stupid man!' I went and rang the front door bell, so my mother could let me in that way. He never came over again! … The maid slept in the top attic, and she called to me to go up to her, and I got up there, I couldn't see her, and I said, 'Where are you, Ada?' She'd got a tin trunk, and she jumped out of this trunk at me! And for years and years and years I would not go up to that top attic! It wasn't till I read in a magazine, if anything like that's happened, it's because you had a fright when you were a child. I instantly, in the dark, walked up to the top of the house. Of course, that maid had to leave, Dad told her to go.

Children's behaviour was firmly controlled, especially on Sundays.

> One day, we went into a very old-fashioned draper's shop on the Banbury Road, and she said, 'I sat behind you in church last night, and you were so good', and she gave me a celluloid duck, and I thought, 'Well, surely, if a child's told to sit still, she sits still.' If I'd moved, I don't know what would have happened. But I loved going to church.

Margaret Twining remembers the restrictiveness of Sundays.

> On Sundays we had stories, Bible stories read to us and things. Sunday had to be a very behave-yourself day! Mother had to be careful what clothes she wore on Sunday. They couldn't be too gay. You didn't do any [sewing or knitting] on Sundays. I don't know what you were supposed to do.

Most families in these roads in the earlier part of the century employed someone to do housework, but it was considered normal, indeed important training, for girls to help with chores, as Gwynneth Twining recalls.

> Iron, air your beds and make your beds. I had the job of dusting the banisters – there were a great many of them, twisty sort of things.

Clare Wagstaff comments that helping with housework wasn't an issue.

We didn't mind, it was just what happened, everybody did it, so you don't mind.

Boys were not usually expected to help – though John Herivel, brought up in Belfast in the 1920s, did not escape.

Mother was always very firm that I should do as much as Elise did. She was very enlightened in that respect. So I was used to doing things. But I did resent it, as a male child, because I'd noticed that Father did nothing at all. But, of course, he worked very hard, and when he came back, he was exhausted. He was entitled to be looked after!

Dorothy Bridge particularly hated helping with the washing.

We used to have a copper for the washing, and oh, I hated it! I had to help my mother fold the sheets. I couldn't bear it!

Friends

Dorothy remembers her childhood as happy, because of good friends in these roads.

They were lovely days. We had such nice friends, young friends. We used to go to tea with the Turners at no.13, they were our great friends. And I had friends in Lonsdale Road [no.6], called the Welfords: he went to London every day, but he had a small firm out at Kidlington, and they had a pony and trap which they kept in Marston Ferry fields at the back of Lonsdale Road. [Mrs Welford] used to make the loveliest cakes! I was great friends with her two daughters, Cicely and Enid Welford. And we used to ride the horse, Snowdrop, in Marston Ferry fields. We used to go to parties at the Twinings, Christmas parties, then they used to come to parties at our house.

Gwynneth Twining's memories of home in the 1920s are similarly happy.

We had this lovely garden to play in. I don't remember any restrictions on friends coming in. We had parties.

Dorothy White's family shared parties with friends: the Georges lived in Lonsdale Road.

We used to have a joint sort of Christmas Party at the Church Hall, with the Twinings and Georges. Mr George was one of the shop walkers at Elliston's.

For the Wagstaffs however friendships were disrupted by schooling in Abingdon.

We had very little contact with other children, because we were boarders at school and we lost touch, really, with a lot of the local children.

During the war they went as day girls, finding their way to school on the buses.

Buses were dreadful. You could queue 40 minutes to get on a bus.

The population of children in the streets has always seemed to ebb and flow. Monica Wagstaff remembers a lot of old people in Hamilton Road.

Quite a lot of elderly people we remember – but of course, when you're very small, anyone seems elderly.

Evacuees enlarged the number of young people around during the war.

We didn't have evacuees because we were full up – but ever so many people had evacuees. Mr and Mrs Butler, they had evacuees and they seemed to get on very well indeed with them, and one of them, another Monica, we were very friendly with. Another lady, she lived right down in Lucerne Road, it's a cottage-like house with lots of wood on it [no.14] – we used to call her the Kitten Lady because she always had lots of kittens – she had a girl there who remained friendly with her for years after the war, and used to come back. The schools had to share. I think you cut out dinner time or something like that – so one school had it in the morning, the other in the afternoon. And of course, teachers worked enormous hours.

Jean Robinson, who was herself evacuated from London with her school, puts in a word for the teachers who accompanied their pupils.

While we were away, the teachers were kind of *in loco parentis*: they didn't just teach you, they made sure you cleaned your teeth and got your hair cut, and things like that. Although I never saw them again, I really have great admiration for what those single, childless women did during the war.

Playing outside

Children spent a lot of time playing outside, as Dorothy Bridge recalls.

On our field, my brother and I, we used to play cricket with a tennis ball! And then when he was eleven, he went to the High School, and had a hard ball. Of course, bowled me on the thumb! All I did was hold it under the cold water tap, you didn't complain.

Dorothy White also remembers playing with boys, in Hamilton Road in the 1920s.

There was a boy who lived just down the road, on the other side, who used to join in our games, and we used to play cricket down the road and so forth. We used to fly kites up and down the road too. I caught somebody's telephone wires. And there it stuck! The telephone people had to come and get it down!

Playing in the road was normal – though it could still annoy the neighbours. A little later Ted Shirley (b.1938) remembers vividly being ticked off by the retired Reverend Raven for kicking his football around in Hamilton Road.

Betty Marshall had lots of friends to play with in Victoria Road in the 1930s. There were tennis courts on the site of Hawkswell Gardens.

I didn't go to school until I was six. The family doctor thought it was utter nonsense, taking a child away from its happy home life, and putting them into school. I liked school, but I was probably just as happy at home. There were a lot of children, up and down the road, to play with. [There were] tennis courts, both grass and bitumen. We used to play ball in the road, we used to play skipping in the road. What a change!

Betty Howes (Marshall) with her pets in the garden of 45 Victoria Road, c.1933. (B. Marshall)

She used to tag along in games at the Paternoster Dairy in Victoria Road, which belonged to the Stanleys.

[They had] very nice parties, and they used to go and play hide and seek and climb up the steps into a sort of hayloft above the dairy part of it, where they bottled the milk and washed the milk bottles. I was always the little one, and I couldn't get up the steps because I was a lot younger than them!

For Geoffrey Paine the family-owned bakery in South Parade was an adventure playground, and there was little anxiety about accidents.

We used to have great fun clambering over the roofs of the bakehouse etc., play hide and seek or things like that, and we had plenty of room to play. Obviously some things went on, but nothing serious, and nobody worried. Life was so different then. It was before television, of course, and certainly before computers, and you made your own fun, and thoroughly enjoyed it.

Alan Knowles was a friend of the Paine twins and has warm memories of the Bakery.

John Rowe on his tricycle in 1934, passing the garden where 10 Victoria Road was built in 1937. (J. Rowe)

Paine's Bakery, that was our basic number one playground, we used to drive poor Roger Paine nuts. The best fun was to get up in the flour loft, and shoot down the chute. If you were able to time it right it was the last one who got caught. One of the goodies which we used to get hold of was a few lardy cakes!

As the grandson of Reg Alden, the local big butcher, Alan also had the attraction of the forbidden slaughterhouse behind Victoria Road on his doorstep.

We weren't allowed to go near it – so of course we did.

He roamed with a gang of friends in the particularly traffic-free days of the war.

We would cycle down the Banbury Road six abreast. All you had to do was miss a bus, and you didn't get many buses. North Oxford was virtually our playground, it was like a great big village and there was quite a large number of us and we would just cycle around wherever we wanted to go.

As Sydney Denton remembers, one thing which would get children indoors throughout the land was 'Dick Barton'.

Every night, the most important thing in anybody's life, empty the streets, was 'Dick Barton – Special Agent'. A radio programme about these detectives. And it was quarter to seven.

The river and roaming

The river has figured large in children's play over the years – especially for those like the Paines, Knowleses and Twinings whose families had river gardens in Lucerne Road.

Margaret and Gwynneth Twining paddling in the River Cherwell, c.1923. (M.&G. Twining)

Gwynneth Twining recalls a particular punting expedition.

We learned to paddle, we learnt to punt, we learnt to swim. Mother used to let us – Margaret and I, and two cousins – go off for the day in this punt, pack us up a lot of sandwiches. Until one day, we went down the river, and we got nearly to the Rollers, and these naughty girls started telling me stories about, if we got to the weir, we would be sucked under, and all the rest of it! So I got in a panic, and said, 'Oh, come on, let's go back! Go back!' And I was paddling! So I sat on the edge of the boat. But unfortunately, of course, I fell in backwards, didn't I! So these girls had to pull me out by my legs! Then, of course, they were scared stiff. They took my clothes off, and dried me with the cushion covers! They dressed me up in their jerseys, one on the top and two tied round my waist, and then we rushed up as fast as we could. It was quite a way to punt up to here. I can remember now, walking up Victoria Road! We trailed up, with all these funny clothes on! They were frightened to death what my mother was going to say! We came in the back door, and there was rather a long passage to the larder, and she was in the larder, and she turned round when she heard us, and she burst out laughing! I think Father wasn't so pleased when he heard! Well, of course, it must have been a bit frightening for them really! And we weren't allowed to go on the river for a bit, not by ourselves.

Geoffrey Paine is nostalgic for the freedom children had before there was so much concern over safety.

We used to have wonderful fun. Parties, or a group of us would come down and we had a punt and a canoe, and we used to swim in the river. We used to get enormous great tyres from large vehicles – all the things that people think, nowadays, are far too dangerous! But we survived, and we had a wonderful time. The river, of course, is far cleaner now than it was when we used to swim in it. But we used to get immune to all the bugs!

Sydney Denton's childhood territory during the war was demarcated by the river – life on his side of the river was rougher than for the middle-class children of these roads.

The Marston Council House boys were at war with the Cutteslowe boys, and we used to go out and raid each other. The river Cherwell used to separate us, and thank goodness it did! How it started, I've no idea. It was territorial, I suppose, and the human race doesn't change very much. We lived on the wrong side of the river – Marston being the wrong side of the river, North Oxford being the right side of the river. I'd recently learnt to swim, and I swam over by the Dragon School, the great famous North Oxford Prep School. And I found, or I stole, might be nearer the truth, a cricket bat, which was split, and it had been abandoned, I told my

Margaret and Betty Twining (second from left and right) with friends on the family punt, c.1919. (M.&G.Twining)

father. Anyway, I swum back with this bat, I bound it beautifully, and I linseed-oiled it, and I got an inner-tube of a bicycle and made a new handle for it, and I thought I was the cat's whiskers with this bat! Anyway, there was a knocking on the door, and it was a policeman. So my father made me go and return the bat. Well, I got outside this school, and there's lots of little boys. And they all spoke with little posh voices! Anyway, eventually, I got to see this [headmaster], Jock Lynam, and he gave me a real dressing down. But I did tell him how well I'd looked after the bat, and I'd repaired it. He said, didn't I realise, that to go swimming on their side, you needed a permit? 'I didn't realise that, sir', I said. So he gave me a swimming permit! And sent me on my way!

The river was accessible from these roads even to those without river gardens: John Rowe used to go fishing in the area round the now vanished Cherwell Arms.

It was open down at the end of the road, at the bottom of Water Eaton Road. There was an old fashioned pub, and a place you could get boats out. We used to sit down there and fish, and put the fish in tubs.

The land owned by Summer Fields to the east of the lane which is now the cycle track was also open, as the Wagstaffs recall.

We could clear off over the fields and go off down to the river – well, everything's barbed wire now. You could get right down to the river, you just walked. I mean, Summer Fields owned it all, but there was no security at all.

They too comment on the different attitude to risk in those days.

There wasn't this awful worry there is now of going lonely places on your own: you can't really let kids do that now. We all had bikes, and we used to clear off. My mother didn't see danger, that was obvious to us, as we're older now. I used to do poling on the river, my younger sister used to do canoeing, and we couldn't even swim – and we didn't have life jackets either.

Certainly bicycles were key possessions, and they gave children an enormous range, as Monica says, remembering the 1930s.

I could cycle a two-wheeler from about the age of three to four – and by five I was on the Banbury Road. There were cars – but they seemed to keep further away from

you and didn't go as fast! We used to clear off on bikes, and one of our haunts was Wood Eaton. There was a small wood there, and we always used to go to the little church there. We used to cycle over to Kidlington, and to Witney. Yes, we were fairly dependent on bikes, I think most people of our age were. We were wild flower enthusiasts, and there were one or two places over at Wood Eaton where we knew orchids were – there's no sign of them now. And I can remember picking that grass, it trembles, it's lovely, over Cassington – there's no sign of that either. Sometimes there was quite a group of us, we used to take a picnic. I don't think anything would have ever happened to you.

John Rowe likewise recalls the freedom of the bicycle – as well as family outings by train.

You'd just go off to explore. Mothers just said 'Don't talk to strange men'. Kidlington was an RAF base and we used to go out there. We bicycled to Witney and Bicester – of course it was just a little road. And years ago before Dr Beeching got in the business you

Clare, Dorothy and Monica Wagstaff out collecting wild flowers, 1937. (C. & M. Wagstaff)

could travel all over the place on the train. You could get a train to Woodstock for a picnic in the Park.

Going for walks was a very standard pastime, as Dorothy White recalls.

We used to walk up the by-pass when they were building that [in the mid 1930s], walk up to Headington. On a Sunday we'd do that.

Toys and treats

Toys were generally simple and few – balls, yo-yo, tennis racquet, etc. Dorothy Bridge has a painful memory of a doll.

My mother wasn't fond of me. She'd do anything for my brother, but she wasn't fond of me. I had a doll, more like what they call a Barbie Doll nowadays, more like a little girl, and my joy was making it clothes. And then when it came that we had to take our exams – when it got to the age of 13, I had to take the preliminary – I thought, 'I mustn't play with my doll for the whole winter', and I made her a gym frock, and put her in my cupboard, and when the exams were all finished, and I'd passed, I went to get her out, but she'd gone. I said to my mother, 'Where is my doll?' She said, 'Oh, you're too old to play with dolls, I've given her away.'

Gwynneth Twining had a camera around 1930.

Wright's coal tar soap we used to have. They had an offer for so many coupons, and I think probably a little bit of money, the Brownie Box Camera. So when I was about nine or ten, I had a camera, and I was thrilled to bits with this camera! And it lasted quite a long time too.

In general, children were expected to amuse themselves. Monica Wagstaff remarks that there was little public provision for them, in relation to her younger sister Dorothy.

She was musical, good at sport, she was good at most things, and there weren't the facilities for sports and things like that. Children have an awful lot going for them today if you look for it. It wasn't there in our day. Tennis clubs were about the only thing.

There was a lot of street entertainment from people begging round the roads, as Dorothy White remembers.

We used to get people round at the door. After the First World War, you got a lot of people singing in the street for money and so forth.

Monica Wagstaff describes a regular visitor from before the Second World War.

Every Friday a man used to come round with a hurdy-gurdy. He had a monkey on his shoulder, and he used to come and collect money. I think he was Italian.

An annual highlight of Dorothy Bridge's childhood was the arrival of Chipperfield's Circus for the St Giles Fair.

Their caravans were not allowed into the city before six o'clock in the morning. My father got to know Mr Chipperfield, and let him put his horses on our fields, so my father got all the manure for the garden! He gave us tickets for his circus.

Betty Grant remembers the St Giles Fair from the 1930s.

That was really good in those days. I don't like it now. Dad used to take us. We used to go down at night, have a look at all the lights and that. There were switchbacks, and Noah's Arks, and dodgems, helter-skelter. There's always been the round-about, the horses.

Geoffrey Paine believes that things were more special against a background of much less material wealth, and that life was easier for children.

As children, we were so naïve, compared with children today [but] the thing which we benefited from – we used to have treats! No such thing as a treat nowadays! When people say to me, 'Is Christmas what it used to be?' I say, 'Of course it isn't.' If you think back, certainly to the 1920s and 30s, where 70 per cent of the population were living on bread and dripping for 51 weeks of the year – for 70 per cent of the population now, it's Christmas Day every day. It's the same with treats. What used to be a treat is now the norm. It's far more difficult for children now, actually.

He mentions some of his childhood treats.

Going to the pantomime or something like that, there was always a pantomime at New Theatre then. Or going up to London. Or even going to the cinema.

John Rowe remembers being taken on 'tourist' visits round the town and colleges during the holidays. Betty Marshall pays tribute to her mother.

She was a wonderful mother. We always managed to do something exciting on half-term – and half-term, in those days, was one day, not a week – and during the holidays.

Childhood in the second half of the century

Martine Honoré came to the far end of Lonsdale Road in 1953 when there were no other families there. It was only a little later that people of a 'younger vintage', like the Tinbergens, moved in and the children had friends to play with. Margaret Willis (then Margaret Helsby) came to 55 Lonsdale Road a year later and also felt constraints on children's behaviour.

> It was quite an elderly sort of road, because I remember, we had to restrain our children from playing outside too much, because it upset people. The only other young family were the Becks, that was the URC Minister and his family.

It was still a very rural environment that her children grew up in.

> That lane, which was just along the back of Summer Fields, was completely countrified. There was a big rotten oak which you could climb into half way along there. And the children all played there a tremendous amount. It was very nice, the farm lane.

Will Helsby outside 55 Lonsdale Road, c.1960. (Margaret Willis)

The site of Hawkswell Gardens was then an open space.

> They dug. They used to dig tremendously, and also when the Cherwell School was built [in the early 1960s], there was an enormous drainage scheme, and all sorts of naughty children got up to all sorts of larks! Little gangs used to form and re-form, you know!

Margaret later came to live in a house right at the bottom of Lonsdale Road: it had been owned when she and her family first lived in Lonsdale Road by Mr Hanks.

> The whole thing was a gigantic garden, and he had a fierce sort of Mr McGregor who looked after it all, and my boys, and many other local boys, used to play a sort of 'Catch as catch can', seeing how far they could get without McGregor catching them!

Mr Hanks had a treasure in his garden, a passenger-carrying railway.

> He was an Old Boy of New College School, and he used to invite the boys, sometimes, to see the model railway that he'd built in the garden. He was an engineer, you see, and he'd actually built it.

Martine Honoré speaks enthusiastically of the railway – and recounts its shocking end.

> He had in his garden a *real* train, with rails, wagons, locomotive – built so that a child or even an adult could ride in it. From time to time he would ask the neighbour children to come and have a ride – it was a great treat. It didn't happen very

often, because it was really a museum thing. It was a treasure. It was his life. It was his pride and glory, beautifully perfected to every little detail. But in 1976 some burglars came at night and stole the train. It was a very stormy night, with lightening, there was thunder. We all presume it must have been done through vans and extremely well plotted. They stole everything. After the theft of this train, which must have been worth a fortune, Mr Hanks developed cardiac trouble and he died.

Parenting

Unfortunately this major incident does not seem to have coincided with publication of the Lonsdalian Mail, *which appeared in about eight issues around 1977. Suddenly there were young academics moving into the roads, and a lot of children living near each other. Jan Martin remembers it as 'a golden age for children' in Lonsdale Road.*

The children meshed. They all got on very well together. And the parents got on well. You either had a house full of children or you had none at all. Two of mine, Lucy and Toby Robinson, Miles [Glyn] to some extent, four Flemmings, oh and Lizzie Sleeper, and Mitchells, all on this side of the road – they did the *Lonsdalian Mail* together. It was circulated among the families. Rebecca typed it out with one finger.

We include a couple of extracts to give the flavour of the publication, which included recipes, advertisements and rather good jokes, alongside insights into life in the roads.

From issue no. 1

St Michael's playgroup had a Jumble sale on Saturday in the church hall there were two of our dashing reporters on the scene. One person was pickpocketed but no one was caught the Jumble Sale made ninety pounds approx this is very good

Smoking

People who smoke are risking their lives people who smoke 40 cigarettes a day smoke 14,600 cigarettes a year this is very expensive. Also 20 cigarettes a day will cost £265 a year. You could buy a car if you saved this money. Why smoke?

From issue no. 7

Lonsdalian cello Group

On Saturday Janet Tinbergans [sic] cello group played in the Music Festival in a non-competitive class. Some of the people taking part live in Lonsdalia, they are Edward Flemming, 52 Lonsdale road, Lizzy Sleeper, 42 Lonsdale road, Elizabeth O'Riordan, 104 Lonsdale road. Also the teacher Janet Tinbergan lives at 88 Lonsdale Road.

While Jean Robinson's children were among the group creating newspapers and performing home pantomimes she expresses reservations about the more excessive child-focussed attitudes she has seen around her.

I was still irritated at this tremendous emphasis on education for children. I can't quite describe what it was that was wrong with it. It was ... oh, 'developing little Hugh's talents', and the kind of preciousness about it.

Pupils of Maretta Grace's ballet classes in *The Dancing Princesses*, 1991. Costumes were designed and made by some of the mothers of the performers.
(Verity Peto)

Children from Lonsdale and Portland Roads creatively occupied in the Fouweathers' house in Portland Road on a day when Wolvercote School was closed in 1992. (Janet Fouweather)

Her own rearing was 'respectable working class' in the 1930s and 40s and she contrasts this with middle-class parenting styles in the 1960s and 70s.

In my background, you never ever praised children because they would get bigheaded, they wouldn't kowtow to the boss and keep a job, or they'd be in trouble at school. Whereas, as I learned, praise is very effective for children, in directing them in the right way, and giving them confidence and so on. It was getting this kind of balance which you try to do. It was a much more self-conscious parenting generation, really, than our parents had been. Our parents' idea was, you kept them clean, you kept them fed, they did as they were told, you made sure the girls didn't get pregnant before they got married, and the boys didn't go to prison.

Establishing parenting boundaries these days is challenging. David Shriger, who brought his family from the United States to Lonsdale Road for 2003–4, gives an interesting and refreshingly positive perspective on life here.

In much of America, the current kind of style of parenting is one where the children are treated like little adults, and included in everything, and there really isn't that much separation between the adult world and the child world. Here, we saw that it's done a little bit differently. Children are still children. And that was very helpful to us, as parents, because we began to mimic some of that behaviour, and we actually liked it. We were happier, the kids were happier. I think we learnt as many parenting things from England as anything else.

Child-minding has of course been co-operatively managed through links with neighbours from early days. Mariele Kuhn remembers this from wartime.

Our children were great friends with the Bielby children, then next to them were the Thorntons, the bookseller. We went babysitting for each other. When one of us would go out, then the children would go, with their ration – milk bottle or whatever, and another day, if I had to go out, Mrs Thornton looked after.

Some houses were preferred to others. The Honoré children had a good garden to play in with their friends in the 1950s.

It was generally my garden because I was less garden proud than some other mothers. For a couple of years children dug an enormous hole at the back of the garden to try to reach Australia. They were a bit muddy, but very peaceful, they dug and they dug and it was right in the back of my garden, I didn't mind in the least.

Swimming in the river, 1987. (Holly Kilpatrick)

Some academic families came with progressive ideals. In the early 1970s Celia Glyn's children played with the Flemmings in Lonsdale Road.

The Flemmings weren't allowed guns and they didn't have television so our house was quite popular!

Children and other adults

Children earlier in the century very often had extended family living in the roads or nearby. Alan Knowles living in Greengates in Hernes Road spent a lot of time with his maternal grandparents the Aldens – their big house West Grove was next door – and also with his paternal grandfather in 13 Victoria Road, who taught him to fish.

He had a workshop in his garage and he and I used to make little boxes which was all great fun. We could walk right the way through from Hernes Road into Victoria Road.

This became rarer as the population of the roads became more mobile. However Helen Holland describes vividly the beloved uncle who lived with her spinster aunt Elizabeth in Portland Road, in the house where she now lives herself.

He was a very witty and endearing fellow, James, very kind and generous. We adored him. We called him 'Juncle' – Uncle James Juncle! His favourite dinner ever consisted of nothing but puddings! He used to wear sock suspenders, and one could say to him, 'Juncle, can I touch you for a fiver?' and he'd roll up his trousers and take out a wadge of pound notes and five pounds notes from his socks, and hand over a tenner! So we were very very fond of him. And Elizabeth stayed on in her role as much less warm, but nonetheless sharp and witty, and rather idiosyncratic maiden aunt. She didn't like to be approached, she'd stick out her hand, very firmly, and say, 'C Y K', which meant, 'Consider yourself kissed', because she didn't like any kind of embrace or warmth. I think the children rather liked having such an idiosyncratic great-aunt, and liked laughing about her latest outrageous statement.

Several people speak of significant relationships between children and neighbouring adults, something which perhaps develops less readily these days. Mariele Kuhn recalls a couple living in 107 Victoria Road who helped her younger son (b.1938).

Mr and Mrs Miles, he was something with the Prudential, and they were very sweet to Nicholas. Nicholas was a bit unhappy at one time.

John Marsh remembers 'Uncle Bert' and Mrs Butler in Hamilton Road.

He worked at the Sorting Office, and she was a Miss Kirner, the jewellers. Our children grew up with them, and they were very very good for children, particularly him – he used to play cricket – and he was then well in his 70s.

Bob Williams' boys got access to the river via a friendly neighbour.

Just across the road from us, which is number 1 Lucerne Road, that house runs down to the bank of the Cherwell itself. Living in that house was a spinster [Jean Paxman]. And she was a very good friend with the boys, and our two boys could, therefore, get down to the river in a rubber dinghy, we could borrow her punt and things like that.

Jelly Williams describes her younger son's friendship with both Jean Paxman and their neighbour Mrs Schepens because of his early interest in furniture: both old ladies had some fine pieces.

When Jean Paxman died, in her will she left a mirror to our younger son John. He

didn't like it at all as a grown man. Eventually he sold it: he got quite a bit of money for it and bought something specific for it, and he still feels a bit guilty about it. But it shows what very good relationships we had, generous.

Paul Wright bicycling in Victoria Road in 1984, when cars were less of a problem. (Sally Wright)

The Morris household in Lucerne Road was practically a second home for Alex Peebles (b.1976), who was an only child until 1982, as his mother Holly Kilpatrick recalls.

He regularly joined them in their 'playroom' which was easily accessed by patio doors from the back of their house. He felt such a part of their lives that when we got back from two weeks away in 1981 he said, 'I'd better pop round and see Professor Morris, he'll have been wondering where I've been!'

Peter Clarke's son, an only child, admired the neighbour across the way.

Andy used to adore that chap! He was very kind of with it, you know, and Andy was young, and he thought he was very groovy!

Activities and constraints

Winter used to be fun for children before snowfall became largely a thing of the past. Paloma Bevir of Hamilton Road remembers the winters of the early 1980s.

I bought some old skis, and some old boots, from Oxfam. When it started snowing, I would go out myself, at dusk, when nobody could see me, to do a bit of up and down with skis. But then the children liked that, and I lent it to the children who wanted to borrow them, and it was quite fun! It was really cold, and after a big snow fall we had very low temperatures, so the ice set in the street. But then winters got milder and milder, and that was the end of it.

With a change in the environment in which children were raised, organised activities became an important way of occupying them safely. We have mentioned elsewhere Mrs Corden's annual pantomime (see
p.191ff). *There have been other youth dramatic groups since then, notably the long-running North Oxford Youth Theatre based in Wolvercote Village Hall. The Portland Road Church Hall has been well used: Cathy Berry remembers going there for 'ballet classes with Maretta Grace, Brownies, Guides, and even karate for a while'. There were plenty of sports activities too, like the Summertown Stars football club. Sometimes this began in the roads: Professor Sir Peter Morris's youngest child Michael (b.1971) was a gifted sportsman, going on to bat for Cambridge University. He had spent endless hours playing street football and cricket in the cul de sac at the end of Lucerne Road, often with Alex Peebles, who also grew up to be a keen cricketer.*

Hamilton Road: playing in the snow of 1981–2. (P. Berry)

Portland Road: children bicycling in the flash flood of July 1994. (Sally Owen)

Increased traffic is now the problem with playing in the street, but some still try. Philippa Berry of Hamilton Road sees this as a good part of the neighbourhood.

There's a young family opposite here, and there is still skateboarding, and bicycling up and down the road. Games, and that sort of thing. And it is lovely.

Sally Bromley says the same of Victoria Road.

I thoroughly enjoy it. I'm never happier than seeing children just playing, on skateboards or bikes and things. I love it.

Other residents are more disapproving, disliking the noise and feeling their parked cars or front gardens threatened by flying balls or frisbees.

Clare and Monica Wagstaff, who spoke above about the freedom with which they roamed as children, clearly feel anxieties for children today, however much more mature they seem. When the Wagstaffs were interviewed in 2000 they had recently had young great-nieces from Canada to stay.

We were on our knees by the end of it. The older one was terribly independent for a 12-year-old. Gosh, when I think what I was like at that age, my word she could look after herself. But a child that age, you've got to go everywhere with them, particularly in a country where they don't know anything.

There is a perception that young people out by themselves in the streets are not as safe as they once were. Helen Holland, who moved to Portland Road in 1997, gives examples from her children's experience.

They were a little shocked by some of the unpleasant behaviour in the street – not from children living here, but from children from Cutteslowe. I remember Eliza having a stone thrown at her as she rode her bicycle home, and Theodore being attacked when he came home with a little friend, being beaten up in the Church Hall car park.

However David Schriger, visiting from the USA, gives a positive view of their daughters' recent experience.

My 11-year old hops on the bus and goes down town, and walks around with friends – that wouldn't happen in Los Angeles, the degree of independence I feel comfortable giving her here. Then the kids here are great. One day she looked at me, recently, and said, 'You know, I think my friends here are nicer than my friends in LA.' The pace here is a little more relaxed, and people devote more of their time to doing things for others. Just taking the time to make a going-away card, even if it's scribbled on a piece of paper, that still takes an effort, and you can either do it or not do it, and I think, in the States, the tendency is not to do it.

Emma Peto and a friend off to school in Lonsdale Road, 2002. (V. Peto)

Most children seem to have had a good experience of growing up here, as Verity Peto says.

Our daughter, Emma, says that growing up in Summertown is like growing up in heaven! She thinks it's absolutely wonderful.

As they get older they enjoy a social life revolving round the proximity of friends and ready access to Oxford's centre. Young adults today tend to disperse to university and to earn their livings, but like Jan Martin's children, who left long since, are often still attached to their home.

They loved it here. They practically cry when I say I'll have to sell the house.

6   *School and University*

People are obsessed with schools. I don't think we've ever been to a dinner party where we haven't heard all the time, and talked all the time, about schools!

Verity Peto

This chapter looks at schooling for those in the roads during the last century. In addition a surprisingly large number of residents today first came to Oxford as students at the University, and we record some of their memories of their education.

Early schooling in the roads

For young children small private schools of variable efficacy were the first choice of residents of these roads in the first half of the century. Dorothy Bridge (b.1907) started school before the First World War.

I first went to school at the corner of Lonsdale Road, and it was lovely. I can remember a book she had there, with a picture of London on it. But the people would not pay the rent, and she had to give up. We went to a school in Victoria Road [no.90] – Miss Bonner – till we were ready to go to a bigger school. My mother told me I could read by the age of four. I had a book of stories: the first one was about fairies. I thought it was stupid.

The Wagstaff sisters recall the period between the wars.

There were so many little private schools in this area in those days – particularly taking very young children. There were State schools, but I don't think anyone in the road went to a State school, a primary school.

Margaret Twining remembers her early education without much enthusiasm.

I was sent to some lady in Portland Road, I think, and I used to be shown books, and supposed to be learning to read, but I don't think I did much! I went to a school run by two Miss Tuckers, down the Woodstock Road, right down by Lathbury Road. I don't think I enjoyed Miss Tucker's School very much.

Her younger sister Gwynneth, like many others in the roads, went to Miss Cooper's in the Church Hall on the corner of Portland Road in the 1920s.

Miss Cooper had a small school there, in the downstairs room. A dozen, or perhaps a few more than that, mixed, boys and girls. Not too bad a school. Taught you to read and write, and arithmetic, but not much else!

Clare Wagstaff remembers vividly starting at Miss Cooper's at the age of five in 1932 – long before the days of decimal currency.

We had our classes between billiard tables. Miss Cooper walked with a crutch, she was slightly lame. I can remember learning arithmetic with pennies and halfpennies and farthings – toy pennies and halfpennies – and learning everything in a very roundabout way. If we were learning pounds, shillings and pence we pulled everything down to pence, then did the sum then got it back up again. That's why I was never any good at sums – it took twice as long as it needed to.

When Clare was about seven and Monica was starting school they went together to a slightly eccentric school.

We went to Sunnymead House, on the corner of Hernes Road, where Ritchie Court is now, that was a big house, and a lovely garden, another little private school. I can remember Mrs West, who was the Head, and the owner. And her friend Miss Lysart with an Eton crop. Miss West had odd ideas, and one of her ideas was toe dancing. You had black shoes, with almost steel caps, and they could dance on their toes. We used to run round the garden at playtime – we all used to have a hoop, according to your size. We all had mouth organs, and the noise was terrible. A lot of it was not very educational at all.

Perhaps more educational was the small Catholic school begun in 1930 in 86 Hamilton Road by Ivy King and Elizabeth Rendall, who lost their jobs when they converted to Catholicism. There were eight pupils including J.R.R.Tolkien's son Christopher: the older ones were taught in the dining room, the younger ones in the drawing room of this little house. Rye St Antony moved the next year to 84 Woodstock Road, and then to its present location in Pullen's Lane, Headington, where it flourishes today with a mixture of day and boarding girl pupils.

Pupils in the garden of 86 Hamilton Road: the first day of Rye St Antony School, 25 September 1930. (Miss A. Jones)

Betty Grant was one of few children in the roads educated at the local state school at this period, as her father taught at 'Summertown Mixed' in buildings next to the old St John's Church on Church Street (now Rogers Street). The family had been living in Kingston Road, but in 1932 her father bought a house in Hamilton Road. She remembers starting aged three or four at Summertown Nursery school in the mid 1920s.

In the afternoons we all had to lie down and go to sleep. When we got to five, six, we came over to Summertown School, and there were two classes for babies.

From there she moved to the main school. The old church was demolished in 1924.

We came on to the big school and there were about six or eight classes in that school. Where the church was, they made a playground, and that's where we went to play. We went to Merton Baths once a week. We all used to parade outside, get on with the teacher, on the bus at South Parade and go into town. Every Remembrance Day, the whole school came up, round the Memorial outside the Church Hall, we had a service. And Empire Day, the whole school used to go in the big playground at the back of the school, and we had a little service then.

Later there was a state Infants School in Hobson Road. Ted Shirley, who lived in Hamilton Road, started there in 1943.

I remember my mother taking me for a walk past the school. I cried, because I wanted to join them. So she asked if I could go and I went to school at 4 ¹/₂.

Boys had a greater choice of well-established schools in the vicinity. The Kuhns, who came to Victoria Road as refugees just before the war, sent their sons, Anton and Nicholas, to the Dragon School, the well-known North Oxford prep school – though not before Anton had experienced the local kindergarten run by Miss Franklin (who earlier taught at Rye St Antony).

She was a Roman Catholic. She told the children about resurrection, lying on the floor, with her big bosom, and then raising herself. She said, 'It's all right. You go to Heaven, it's wonderful. You have ice cream, balloons.' That was during the war. And Anton said, 'How did she know? Had she been here, in Heaven?' And we said, 'Of course not.' Then he said, 'Then she's telling us a lie.'

Mariele found the Dragon School very competitive.

Nicholas liked Latin, but other things he didn't. So they moved Nicholas to something called the 'Dud Form', can you imagine? The Dud Form! After, they realised he was too intelligent. But what a thing to do to a child! I never thought really highly of it, they just pushed them, to get him into Eton.

Geoffrey Paine, son of the local bakery business, loved the Dragon when he went there in 1942, having soon moved with his twin brother David from the state to the private education system.

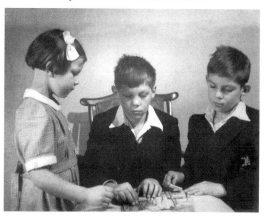

The Paine children in their school uniforms, c.1944. Josephine was at the High School and David and Geoffrey at the Dragon School. (David Paine)

We started off at the [Infants] school in what is now Hobson Road – it was Albert Street in those days – and then went from there to Woodstock House School, which could best be described as a 'Dame School', and then at the age of nine, went on to the Dragon School. We had an enormous amount of freedom. Far more freedom then than they do now. You could go into North Parade. The Dragon, then, was about 15 years ahead of its time. Out of class you called masters by their nicknames. There was a mix of business people and University people.

Secondary schooling before the war

Secondary education for girls from these roads at this period was usually at one of the private day schools, as in Dorothy Bridge's case.

I went to St Faith's School, an Anglican Convent School, the best school in Oxford. I could have gone to the High School. When I started, it was 1918, just before war ended. It was a wonderful school. They had three schools. They had a boarding school for mostly clergymen's daughters, who lived in the Convent buildings. Our school was on the Woodstock Road, next to Leckford Road – 115. And then they had a school in Winchester Road [St Denys's], where you didn't have to pay to go, and that produced some wonderful girls.

After leaving school Dorothy went to train as a secretary.

I started to learn shorthand and typewriting, and it was September, and I was going down on my bicycle. It was half an hour later than we had to get to school, and the weather was hot, and I thought, 'This is perfect!' Then after a week, I thought, 'It isn't perfect. I'm missing something.' And it came to me that I was missing Sister Muriel's New Testament lessons. I always regret I didn't write to thank her.

Dorothy White went to St Faith's a little later, in the 1920s, but when she was eleven moved to Milham Ford.

The Headmistress was Miss Joan McCabe, she was wonderful. Absolutely crippled with rheumatoid arthritis, but she ruled with a rod of iron!

Milham Ford was a girls' grammar school attended by many girls from these roads over the years. Betty Grant won a free place there from Summertown School in the early 1930s. Betty Marshall went a little later, but was happier at St Faith's.

Milham Ford, in those days, was in Cowley Place, at the back of Magdalen College School. I stayed there for four terms, not terribly happy, for all sorts of reasons. When they moved to Marston, I left, and went to St Faith's, which was on Woodstock Road. It was a Protestant Convent, not Catholic. Oh, it was fun! I liked it very much. My mother went to the sister school – St Denys – and I was taught sewing by the same nun who taught my mother to sew! Sister Lydia. She was as old as the hills. My mother said she was old when she taught her! She really was old. It wasn't just a child thinking somebody was old, she was <u>old</u>!

The Wagstaffs were sent to a Catholic convent school in Abingdon, as Clare recalls, when she was about nine, and her sister six. They were too young to enjoy it, and felt it deprived them of local friends.

We went to Our Lady's Convent at Abingdon, as boarders. So we rather lost touch with other children in the road. We were never close friends with any other children.

Gwynneth Twining went like her sister Margaret to the High School, part of the Girls' Public Day School Trust, seen then as now as the most academic girls' school.

It was down the Banbury Road – it's rather a nice big house. It was purpose-built [21 Banbury Road, to which the school moved in 1880].

Margaret was lukewarm about the experience.

Some moments were better, some years were better than others. We had morning school only. Came home at one o'clock, unless you were coming from the country, and then they were given lunch. We played games in the afternoon, if you wanted to. And we had hours of homework, because we didn't have afternoon school. We had Panama hats, and you had to wear them, you had to wear your uniform properly. You weren't allowed to cycle more than two abreast down the Banbury Road. We weren't allowed to eat ice creams on the street, in your uniform. A contrast to children these days, with their packets of this and that!

Gwynneth, who went a little later, did have some afternoon school.

We had subjects like art or domestic science. And some of the afternoons we were playing games. The only things I liked about school was the games and the Girl Guides. Lovely. The Girl Guides, we had great fun! Games, played hockey, cricket, lacrosse, tennis, and netball for a little while.

Vic Brown, now living in Lucerne Road, gained a free education through a scholarship at Magdalen College School. Born in Jericho to an Oxford family in 1919, he started at St Barnabas' School.

In 1930, I took what was called the 'Scholarship Exam' then – later it would have been called the 11+, I think – and I got a free place at Magdalen College School, and I stayed there until 1935.

He went into the accounts department of the County Council but did not like it. Through the University printer Dr John Johnson, another old MCS boy, he got a job at the University Press, before the war sent him into the army.

Above: Guide camp 1936, Gwynneth Twining centre with hat. (M. & G. Twining)

Below: The High School hockey eleven, Gwynneth front right. (M. & G. Twining)

Several boys from the roads went to Oxford High School for Boys in George Street, like John Rowe during the war. He cycled down with others.

There used to be a race to the High School, all the little boys down the Banbury Road, gangs of them. From Victoria Road it used to be about nine minutes.

The Paine twins moved on in 1947 from the Dragon to the local public school St Edward's, at the end of South Parade, and found it quite restrictive by comparison.

We boarded at St Edward's. We didn't live very far away, because we lived at the other end of South Parade! If you wanted to go to Summertown, you had to get a pass. It was very much an enclosed institution in those days. But, in fact, you didn't have much spare time, particularly if you played games in one of the teams. In the last winter term, both David and I were in the First XV, and on a Saturday, playing rugby, and school in the morning, etc, by about 9 o'clock, I was absolutely worn out!

St Edward's still expects day pupils to stay and have their supper at the school. Sydney Denton, who later sent his son Shaun to the school, remembers St Edward's pupils when he first worked in Summertown.

[St Edward's School] were fairly big employers of domestic staff, that sort of thing. The boys all used to wear boaters, and they all had to be very very smart. It was a very Christian school. We thought it was very social elite.

Education after the war

Sally Bromley, born in 1948 in Carlton Road, started going to Cutteslowe School at the age of three.

My brother would push me there; my brother and I fought like cat and dog, so my mother was never sure whether he'd actually pushed me out of the push-chair or pushed me until I got to the school! I have extremely warm memories of that school. I can remember playing in the sandpit there in the nursery, and the paddling pool – both quite recently filled in.

Sally, centre, in the sandpit at Cutteslowe Nursery School, c.1953. (Sally Bromley)

Sally remembers hearing from her classmate Kit Villiers about the voyage of the replica of the Mayflower, in 1957 (p.91f).

I vividly remember him coming out to the front and telling us the latest story of where his father was, sailing across the Atlantic, in the *Mayflower*. So that's one of the gifts of living in North Oxford.

Many residents of the seven roads used Cutteslowe School. Margaret Willis has good memories of it when she lived in Lonsdale Road as Margaret Helsby from 1954 until 1967.

All four went to Cutteslowe School. It had a simply splendid, extremely strict Headmistress who assessed those children absolutely magnificently. They learned to read so fast and so on. It was very good. There was that recreation ground outside, where they larked about, coming out. I used to meet them there, because there was a quarter of an hour in between when the little ones came out and the big ones. I remember making a song with the Council, about the lack of seats for us to sit about and wait! We got a seat in the end. But, unfortunately, it was vandalised in next to no time, so we didn't get another!

The 1944 Butler Education Act expanding secondary education for all and giving new life to grammar schools brought more enthusiasm for state education among the middle classes. Margaret's daughter Mary, like many girls from these roads, went to Milham Ford.

They had special permission to ride their bicycles through the Parks. That was very nice. Mary was telling me recently, it was a wonderful bonding thing, if you all rode to school together.

Margaret, who had been educated at a grammar school in Putney, knew Milham Ford also as a teacher (p.135).

[It] was exactly the kind of school where I'd been myself, and had this magnificent Head called Mary Price, who was really quite famous. Very good.

The High School for Girls had become a direct grant school in 1945. It moved to its present site on Belbroughton Road in 1957. One of Elsie Hill's daughters went there.

Barbara first went to the High School. [She] got a free place under the 11+ examination. Then Tricia got a place at Milham Ford, which was then a girls' grammar school. They were a very old-fashioned classic type of girls' school; and the High School, much as it is now – pretty strict and achievement-related.

Janet Tinbergen moved from the High School to Milham Ford in 1960.

I was at the High School to begin with, then I switched half way through to Milham Ford, because the High School was very inflexible about time off for music. It turned out to be a much better school. At that time Milham Ford was absolutely at its best. Miss Price was an exceptional head. Nearly every girl in my class was first generation grammar school and about a third of us went to university. In the early 60s that was an extraordinary achievement. And my parents saved money on the fees. Why pay for education when it was better!

With the baby boom after the war there was a pressing need for provision of new schools by the 1960s. Sally Bromley went from Cutteslowe to St Denys's convent school, and then to one of the newly built schools, the Central School for Girls, which had moved to Cheney Lane in 1959 and been renamed.

I passed my 11+ and went on to Cheney Girls' Grammar School as it was then.

The new Cherwell Secondary Modern School on the Marston Ferry Road was opened in 1963. Eric Baldwin of Lucerne Road came to Oxford as its first headmaster. He was from a working-class family in Middlesborough, and had left school himself the day he was 14, to become an errand boy, before being apprenticed at an iron and steel works. It was during the war that he decided to go into teaching.

At that time, there was a desperate shortage of teachers, particularly men teachers, and some of my friends were teachers, and they pushed me into teaching, because I was so interested in music and drama, and reading. So I applied to become part of the teaching force, by means of the Emergency Training Scheme.

He got his matriculation and was accepted at Durham University, a source of pride to his parents.

I'd lifted myself out of the working class, and crawled into the middle class!

He spoke with justifiable pride about his pupils at Cherwell Secondary Modern, which took those children not skimmed off at eleven to go to the more academic grammar schools.

Eric and Dorothy Baldwin talking to Eric's ex-pupil Caroline Fosdike, the vicar's daughter, at her wedding reception in the Church Hall, May 1990. (D. Baldwin)

Most of them were from places like Cutteslowe, and West Oxford, and Wolvercote, and most of them were working-class, but there was quite a sprinkling of academic idealistic people who deliberately sent their children to this secondary modern school, this new one. I let them know that we would enter them for national examinations at the highest point that we could reach with them, 'O' followed by 'A'. We started taking the odd 'A' level, in about 1967. I'd got a grand squad of teachers around me, and if they wanted to do 'A' level, I made it possible, if I could. We finished up with quite a number of sixth-formers. We got two kids into Oxford, whilst it was still a secondary modern school. I wanted to go on to 'A' level as much as possible, because I believed in people. I was bound to, with my own experience – I left school at 14, I was 29 years old when I was fully qualified.

Throughout the whole of my time at the Cherwell School, we had a very good sprinkling of people from abroad, and academics coming to Oxford. For instance, the two who got into Oxford had never taken an 11+, were just sent to our school. I was very pleased and proud to receive that sort of parent, who could have gone, easily, to Oxford School or Magdalen. It was a very good school from the beginning. We were quite famous, and visited by a number of people from foreign countries – even Russia – because it was state of the art at first.

Problems were not worse than elsewhere.

The main problem was always the parents. I've always said this, that bad kids come from bad parents. We had a fair share of problems – in the 1960s, don't forget – where kids used to get 'fuelled up', as they called it then – although many schools, most secondary schools in Oxford, if not all, had problems [with drugs]. Cherwell School had very little in the way of real confrontations.

Schooling from the 1970s

Eric saw Cherwell School through its change to a mixed comprehensive in 1973, when a major shake-up of education under the Labour government did away with most grammar schools.

I was able to stay until the transition from secondary mod to full-scale compre-

hensive school. So I feel that I really completed the job. I saw the first two comprehensive cohorts through the school, and since I happened to be 60 at that time, I
decided quite suddenly to retire.

*Eric still favoured the three-tier system introduced in Oxford in 1973, which was dis-
mantled recently, in 2003, and replaced by a two-tier primary and secondary system.*

I believe that the system we had, 5–9, 9–13, 13–18, was a far better system than
the one that we've just got. I think the middle school is a splendid conception and
I'm just sorry to see it go.

*Many residents of the roads have experience of the local education system from the
1970s on. A lot of children of course still started at a local playgroup or nursery, as
Celia Glyn says.*

There was a very good state nursery attached to Cutteslowe School; and one at
Wolvercote which was quite popular. My children went to St Michael's playgroup.

*St Michael's playgroup in the Portland Road Church Hall, like Mrs Brown's in the
United Reformed Church Hall, was a private enterprise used by many local families.
Celia herself ran it from 1977 to 1983 with two paid helpers and a volunteer mother:
she began on a wage of £12.50 a
week for five mornings.*

It was a very local population
and a very supportive group
of mothers and I enjoyed it
enormously.

*Her son Miles went on to Phil &
Jim (St Philip and James Primary
School). She and her husband, the
economist Andrew Glyn, who was
an Old Etonian, used the state
system on principle, as members
of the local Labour Party.*

We'd put him down on a wait-
ing list when we were living in
Polstead Road and been told
we'd have no chance, but he

The 'boys' corner' in the St Michael's playgroup in the Portland
Road Church Hall, 1978. (C. Glyn, © R. Marken)

got in terribly quickly, and I think they picked academic parents. It was a good
school. Then it was the first year they brought in middle school, so Miles went to
[Summertown] Middle School – but a lot of his friends left to go to private schools.

*Many parents in the roads began to opt for private schooling at this period. Kate Jones
Finer describes her neighbours in Lonsdale Road when they arrived in 1977.*

They were the sort of academics that were broke, bringing up children and usually spending a fortune, all against their principles, paying for private education –
against their principles, because they were mostly left-wing, but worried about
their children's education.

Holly Kilpatrick's children went on to the private Dragon School after starting at Phil &

Jim's, the first school in favour at the time – where she had found endemic head lice.

I found that a lot of the mothers there, who were, perhaps, working in academic posts, were leaving the children with quite unsuitable babysitters. Certainly the head lice problem was absolutely shocking, always! I used to check the children every night, but so many children just weren't checked, and they were alive!

Celia Glyn's daughter Lucy went to Bishop Kirk, built in 1966 as a primary school on the site of one of Summertown's old houses, the Avenue, between Middle Way and the Woodstock Road, and extended in 1973 to become a middle school. Here she was taught by one of Oxford's famous writers, Philip Pullman, then head of English.

Lucy Glyn (second from right) starring in one of the plays written by Philip Pullman for his Bishop Kirk pupils, 1981. (Newsquest Oxfordshire Ltd)

He wrote plays for the children, Victorian melodramas that had parts for everyone, enormously enjoyable for them. She was in two of his plays: *Count Carlstein* was the first one, in 1980. In *Count Carlstein* I remember Carl Gombrich [from Portland Road] being a very good baddy. It was brilliant, it was really good. I still bump into [Philip] occasionally and he still asks after Lucy, how she's doing, and knows what a lot of the other children from middle school are doing now. A brilliant English teacher. He sent Lucy a copy of the book of one of the plays when it came out, *The Ruby and the Smoke*, with a dedication.

Bishop Kirk, a Church of England state school, was favoured by many parents in the roads, like the Berrys.

We wanted our children to go to BK – it was supposed to stand for 'Brilliant Kids' – because the education there was far more structured than at Summertown Middle, which was about letting the children 'discover things' and just be creative. Though in fact we had moved our daughters from Greycotes in about 1983 because we found that school too rigid. We had to get a letter from our church, which was Blackfriars, to say we were church-goers, as indeed we were.

The two middle schools were later amalgamated: the Bishop Kirk site was sold for residential building, while a new school was developed on the site of Summertown Middle

'Victorian Day' at Bishop Kirk School, 1989.
(Philippa Berry)

and the Catholic school St Gregory's, which moved to another site. Sally Bromley taught at Bishop Kirk and then at Frideswide.

There was a great deal of vying for which school your child went to, because Bishop Kirk had, historically, been a very academic school, and Summertown had been a very practical applications school. It was suggested that we link up with Summertown Middle, and we were quite happy about that, because we were all quite realistic that there was this quite unnecessary division. We actually opened to children in September 1990, opened up as Frideswide School.

Bill Fosdike, vicar of St Michael's Church, put a lot of work into the establishment of Frideswide's. Despite some questioning of continuing church involvement in state schooling it maintained the traditional connection.

We very firmly offered that it needn't be an aided school, but people said, 'No, let's keep it. That's why it's called 'Frideswide': for churchy people, it's obviously named after St Frideswide; for non-churchy people, Frideswide is a nice Oxford name. But it wasn't a school for the Church, it was a school that the Church was helping to maintain in the community.

Sally speaks warmly of her years at Frideswide, until it too was closed and the buildings absorbed into Cherwell in the reorganisation of 2003.

It was probably the happiest place I've worked at in my life. It was amazing. A huge amount of fun, laughter, lots of driving of children to help them to excel, and this was just part of the ethos – partly instigated by Mari Powell, she's very well known, followed by Anne Freeney.

Reorganisation came through in 2000, but we went out on a high. I am proud to say that the SATS results for that school year were just superb. Nobody wants to change. The last thing I wanted was Frideswide to close. It was one of the really saddest days I can remember, because it was so happy, so successful, and so high-achieving. However, one has to accept it, and keep the things that you liked, in your heart. I decided to pull out and do my own early retirement thing.

Since retirement Sally has been drawn back into part-time work.

Sally Bromley was given a day off teaching at Frideswide to appear as an extra in *Shadowlands* (1993), filming here in Magdalen College. She was the Lady Mayoress. (S. Bromley)

Now I'm Advisory Teacher for PSHE/SRE (Personal, Social and Health Education / Sex and Relationships Education) – what a mouthful!

Verity Peto, who sent three daughters to local state schools in the 1980s and 90s, speaks eloquently about parental anxieties over choice in schooling.

We sent our children to Wolvercote First School. For historic reasons, although we were in the catchment area for Cutteslowe School, there were no children living in any of these seven roads, who actually went to Cutteslowe School. All the children who went to state school, either went to Phil & Jim, a few went to St Barnabas School, but by far the majority went to Wolvercote School. So when Philippa was due to start school in January 1984 we appealed against the Local Authority's decision that she should attend Cutteslowe School, on the basis that she would find it difficult to find friends to play with out of school, or to travel to and from school with. As a result of our successful appeal, we ended up being informal advisors to quite a few parents who wanted to negotiate this very complicated system of appeals. Our children were at Wolvercote

Maypole dance at Wolvercote First School, 1981. (Lynn Ahmed)

while there were two very good Head Teachers. I think that, whether or not your child is happy at school and achieves a lot, often has a lot to do with the Head Teacher.

[Schooling is] a very Summertown/North Oxford obsession. It probably is in a lot of other towns, but probably particularly so here, because people move here having an expectation that the schools are going to be good – partly because there are some very well known private schools here – there's the Dragon School, and on the other side of Lonsdale Road there are the grounds of Summer Fields School, which is an even more expensive prep school for boys. But also, there is an expectation that the state schools are going to be good, probably because of the University. We've had a good experience of the local schools here. But as a recent [2002] survey pointed out, if you look at the league tables there are no Oxfordshire schools in the top 50 State Secondary Schools in the country, for academic achievement, except for the Cherwell School, where our children went. It's probably more that there's an expectation that the schools will be good, rather than an actuality.

Peter Thompson describes the educational paths of his stepson Marios (b.1973), which included private education, and his son Joe (b.1981), who went entirely through the state system.

Marios went [to] Hobson Road School originally, which has long since been redeveloped into housing, and subsequently Wolvercote Primary School. The Cutteslowe School was the preferred school, at the time, but it was full up, so he went to Wolvercote, and was very happy there. [Then Sonja] sent him to Magdalen College School. Joe went to Wolvercote School, from there to Frideswide, and from there, went to Cherwell. He knew what he wanted to do, and, in fact, he was doing computer consultancy, such as designing web pages and fixing people's computers, while he was in the sixth form. He was absolutely certain that he didn't want to go to university, because it didn't accord with any of his interests. And to this day he has never opened the envelope containing his 'A' level exam results, he's never found it relevant to know what those results were.

I certainly didn't consider that [private education] represented value for money. My view of education is that its purpose is simply to develop self-confidence and appreciation of the opportunities that are available among children, rather than to tick the boxes against a number of specific academic hurdles. I had always felt, particularly since I went through private education, that there was a positive disadvantage, in that possibly ten of one's most formative years are spent in a

Louisa Peto, centre, at Cherwell School, 1996. (V. Peto)

period of isolation from the kind of people that you encounter in 95 per cent of the population. Marios certainly bore that out – he reckoned it had taken him two years at Sheffield, to be able to relate to people that came from a non-selective walk of life. And that was people at university, so they are still fairly selective. Joe was very happy, he never did have tremendous academic ambitions. I think it's significant that all the friends that he developed in Cherwell, pretty well exclusively, ended up going to Cambridge.

Schools rise and fall in reputation. Bob Williams wants energies now to be thrown into the improvement of Cutteslowe School to counteract the social gulf between these roads and the Cutteslowe Estate.

The Cutteslowe Primary School is not a very attractive school for our neighbourhood, in many ways, and anything you can do to improve it as a centre, as a school, is going to be very welcome; at the moment, everybody who's got any money in our four roads or so, are sending their kids into the private sector – or they may go to Cherwell, but they don't go to Cutteslowe Primary School, most of them.

The Schrigers, spending a year in Lonsdale Road in 2003–4, sent their daughters to private schools – Greycotes and the High School – primarily for ease of organising the places. David gives an interesting angle on the more formal education which many who choose to pay for their children's education are looking for, and the general difficulty of selecting the right kind of school for a child.

Things were a little rocky at the beginning but they both had wonderful years, and I was very impressed by the schools. The school in the States is all experiential learning, and no competition, and teamwork, and not rushing towards any particular goals too quickly. We had [my older daughter] in this very kind of relaxed school, because (1) having had the opposite in my education, I thought, 'This is probably a better way to go', and (2), for that particular child, we thought it was right. And I tell you, we were probably wrong. But, like much parenting, you only learn what the right thing to do was after it's too late to correct it! She loved the structure, she loved the fact that she knew that two weeks from now, on a Tuesday, she had her geography homework done, and it had to be three pages ... that was very comforting to her – more so than her old school, when they gave her a blank piece of paper and said, 'Do what you want', which creates a whole different set of anxieties.

Private schools like the Dragon and St Edward's now take a high proportion of girls alongside the boys for whom they were founded, but single sex education – as at Greycotes and the High School – can still be chosen by going private.

St Edward's has made efforts to reach out to the wider community in Summertown, making its lavish facilities available – the Esporta Health Club is on its premises, and a concert hall is being planned. Kathy Clarke mentions the benefit to their elderly neighbour of visits from a St Edward's boy back in the 1980s.

They have their community service programme there and he had this delightful young man used to come every week and do the garden and have a long chat with Arthur as well, and Arthur always enjoyed seeing him.

Another feature of the educational scene has been the privately run sixth-form colleges and foreign language schools in the area, which lodge their students with local families. Beryl Phillips has taken student lodgers in Lonsdale Road since 1965.

When the boys left home I missed the company. Of course the money was nice as well. I've been very lucky, always had very nice students, never had any problems or anything. University to start, and then the schools of English – Swan School and Regent. It's very nice having students from other countries, very interesting.

Peter Thompson and his wife Sonja Drexler have also enjoyed hosting these students.

In recent years, the Language School students tend to be fairly short-term, anything from two or three to six, or a maximum of ten weeks. From D'Overbroek's, in the last three years, we've had students who have done their complete 'A' level course, i.e. they've stayed two complete academic years. The first of those was a lovely girl from Botswana, who's now at university in Liverpool; and the other is Mercedes, an equally lovely girl from Angola, who has overcome language difficulties from her native Portuguese, and has won a place at Imperial College, studying geology, which I think is an absolutely amazing achievement.

Students at the University

Oxford University figures importantly in the life of the roads, as many residents are or have been employed there, as teachers, researchers or support staff. However our interviews also collected many interesting insights into the educational paths of people who first came here as students.

Maurice Cardiff (b.1915), who came to Hamilton Road in retirement in 1998, gave a glimpse of pre-war Oxford as a place of glamour and privilege – but felt he had little

*educational benefit from it. Earlier his friendship with the son of John Buchan and visits
to the Buchan family at Elsfield were more stimulating than his expensive education at
Eton.*

I was very excited to find myself with a family who were listening to music and
talking about poetry, and had a wonderful library. Eton was only interested in
games, as indeed, Oxford colleges were.

*Even as an Etonian Maurice had difficulty with the Latin requirement for entry to Ox-
ford at the time, and found himself taking an eye-opening year off – which made return
to Oxford life very difficult.*

Worcester College, rather through, I think, the influence of John Buchan, said they
would take me the next year, providing I passed the Latin paper. So I did what was,
then, very unusual, and very common now, I took a gap between school and coming to university. I spent a month in Paris, three months in Aix-en-Provence, two
months in Florence ... The trouble was, that after all this freedom and rather exciting adventures I'd had, Oxford, when you were gated, if you weren't in by eleven?
ten? – was too much like going back to school. Also, the only thing I was interested in studying was English literature and, perhaps, French literature. But English Literature, at that time, the course ended you up with Middle English and no
further. So I did history, and started off with the Roman occupation of England,
which I wasn't at all interested in. So I was rather bored! Oxford, at my time, was,
I think, going through a bad period. The war was looming. Politics was everything,
you had to be either Right or Left – no, Communist, or a Catholic. Father D'Arcy,
who'd converted Evelyn Waugh, was still going round looking for likely aristocrats
to turn into Catholics! And, of course, there was a strong Communist Movement
as well.

*Maurice's connections with interesting people on the fringes of Oxford life – like the art-
ists Leonard Huskinson and later Paul Nash, and the writers Rosamond Lehmann and
Elizabeth Bowen – were more important, not to mention his love life.*

Leonard was a painter, and he looked like Mr Toad, and he drove a wonderful yellow Rolls-Royce! He was a very nice man. There was Rosamond Lehmann who I
became friendly with. She was a great beauty, and a very good novelist. They used
to come to lunch with me, and I used to go to lunch with them. I had one other
attraction outside Oxford – I was madly in love with an actress who was in the
Royal Shakespeare Company in Stratford-on-Avon. I was not a good student! So I
had all these external attractions, and found Oxford very stupid.

*Several of our interviewees were students during the war years and came from much
less privileged backgrounds. Joan Crow came up to Lady Margaret Hall from Long Eaton
County Secondary School in 1937 and took her Modern Languages degree in 1941.
There were of course few women at Oxford, and all colleges were much smaller.*

The total intake at Lady Margaret Hall was about 150 and now it is over 400, so
that measures the way the college like other colleges has increased since the war;
so I was one of an annual intake of about 50.

*After war work Joan returned to Lady Margaret Hall as a tutor, and met her husband, a
fellow of Oriel.*

I had already met him in a sense in 1939 to 1940 when I went to his lectures, but I was simply somebody scribbling away for dear life sat in the front row.

They spent the rest of their working lives in the University, moving to Victoria Road in 1980.

I continued at LMH until I retired in 1984 and my husband retired in 1979, so we were both totally committed to the College for the whole of our careers. It was a very interesting time, a time for great changes especially for the women's colleges which became mixed. Oriel was the last men's college to go mixed.

Margaret Willis (then Margaret Andrews) came up in 1940. The only child of parents who were not well-off but were ambitious for her to achieve her potential, she had been at Putney County Secondary School, and had studied German and French.

Under certain pressures from my parents, who were very keen I should get on with this – they'd only heard of Oxford and Cambridge, so they said it must be one of those – I did Oxford Entrance and came up to Somerville. Everything was blacked out. We did fire-watching in the Museum. That was bizarre! There were a lot of students in uniform: if they were officer material, I think it was, they had six months at Oxford, and they used to come to lectures and so on with us. On the whole, very young men, and a lot of girls who were on short-term degrees, allowed to do it in two years, and then released into the Forces, and a lot who went to the Foreign Office. A lot went to Bletchley Park. We were supposed to do a few hours' work to justify our continuing presence. Somerville set up one or two extraordinary projects. One was working in the laundry of the Radcliffe Infirmary – they didn't know what to do with us! At the very top of the New Bodleian, there was a department for sending books to prisoners-of-war. Blackwell's would supply anything that prisoners-of-war asked for, and we used to go through their requests.

The fees of £150 a year were made up from various sources.

I had a very small grant from Somerville, almost nothing; a Scholarship was given by the Drapers' Company; I had one from my school, which gave a very small scholarship. And by committing myself to teaching after the war, I got another grant. And by that means, I got the lot.

Like other students of the time she recalls being very cold.

We used to gather in each other's rooms, because we could have the fire on for so many hours a day. And we had gloves with free fingers, so that we could write. It wasn't bad. All the clubs and so on all went on just the same. And the Bach Choir went on. We rehearsed at the Sheldonian. Wonderful!

Margaret went on to teach. Having married a dentist she returned to Oxford in 1949 and has been here ever since.

Professor Bob Williams (b.1926) of Victoria Road came to Oxford like Joan and Margaret through an excellent grammar school education, in his case at Wallasey Grammar School.

We had, at school, some very very fine teachers – two, in particular, I remember. One was the chemistry master: he had a First from Cambridge, but he'd been thrown out in the Depression from industry, and so he came into school teaching. He was an excellent school teacher – provided you were prepared to work. He was a better tutor than I ever had at Oxford. He should have been a university man. The other person was a quite different character. He taught mathematics, again, a Cambridge man. He used to give us books to read, from his shelves. He introduced me to quantum mechanics, which hardly anybody, at that time, knew, and I read that sort of stuff. And because, now, my interest had been touched, I fought with these things, so that I tried very hard to learn.

Having met Oxford's requirement that he do a crash school certificate in Latin Bob put together enough funds from various scholarships to take up a place at Merton in 1944. He describes vividly a very difficult experience.

From the very first day, I was lost. I was lost socially. Merton was a very strange place at that time, there weren't very many undergraduates, because a lot of them had gone to the war, most of the under-graduates came from public schools. My room was, basically, unheated. There was a very small electric bar fire, but that gave up every now and again, it was cut off. Not only was it cold, it was damp, and the inside walls of that room, actu-ally water ran down them. It was so mis-erable! You had no supply of hot water, no lavatory, except across a quad. The hot water was supplied by a scout who woke you at seven in the morning, with a tin can of hot water, which you had to use to shave – as quickly as possible. Now, this is a complete contrast to where I'd lived, because we were not poor, we always had heating, we always had hot wa-ter. Never in the wildest moments, would we think there would be water trickling down the inside of a room!

Bob Williams as a young chemistry lecturer, 1957. (R.J.P. Williams)

The third thing that really knocked me sideways was my tutor. He was a dear old man. He knew no modern chemistry, his chemistry finished in the 1920s, and this was the 1940s, coming 1950s; and the main source of chemistry had been in two areas, thermodynamics and quantum mechanics. He knew neither, because they'd both been developed in the 1930s, as far as chemistry is concerned. So his idea was basically to be a father figure, and to try to interest you in subjects which were dead. Some time in January, I decided, 'Right. I can chuck this and go to Liv-erpool University', which I'm sure I could have got into. 'Or I can go and fight'.

Eventually he began to find his feet, and found a way towards his main interests.

I studied basically on my own for one year, until I said to my tutor, rather bluntly, in the third term, 'I'm sorry, I have to have another tutor, somebody modern. I want to do what is a biological topic, with chemistry in biology'. There was nobody who would take that on, the sort of chemistry that I wanted to do. But there was one man, a man called Dr Irvine, who by nature, had been an organic chemist. And then ... it was candid good luck! Because when I started to study the organic com-binations with various things in the soil, I discovered that there was a system to it

127

all, to the way in which the organic and inorganic things combined. I'd published a paper in *Nature*, before I'd got a degree at all! Given the opportunity to go on and do a DPhil, I took that opportunity. And I then discovered that by doing this I was actually excused military service!

Bob went on to a distinguished career at Oxford in this particular field of chemistry.

Bertram Mandelbrote, who came as a Rhodes Scholar from South Africa to Merton to do medicine, confirms Bob's account of primitive living conditions.

I was 23. I came in October '46 and it merged into the year of '47 when we had the worst winter. In Merton I was in the Grove Quad. All the bathrooms were frozen so there was no scope for getting a bath – there weren't showers anyway. The scout, Baskerville, used to come in with a bowl and a jug full of water which was supposedly hot, but by the time you got out of bed it was frozen virtually. You had to take the little one-bar heater and defrost your sheets. We had snow for three months solid, and it was in the days of the pea soup fog as well. My parents sent me food parcels. We tended to eat in British restaurants – all stodge and pretty grim.

The work he was doing however made it 'all a very exciting time'.

Jean Robinson, from a working-class background in Southwark, came to Oxford a little later, in 1953. Unlike those mentioned previously she did not have support from her parents or her teachers for her academic gifts, though she feels she got a thorough basic education.

I had always had this passion for books, and my mother had found this rather irritating, to be stuck with a daughter who always had her nose stuck in a book when she ought to be helping with the ironing or whatever. This wasn't the attitude to my brothers, but it was to me. School work, in those days, was pretty boring, compared with school work now. A lot of books, a lot of writing précis, spelling, grammatical exercises, learning history by rote – but it was thorough. We got a good basic grounding – something that my daughter, much later, never did. It was boring, but then life, generally, in those days, was boring, and you didn't expect it to be anything else. The only excitement in your life was Hollywood films, there wasn't any television. [I got] what was then called School Certificate, with Matriculation exemption, which meant you could have gone on to university: that never occurred to me or my family, that I could have gone into the sixth form.

While she worked as a secretary at the Daily Herald *and then for Members of Parliament, she went to Workers Educational Association (WEA) evening classes and was eventually encouraged to apply to Ruskin College. She speaks movingly of gaining access to these transforming opportunities.*

I was terribly serious, read serious books and went to lectures. In 1953, I went to Ruskin. I was still living at home, which is what one did. By going to Ruskin, I actually was able to leave home at the age of 23. I had a Local Authority Grant. And, let me tell you, I had never been so well-off in my life! Everything was paid for, I was not expected to do anything, except make my bed. There were no words to describe this, but I remember going into the Bodleian Library, and feeling overwhelmed with riches. If you'd put me in a room full of jewels, if you had surrounded me with piles of diamonds and pearls and emeralds, it could not have matched what I felt, that there was all this, and it was at my disposal. And the teaching was so good. I did not realise, then, what a fantastic bunch of tutors we had. The standard at Ruskin, in those days, was just incredible. It was all adult students, the age range was from 21 to 40, who came from all walks of life.

At Ruskin she met her husband Derek, a miner's son who went on to get a First in PPE and later returned to Oxford to an academic job. There is more about Jean on p.88f. A passion for truth has never left her.

If you are doing academic research, you should have a passion for the truth, not to prove a party line. And by that, I don't mean a political party line, I mean a particular line in medical research, or sociological research, or whatever.

She did not go on from her Ruskin course in Labour History to do a full degree, partly for economic reasons after her marriage, but also because Oxford did not offer sociology.

Sociology was up and coming, and sociology, in Oxford, just wasn't on.

Mary and Marguerite Tibbetts (b.1916 and 1918) of Victoria Road, daughters of a Deddington blacksmith, exemplify others who missed out on further education after school but came to it later: Mary took an early Open University degree and went on to be a founder member of U3A; Marguerite did a diploma at Oxford University's Department of External Studies in Social Policy and Administration in 1969–72 and had a long association with the WEA, only recently retiring as chair of the Oxford branch.

Kate Jones arrived at a career in sociology via a degree in history at St Anne's. She came up in 1960 from a grammar school in Wales, and like Jean Robinson felt very well off on her grant.

I think my parents were assessed to pay £12 a year. I saved money! I used to have £5 spare, I remember, I used to aim at that. And I only went out with men who would pay! It was an absolute luxury for me! I mean, after North Wales there was six to one here. I think I really had my teenage in Oxford. In North Wales, I was regarded as too clever for boys.

She went into social work and then to further study at LSE and an academic career. She married Sam Finer, who became Professor of Government and Public Administration at Oxford (p.86) – though Kate had to pursue her own career at Birmingham University as her field was not covered at Oxford.

When Mary Tregear came from Hong Kong in 1962 to work at the Ashmolean she found Oxford very strange.

Oxford was still really coming out of all that period when students wore gowns, and that sort of thing. Bulldogs and people around, and undergraduates were not allowed to drive cars. It really seemed extraordinary in many ways! Into colleges before eleven. Taking students along, them telling you where's the place to climb in, so you stop the car and let them out, and drive off as quickly as possible! Oxford, itself, was very informal. After being in Hong Kong, I thought everybody looked as if they'd just walked out of the kitchen! Because, in Hong Kong, people are very smart.

Peter Clarke came up at around this time to read history, having attended a Catholic boarding school and then studied in France. He was at Trinity from 1963 to 1966.

Of course, it was before the Colleges became mixed, and so I think there was a ratio of about eight male to one female student, and it was very strange, really. The city was smaller, the students seemed to be more in evidence. There was a great deal of separation between the University and the town, which seems, to me, to be less so now.

After doing a doctorate on Islam in London, teaching in a university in Nigeria and then working for the BBC World Service, Peter got a job at King's College London and lived in Lonsdale Road for many years as one of those academics who commuted to other universities from Oxford. He has now semi-retired to a post in Oxford, and makes other comparisons with what he sees today.

The whole attitude towards dress has changed. Everything's much more casual now, and much less formal. Tutors and students are, in the way they interact. Much less kind of privileged, it seems.

Philippa and Martin Berry at their graduation in 1970. (P. Berry)

Philippa Berry first came to Oxford aged 10 as a boarder at Rye St Antony School, because it was the only Catholic girls' boarding school not run by nuns. After a spell in Paris and some secretarial work, she suddenly realised that her ambition was to be at Oxford University.

I was in the process of trying to get a visa to go to America, and setting up a secretarial job in Chicago. I would have hated that! Anyway my brother said, 'OK. What would you really like to do, if you were handed it on a plate?' And I said, 'Well, I'll go to Oxford University and read English' – it just came straight out! So he said, 'Well, get on with it, then!' So I did. I went back to Rye St Anthony and worked as an Assistant Matron, and had lessons with my old English teacher, and wrote essays, and got back into it. I arrived in Oxford in October 1967, and absolutely loved every minute! Flying round Oxford on a bicycle, with my gown, we had to wear gowns.

While Philippa was at St Hilda's she met her husband Martin, who had grown up in Oxford and gone via St Edward's School to read Law at Pembroke College. They graduated in 1970, married the following year and have lived here ever since. They are one of numerous 'Oxford couples' living in the roads today.

7 Working Lives

Quite a lot of wives didn't go out to work, because they worked at home. But, my golly, they worked!

Betty Marshall

Men's work, the husband's job, has of course long been a definer of social status, and the kind of work done by male householders in these roads is touched on in other chapters. The emphasis here is on women's work in and out of the home, unpaid and paid, which gives insights into key social changes in the 20th century. We also include some extracts reflecting general experience of the world of work.

Women and housework

Until the Second World War social convention decreed that women 'gave up' work on marriage to look after home and family, but as Betty Marshall points out, before the widespread availablity of labour-saving appliances those without domestic help certainly worked.

They had coal fires because, of course, you didn't have central heating, not many people had electric fires either. My mother would clear the grate, she'd lay the fire, she'd fill the coal bucket, but my father brought it in at lunchtime. She did their washing and ironing. She made all my clothes. She knitted all the jumpers and my school socks. She made her own clothes. How she ever had time to do anything else, I can't imagine.

Kate Jones Finer says the same of her mother after the war.

She got married and she didn't work then. I mean, she did, she worked like anything, but not paid.

In the earlier part of the century even modest middle-class people like those living in these roads had help with the housework. The Bridges had a live-in maid – partly to help look after an old aunt who lived with them – though Mrs Bridge worked in the house herself in the mornings.

We had a very nice maid from Water Eaton, by the name of Pledge. That was a lovely family. Most people had a woman, or somebody to help them do the housework. My mother always helped with the housework, and after lunch she went upstairs and changed all her clothes. My mother used to work quite hard herself, and she was a wonderful cook.

Some better-off families continued to have live-in servants between the wars, though they were becoming scarcer. Monica Wagstaff speaks of neighbours in Hamilton Road, including the managing director of the department store Elliston & Cavell (now Debenham's), who lived next door.

They had a proper maid, she even had a uniform. The people in [no.56], that was a very nice establishment at one time, they had a maid. The one next door was in black and white, like the waitresses in Lyons used to be, and the other one was in brown and coffee coloured. There were quite a few people who had a living-in maid round here. She helped prepare meals, she would get the breakfast, answer the door, do the fires, answer the telephone if you had one – not everyone had a telephone then – went shopping to a certain extent. An old lady, Miss Ward, she had a companion help, you could get people like that. And the Miss Walkers did, two sisters, they had their living-in. She was living-in everything – nurse, maid, everything – and she came from the country. As the person got older, you couldn't replace them, people just didn't want to do that sort of work any longer. Also, I expect, the amount of money you had to pay them went up alarmingly. The fact you gave them a home, a place to live, you probably didn't have to pay them very much [earlier].

It was more common between the wars to have a 'daily', generally a woman who lived in one of the older parts of Summertown. Dorothy White remembers their Mrs Tappett.

We had an old charlady who used to come in quite frequently during the week. She lived down the bottom of Church [now Rogers] Street.

Later they came from the nearby estates, as the Wagstaffs remember.

The lady who did our washing and ironing lived on the Cutteslowe Estate, and so did the lady who used to come and clean. One came from Wolvercote Estate – but most came from Cutteslowe Estate.

Gwynneth Twining describes the help her mother had, including assistance with the particularly heavy work of washing in the days before washing machines.

We had a sort of friend person, whom we called 'Auntie Eff', who lived in for a time when I was small, and she looked after me and took me out and things. Besides that, we had a daily woman, Mrs Hill – 'Hilly' we used to call her. She lived in Grove Street. Her niece, Gladys, came at one time too. Then there was another funny little lady who used to come on a Monday to do the washing. That was her business. The scullery had a big sink, and this great thing [a copper] in the corner. And it was all steamy on a Monday.

Monica Wagstaff recalls similar arrangements – though their laundry went out (there were several laundry businesses in neighbouring roads, including the Electric Laundry opened by Reginald Alden the butcher at 6 Harpes Road at the end of the 1920s).

We had a girl who used to come here to look after us, plus one who used to come and do housework. But someone used to collect the washing and ironing and bring it back: we just did hand washing.

Help might come in for other tasks too, as Margaret Twining remembers.

We had a lady came in and spend the whole day making summer frocks for us. She'd cut this out, and then she'd tack it up, and we had to try it on, and then she'd sit there with her machine, stitching them. By the end of the day, that frock was nearly made. I suppose Mother finished it off.

Making clothes at home was very common, part of women's contribution to the family economy, and a way of keeping hands usefully occupied. The Twinings' mother did that embarrassing thing of making school uniform which could have been bought, as Gwynneth remembers.

When I went to the High School, she made blouses. At that time, we had square-necked things, with dots and dashes round. She copied the design, but it wasn't the same as the one my friends were wearing, was it! I didn't like it a bit! She used to knit the jerseys too, which were perfectly nice, probably better than the ones that you bought, but it wasn't quite right to a child.

The Second World War, when women were needed to work in factories and elsewhere and were relatively well paid, was a great catalyst for change, as Monica Wagstaff remarks.

The war definitely freed women, because most women worked, munitions or something like that. I met people who were working in offices and would go and do two or three hours in a factory with munitions – it was very good money. In the evening, you could get jobs any time. And during the war, there must have been hundreds of [women] working at Osberton Radiators and places like that. I think they stayed to work in factories: they'd earned good money during the war, some of them. After the war it got more and more difficult to get help, because women were going out to work and they didn't want these house cleaning jobs.

Many households here continued to have help after the war, but it now often came from further afield. Margaret Willis, who went back to teaching after her children went to school, lived in Lonsdale Road twice.

I always had some help. Very nice person who used to come up, was paid something ridiculous, two shillings an hour or something! She lived in Cowley. Came up on the bus, twice a week, I suppose. Then many of us had Mrs Morton, who came in from Stonesfield, on the bus, and served any number of us. And when she became 80, the dream of her life had been to have a greenhouse, so we all bought her a greenhouse, and we thought that would be the finish. Have a little lunch, goodbye Mrs Morton, 80 years old – and the next Monday, she was here again! She went on for years and years. She must have been 85 or so when she was finally told that she was not to travel, after having a cataract operation – she did finally cave in then! She was very small, and she was very short-sighted, so the limit of her powers was considerable – but loyal beyond words! She worked for me here in Lonsdale Road, she worked for me in Bainton Road, and back here again, and never never failed.

Jean Robinson, who grew up in a small working-class terrace house where she automatically helped her mother, found herself in the 1970s and 80s in the trap of the post-war middle-class wife with a much bigger house but no help. Au pairs were a popular solution at the time.

Somehow, I end up with more and more work, and more difficult work, than my grandmother and my mother. And domestic help simply was not available, or not at the amount of money that we had. For a time, we had au pairs, when the children were small. We had a girl from Ecuador, who was beautiful – long green fingernails, when nobody had that kind of thing, and the curtains twitched when she walked down the street! They didn't earn very much, but I was, therefore, fran-

tic to see that they didn't do very much. I remember being at some academic social gathering, and one of the male dons said, 'Oh, this is so that middle-class
women can have cheap servants'. And I said, 'Well, one of the things about au
pairs is that the women in the family can actually join the middle classes, instead
of staying in the working classes and doing nothing but manual work for most of
the day.'

Others like Geoffrey Paine and his wife have always done without help. Geoffrey's ma-
ternal grandmother had been a lady's maid herself.

When asked by some snooty lady, 'Oh, Mrs Dobson, do you have a maid?' she replied, 'I've had many things in my life to put up with, but having a maid was not
one of them.' If you go back a few years, when people had live-in maids, there's an
awful lot of truth in that! We've never had any help in the house.

Jean Robinson's solution now is more radical.

I just don't do it! Occasionally I'll have a little blitz, but I realised that life was very
short, and getting shorter! There were other things that I did that lasted, and had
an effect. I know that the column I write in the *British Journal of Midwifery* has an
effect, because I get the feedback. I feel, 'Well, I've done my job. My kids are reared,
they're happy, they're doing well. I make sure my husband's fed well and has
good clean clothes. And as for the rest this is not where my time and energy is going.'

With freely accessible labour-saving appliances and more casual lifestyles, help in the
house has become less important for most people. If they have it, it is now typically pro-
vided by foreign students, or by small businesses fielding pairs of women with yellow T-
shirts and their own equipment.

Married women working

The Wagstaffs' mother had worked before marriage but never afterwards.

Not many women did: it wasn't acceptable. She had three sisters – they all gave up
when they married.

It was exceptional circumstances that would bring a married middle-class woman to
work for money before the Second World War – as with the death of Dorothy White's
father, which led to her mother establishing a knitting business (p.63).

The expectation, or indeed requirement, that women should stop work when they
married began to break down after the Second World War, more quickly in some profes-
sions than others. Joan Crow went into the Civil Service during the war.

I was drafted into, of all things, the Ministry of Agriculture. I knew nothing about
agriculture but one learns, and I was there from 1941 until 1946.

She then returned to Oxford and taught at Lady Margaret Hall. She married a fellow
academic, which was not uncommon.

I was fortunate enough to be called back to Oxford by my old college because
my tutor had retired and they needed a replacement. I know that if one stayed in
the Civil Service you had to resign if you got married, but LMH was much more
forward-looking in that respect and already had one or two married women who

wished to continue with their academic work and were able to do so. I think that in LMH all my married colleagues were people who were married to dons or university employees.

Joan achieved the more unusual feat of working round a baby, in the mid 1950s.

Fortunately at that time LMH had acquired some property in Fyfield Road and were turning it into flats for its Fellows, and I was able to have one of those, and that made life very much easier because I was near my place of work and could carry on while looking after the baby, with help of course.

Margaret Willis, who married John Helsby, a dentist, in 1946, managed the same thing after the birth of her first son, as teachers were so much in demand.

I taught [in London] for a year. And then Richard, my eldest son, was born. And the following summer they invited me back, which was a halcyon period, because I said, grandly, that I couldn't mark any books! I was teaching and looking after a baby. We were living at home, and my mother was making supper, and it was quite easy. I was given transport, and somewhere to feed him in the middle of the day! They needed me!

After returning to Oxford she concentrated on raising her children but then went back to teaching part time.

I taught at Greycotes for a bit. And then I had a lovely chance, I was asked to go and fill in for somebody at Milham Ford. I taught there for a term and then I was invited to go back, half time, to help in

Margaret Willis, centre, in a photo of pupils and staff, several of whom lived in the seven roads, at Beechlawn, 1980s. Pupils were taught in teachers' homes. (Margaret Willis)

the Modern Language Department. I taught at Beechlawn for a long time, so does almost everybody else! All the women in Oxford who have got degrees, have taught at Beechlawn at one time or other!

It was still the case after the war that most married women would focus on home life. Yvonne Hands came to Portland Road in 1956, married to a young archaeologist, and feels that it would have been better for many women to have worked.

We had little children, we were all busy, in a sense, but I think I ... they'd have been better working. I don't think any of them worked. If you didn't need to, financially, unless you were a rather dedicated professional woman, like a doctor, on the whole, women didn't work.

Joan Gurden was widowed at 37 with three children and thus forced back into work: she came to Oxford to teach.

Fortunately, I had a degree in Modern Languages, and an Oxford Diploma in Education. I hadn't taught, except for two years before I was married. So the children had to go to boarding school, and I lived in Headington. And eventually, with the help of an uncle, I managed to buy a house in Portland Road, and I left Headington and worked at Milham Ford for nearly two years, where Miss Price was the wonderful Headmistress.

She then went to be headmistress of a small boarding school in Northamptonshire (1962–8), when a friend lived in the house, and the children returned for holidays. She taught again at Headington, and after retirement married Sir Harold Gurden, MP.

Women living by themselves were often not very well off, and frequently, as mentioned in chapter 2, supported themselves by taking lodgers. Breaking into the serious job market was not easy or attractive for older married women. Margaret Willis remembers Mrs Lander at 46 Lonsdale Road and her methods of making a little extra money.

She was the widow of an academic, and she made part of her pin money by looking after households where there was a new baby, and when we had our Mary and Will, she came across the road to us, and took over the housekeeping for two weeks, three weeks, whatever. Wonderful woman! She only went to people she quite liked! She let a flat in her house. She was a great lady. A lot older than us, but she was a graduate scientist, in fact quite an early graduate of Royal Holloway College.

John Herivel talks about the power of convention in the case of his wife Elizabeth, an Oxford graduate whom he met working at Bletchley Park during the war.

She had a job before we got married. We made a bad mistake there, because she should have gone on with it. But it was at a time when people got married, it was just the normal thing that the woman should stay in the house and have children, just what had been going on for a very long time. But I think when she looked back, she was sad that she didn't go on with that.

Beryl Phillips got married just after the war. She was someone who enjoyed working, but when she wanted to get a job she was surprised to find she couldn't return to hairdressing.

You had to take either factory work or food shop or nurse or something. So I worked in Sainsbury's at the top of the High Street. They used to do the butter pats, you cut up the butter and shaped it, and did it all up and weighed it, oh it was lovely!

She gave up work when she had her first son. When her younger son was about 13, she took a part-time job in Bonner's, a specialist grocery on South Parade, for 'something to do, get out and meet people'.

Betty Marshall, returning to Victoria Road from Kenya in 1985, found difficulty finding a part-time job. For many years she was a familiar figure delivering newspapers in the roads.

I wanted to work, but I couldn't, because my husband wasn't well, and I didn't really want to work full time. It was difficult. I went after one job in a shop, that wanted somebody part time, and I was 59, and they said, 'Oh! Well, the only thing is, we retire people at 60, and we've no means of paying you a pension.' And I said, 'Well, I'm not after a pension. I would like to work three afternoons a week, or whatever your part time is.' No, there was no way.

Margaret Willis comments on the change in women's expectations since her youth.

When I was brought up, one was, on the whole, trained to expect to be somebody's wife and helper, and being quietly at home. And when I was about 20-something, 25, a book came out called *Wives Who Went to College*, which was the first disquieting murmur that educated women might start to make themselves felt, and they've gone on from there, of course. Now the position of men has altered, in the sense that the balance between the sexes has altered.

With more choices available to women from the 1970s onwards it is now having children, rather than marriage in itself, that tends to halt or interrupt a working life for women. Verity Peto was a solicitor before having children but stopped to be at home with them, later returning to work part time.

I really enjoyed being with them when they were little and at primary school, so that was a very nice thing for me to do. But our house was not very expensive, we paid £21,000 for it in 1978. I'd saved up for a deposit, because I was the breadwinner while Tim was a medical student, and so it wasn't essential for me to work, and I was happy not to. But I think, nowadays, it's essential for people to have quite a high income, to buy houses round here.

Verity Peto and baby Philippa at home in Lonsdale Road, 1979. (J. Silverman)

Jocelyn Morris, a doctor, had been assisted back to work in 1975 at the Radcliffe Infirmary and then the Churchill by an enlightened scheme.

I went back to work quite quickly. I was very lucky, because Rosemary Rue, who was the chief medical officer for Oxford, had this scheme for funding married women doctors to go back to work part time, which was really way ahead of its time. So it wasn't difficult. I used to work five mornings but then I changed to two-and-a-half days.

Elsie Hill, who moved into Portland Road in 1965 and worked full time in her husband's publishing business, has noticed the difference in women's working.

That has certainly increased during the time I've been here, until there are very few who don't. I mean, they may stay at home with their children for the first five years, or the first ten years, but after that, almost take it for granted that they work.

The situation has reversed to the point that Peter Thompson's wife Sonja Drexler is unusual in following the old pattern of staying at home and making a little extra income by looking after lodgers.

Sonja is one of the few people that I know, who, since Joe was born, has never had a job. It hasn't been an economic necessity. It might have been if we'd decided to send Joe to private education. In fact, she decided that she would rather stay at home, run the domestic affairs. We've provided lodgings for foreign students for the whole time we've been here. It's been a very interesting experience doing that. Meeting people from all over the world.

Single women working

As we saw in chapter 3 the roads have been home to many women who did not marry but had long independent working lives. In the light of comments above, unmarried middle-class women whose working was not questioned might seem to have had more fulfilling lives – though until the last quarter of the century the jobs open to them were limited. They were typically secretaries, nurses or teachers.

Clare Wagstaff worked as a secretary, while her sister Monica trained as a teacher. For them it was natural to continue living at home.

On your £2 a week – even though it went a lot further in those days, it didn't stretch to living away from home. People who lived away from home were usually in hostels. Big shops like Elliston's, that had a hostel for a lot of their girls on the corner of Keble Road. These big companies seemed to look after their employees a lot more.

Monica, Dorothy and Clare Wagstaff, 1948. (C. & M. Wagstaff)

Clare, like Monica, stayed working in Oxford for this reason. She had begun with the British Council during the war, when it was based in Oriel College, but left when it returned to London.

We were only earning sort of £3 a week, you couldn't really think of living in London, so then I went to the Clarendon Laboratory, where I stayed about 23 years, and then I transferred to the Department of Atmospheric Physics, which was just next door, for the rest of my time.

The war opened doors for many women to more exciting lives than they might have expected. John Marsh remembers Miss Chavasse of 49 Hamilton Road.

I think she was a Matron, and she'd served in the Army Medical Corps, or whatever. She'd been through the war in the Middle East, and she'd stayed on, I think, way beyond what she should have done, through some oversight, and she thoroughly enjoyed it. When she retired, she came back to Oxford, where she'd been brought up. Her father had been a Bishop of Liverpool. She never married. She was a very nice person, a very matter-of-fact, down-to-earth sort of person. She had a twin sister, who did marry, her husband was a Dean of Windsor, and they both lived to be over a hundred.

Betty Grant (b.1922) spent her long working life in one area.

I left school and went straight to work in the Public Health Department, looking after the school medicals. All my life. Forty years. I worked up and up and up, and in the end I was doing the arranging for all the doctors' work, and all the school medicals and all that.

Marguerite Tibbetts of Victoria Road also worked as a secretary in the health service, from 1946 to retirement in 1983. When she wanted to take a diploma in the 1960s she was steered into social administration.

I wanted to do hospital administration, but the man said 'There's no place for women in the health service'.

Her sister Mary worked as a secretary from 1946 to her retirement in 1981 for John Brookes and in other roles at the College of Technology (from 1970 Oxford Polytechnic; from 1992 Oxford Brookes University). Such long-term connection with one employer was typical of this generation, and markedly different from later experience.

Mary and Marguerite Tibbetts on the right, working as secretaries in the Chief Engineer's office in South Parks Road, 1942. (M. & M. Tibbetts)

While Clare Wagstaff stayed working with the same employer – the University – the changes she saw are characteristic.

At one time we knew everybody in the lab. Now they've built on and on and on, and extended and taken in departments all over the place. By the time I left you could walk round and hardly be saying hello to anyone. The community spirit wasn't quite the same – but it was still a very nice place to work and lots of fun from time to time. But it did change, it changed a lot.

Caring

Family obligations in earlier years usually took precedence over work outside the home for women. Margaret Willis's spinster neighbour Cicely Davies was a teacher.

She was an English graduate, and she had taught at Headington School, and then just before we came [1954] she had her elderly mother living with her, and she'd given up Headington, and the High School – she'd taught at the High School as well.

More social services or agencies now ease some of the caring burden. Monica Wagstaff describes the sisters' difficulties caring for their mother and working at the same time.

It was one of the reasons I got early retirement, just to be at home with her, it was getting very difficult. Clare had to rush home every dinnertime and check on her and get a meal, and I was home early, but we realised we couldn't go on like that. The last two to three years of her life she had some form of dementia, you couldn't leave her for long at all.

They give a salutary reminder of general feelings of gratitude at the advent of the National Health Service.

> 1948 the health service came in. I know people grumble about it, but it wasn't there [before]. My father had to pay for all medical bills – my mother had to have tablets and things which were all very expensive.

In the later years of the century women had more of a choice over whether they worked or devoted themselves to caring for their family. Celia Glyn's decision not to work while her children were growing up in the 1970s and 80s was affected by her own experience as the daughter of a working mother, but was not uncommon.

> I had very decided views about young children, about how they should be brought up. I was overcompensating I think for my upbringing, since I had had a mother who worked and we'd had au pair girls and rather unsatisfactory childcare. Also I felt it was terribly important, the pre-school years. I think a lot of [my friends] weren't working during pre-school years. A lot went back later. We didn't financially need to work. Society has changed so much since then. I hadn't done a job that I really felt involved with, I hadn't gone to university. I still felt a failure from that point of view, and I think I was trying not to be like my mother. Possibly I would have been happier if I had gone back to work sooner.

Celia ran the St Michael's playgroup for seven years from 1977, during which time her husband left. A lot of her friends' relationships broke up at around that time. She has taken lodgers and since 1989 has worked part time as secretary to the director at the Phonetics Laboratory.

> My brain is not completely engaged but it's a very good place to work. It's a small research lab. I can choose my time.

This flexibility was important during the years when she was involved in the care of her mother, who had moved to live in Oxford.

> Towards the end the fact that my hours were flexible was very helpful, because I could go on what I used to call a 'death run' – when her alarm went off I would be rung, and go across and not know if I was going to pick her up off the floor, whether she'd be dead or alive, which was awful. For a while I did two part-time jobs.

Voluntary work

Voluntary work has traditionally depended on women with no financial need to work but a desire for socially useful employment. Mariele Kuhn was an early and very loyal volunteer for Oxfam, which was originally founded as the Oxford Committee for Famine Relief in 1942.

> There was a meeting in the Church Hall, and they told us about the idea of Oxfam, and who was willing, so I stuck up my hand. I worked at Oxfam for 50 years!

Sally Bromley remembers the Oxfam headquarters being built in Summertown in the 1960s and did volunteer work there as a teenager.

> I used to have to lick and stick labels, and write addresses to donors, and I remember writing one to Enid Blyton, who is so wonderful! And this is all at the contro-

versy of whether Noddy should or should not be allowed in libraries, and I was thinking, 'Noddy lives!' but I can't write it on the envelope!

Sally pays tribute to Susan Heaton, who grew up in Hamilton Road.

We all know her now as Sue Smith, and she's a very important character within the church, and does a lot of fostering. She's quite a remarkable girl who does a lot of caring.

Elizabeth, Lady Johnston came to Victoria Road in 1978 when her husband retired from the diplomatic service, and used to help at various places.

I got involved with the Lunch Club [at the Ferry Centre], and the other people with me, who did the cooking, are great friends. I had a hilarious time! And our clients, I think, rather enjoyed having their lunch cooked by a Lady, though I don't care for being called 'Lady' very much, but we stuck to it for the lunch club anyway. I also helped, sometimes, doing the food at St Michael's at the Northgate, in the City Centre. That was where I had the very nicest thing said to me. One day, an old tramp came in, and he had his cup of tea, and he made it last as long as possible, so he could stay in the warm. While nobody was looking, I filled up his cup, and he said to me, 'Oh, thank you, dear. You're a real Lady in disguise!' I also helped at the Gatehouse, which was a drop-in centre for homeless people. It was only open for two hours every evening, 5 till 7. It was interesting, but also rather sad, so many people depended on it.

Margaret Willis worked for the Citizens' Advice Bureau, then in George Street.

We did two sessions a week, and that was really an absolute commitment. It was absolutely rigid, as, of course, a proper voluntary job is. It dealt – <u>deals</u> – with everything that you can possibly think of: people who can't manage, whose Giro hasn't come – that's a very frequent complaint; people wanting to know how you set about getting divorced – especially after Christmas! Oh, anything at all.

From 1974 she served as a magistrate for 18 years.

It was extremely interesting, and it dovetailed beautifully with the CAB work, because you'd find yourself sitting on people with problems, from a completely different angle. Very absorbing. You work in threes, and you meet people that you never would have met from other walks of life. I loved it.

An outstanding example of someone who has made a challenging career from voluntary work is Jean Robinson (p.88f). She followed her husband to his first job in Sheffield, then back to Oxford.

He got a job at the Institute of Economics and Statistics and he had a Lectureship at Balliol, and then he got a Fellowship at Magdalen, where he's been ever since. The difficulty with coming back to Oxford, at that time, was what did I do? I soon discovered that Oxford was full of wives, full of frustrated, brilliant, academic women with no jobs. At that time, of course, there were only a few women's colleges, there were no women teaching in the men's colleges. Oxford is, or was then, a very limited job market anyway. It was the colleges or it was the car factory.

She joined the Regional Hospital Board in 1966.

They were looking for people to sit on Hospital Boards. I think they wanted a token housewife. It was a quite extraordinary experience. The Regional Hospital Board, as it was at that time, controlled major hospital expenditure, throughout the Region. I thought it went through a kind of ritual, that there were things going on elsewhere, but what we did was a ritualistic rubber-stamping process.

She proved herself far from a token housewife, by challenging things she thought were wrong.

This, of course, was a voluntary job, like all my jobs at the time. What I learned was, if you were willing to work for nothing, as a woman you can work at a very much higher grade, and get very much more experience than ever you would in a paid job. Looking back, that's what a lot of women in Oxford did. I cared what my friends thought about me, I cared what my family thought, and if they thought I was OK, it really didn't matter what the rest of the world thought. And what did I have to lose but a voluntary job?

She became Chair of the pioneering Patients Association alongside other voluntary jobs.

That was the real fast learning curve, the most educational experience of my life, really. There wasn't any consumer voice in the Health Service. We were getting a hundred, about a hundred complaints and enquiries a week, and I had a staff of one, who was a full-time paid secretary, who was very good, and some volunteers.

Voluntary work can be exceedingly challenging. Jean speaks movingly of her ultimately too draining work with victims of sexual abuse through the Prevention of Professional Abuse Network.

It's like a bonsai tree, when you distort the roots, it becomes something like a tree, but it doesn't become the tree it should have been. I found that painful beyond belief. Suffering I can deal with. Loss, those things I can deal with. But this seeing the shadow, or glimpses of what that person should have been, and did not become, and would never be. It was like the murder of the soul. It became so painful to me, I could not go on doing it.

Many cultural activities of course have depended on women's voluntary commitments – as Joan Crow commented of the pantomimes put on by Mrs Corden (p.191f).

I wouldn't think it would be possible for her if she had a job because it really was a full-time occupation for months. Any proceeds of the show went to charity.

Jelly Williams, who worked for many years for the League of Friends of Littlemore, Warneford and Park Hospitals, and as a trustee of the Oxfordshire Group Homes pioneered by another resident of the roads (p.87), belongs to a generation of highly educated and capable wives who often combined part-time jobs, in her case working on the Oxford Dictionary and teaching at Beechlawn, with voluntary work.

I could say that everybody one knows is involved in something or other. People have a social awareness on the whole, certainly then I think.

A major social change over the last decades has been the number of women in regular employment, and a focus on money-earning, to the great detriment of the voluntary sector, as Margaret Willis notes.

It gets more and more difficult to fill any of these voluntary jobs. Most of the voluntary charities and so on have great difficulty now, getting people to work there.

Business and beyond

As discussed in chapter 2 these roads were full in earlier days of people with all kinds of business interests in Oxford. This is not now so common, as Philip Gilbert of Portland Road commented when he was interviewed in 2001.

My background is entirely non-academic, and most of the people who live in this street are academic or professional people.

He grew up in the Jewish community in Stepney and met his wife, an artist, as a Young Communist.

It was a world that was completely enclosed. Most of the adults spoke in Yiddish. I was very active from the age of 14 in the Young Communist League, and latterly, in the Communist Party. Ruth was also in the Young Communist League. Her father was almost a founding member of the Communist Party.

After a couple of dead ends Philip opened a bookshop on the covered market in 1977.

I compounded my errors by going into partnership with my brother, and opening a hairdressing salon in Oxford, which lasted all of three years. It folded, and I got a job working at the University Examination Schools in the High Street. Extremely poorly paid. But the holidays were very good. I was always a lover of books, and a very good friend of mine had said to me, 'Why don't you open a second-hand bookshop?' I eventually found a shop in the covered market. This chap took it over as a record shop, and we ran it together, a third of it was books. It must have been the smallest bookshop ever. If I had more than five or six people in the shop, I had to stand in the alleyway, to give them room to walk round the books. Then the chance came of acquiring the shop next door, and I took it, still calling it 'The Little Bookshop'. We certainly haven't made a fortune, but we've made a living, been able to buy this house. I think of retiring, but I just haven't got around to it yet.

We gave a flavour of the earlier life of Sydney Denton on p.69ff. His interviews give a revealing insight into the life of a hard-working selfmade businessman. He began his cycle business when he was working at Morris Motors during the day, alongside other enterprises.

I used to go and help Harper's of Cowley, they were a cycle dealers, and then moved into mopeds and motorcycles. I used to assemble small Holden motorcycles for them: I could put three together in my lunch break. They used to pay me in old bicycles – that's what I earned, an old bicycle. I would then climb aboard my moped, and moped home to Wheatley, which is roughly five, seven miles, with this blasted bicycle on my shoulder, nearly breaking my arm! Flat out, I was! Flat out! I would deposit the bicycle down the garden shed, and having had my dinner, I would go and work on that bicycle, and turn that dirty old bicycle into a well-presented bicycle, ready for sale at the weekend. That's what I did every night of the week. And I could sell anything I could produce. But I only had one pair of hands. So then I started employing everybody who lived and worked in the cul-de-sac. I suppose you'd call it a cottage industry. We were doing up bicycles as fast as we could go. Virtually everybody in the cul-de-sac worked for me. Some operated cleaning up and restoring bicycles, others delivered the concrete mixers which we hired out. The touring caravans, people would be cleaning those. They were

'Mr D' in his bicycle shop at 294 Banbury Road, 1982. (Sydney Denton)

mowing my lawn and cleaning my windows, and everybody was getting paid! We were all desperate for money, we all had a mortgage, it seemed a millstone round one's neck at those times. So then it was getting to a size where I was actually earning more money part time – by part time, that's a laugh! I actually worked from five o'clock at night, often to 12, one o'clock in the morning, and then I worked all weekends.

He took over a tiny bicycle shop in Magdalen Road.

The rent was £3 10s 0d a week. Well, on the first week, I took £149-something. I netted £80. £80! I mean, that was a bloody fortune! £80! And I'd still got all the evenings to work! So we were singing, really really singing!

His first bicycle shop in Summertown was opened in 1970 at 194 Banbury Road. Bond's Cycles, which had refused to sell to him, closed down soon afterwards.

Although it wasn't a prime site, I now had the whole area to myself. I was up and running. Big time we are now, big time!

He bought the freehold of 294 Banbury Road, the premises of the old Twining shop, in 1978 and ran a very successful business there and at four other branches, as well as building up a substantial property portfolio.

I was always good at mental arithmetic. When I left school, I could hardly read and write. I mean, I know now how to spell 'business', I find that reasonably easy to spell! I found ways round things. What I do, I carry my strengths, and all my weaknesses I have somebody to carry out, so I had a secretary to look after my weakness.

Business at a high corporate level is represented in the roads by John Leighfield. He was born in Cowley, where his father worked for Pressed Steel, and educated via the 11+ at Magdalen College School. He then went to Exeter College, where he read Greats. Like many classicists John went early into the newly developing field of computers, beginning with the Ford Motor Company in 1962. He later moved to British Leyland, which is what brought him to Victoria Road in 1972. Chairmanships, Directorships and Presidencies have followed, covering IT, banking, education and music, and he was awarded a CBE in 1998. John's private passion is the collection of maps of Oxford and Oxfordshire which he began in 1966 – he is also now a director of Getmapping plc.

John Leighfield in his finery as Master of the Worshipful Company of Information Technologists, greeting his guests, the headmaster of Magdalen College School Andrew Halls and his wife, at a dinner at the Mansion House in 2006. (John Leighfield)

Another resident of Victoria Road who went early into computers is Sam Clarke, whose career is representative of the complex working lives now common in the roads. After coming up to Pembroke College in 1967 to read engineering and economics he went off to work for IBM.

> I'd hardly used a computer at all by the time I'd left [Oxford]. I'd heard of them. And I knew you fed bits of paper tape into them and got things out. But that was about as far as it went. I thought computer companies would help me get experience of a range of companies and would help me migrate into management of some sort.

After three-and-a-bit years he resigned. He heard of Oxfam through a friend of a friend in 1974.

> Somebody directed me to one of the senior staff in Oxfam, Guy Stringer. He was looking for somebody who knew about computers. I arrived that February to find Oxfam without lights, because it was in the middle of the three-day week. I had thought coming back to Oxford would be nice to be out of London, nice not have to wear a pin-striped suit all the time. What I hadn't realised was that I'd be working in a cold building, having to start at 8 o'clock because that's when it got light – and I think there was some reason why I had to be well-dressed in the early weeks!
>
> It was quite small and clubby. I remember everyone feeling much older. They didn't have computers there. The nearest computer was Birmingham – a computer bureau. At the time of my arrival they had a whole room which was called the Registry Room, in which there were lots of little plastic frames, and in the middle of the frame is a piece of paper with someone's name and address on it and lots of

holes punched round the frame and colour coding. And a whole team of people who lived, worked, ate and thought names and addresses. Every time you wanted to send something you had to pull out these thousands of drawers of little frames. This is what the computer was taking over. And gradually my work caused those people to move from those frames, which they were very reluctant to give up, to checking computer printout, which was very boring for them really.

Oxfam was growing rapidly thoughout that period and I just happened to be in the right place at the right time. Within a year I was asked to become a fund-raising manager. They had never quite had anybody in that role before. It was completely new stuff to me. I was an energetic young thing who was around and just happened to be there at the right time. I must have caused to be sent out literally millions and millions of letters, begging letters basically, the sort that people don't like to receive terribly much, but surprisingly large numbers of people responded. There was quite a lot of strategy behind it. There was a growing science of fund-raising.

In 1983 Sam took up the new post of Fund-Raising Director.

That took me to the top table in Oxfam, and you then began to share some of the decisions that the top people were having to take, which was truly fascinating.

By the time he left in 1988 Oxfam was much bigger.

It had grown consistently. It had been very successful in being there or getting there in times of disaster, and it had built its reputation and its capacity for doing things. It had built its base of supporters. It had started campaigning. It had started putting together the other side of changing people's lives.

Sam wrote The Complete Fund-Raising Handbook, *while he did consultancy for other voluntary organisations and an MBA at Cranfield. He became the first director of Oxford Mind, and then in 1992 went to the World University Service in London, an organisation working with refugees. This meant commuting four days a week, which was unwelcome. From 1996 Sam resumed working freelance with voluntary organisations (p.90).*

I've shifted emphasis to the environment now and work with three different environmental organisations – Friends of the Earth in this country; Friends of the Earth in Ireland which I sort of reconstituted and built up; and founded something [in 2005] called 'Stop Climate Chaos', a coalition of organisations. And those things and some others are what fill my time now.

Working from home

Francis Twining made covenants to restrict 'trade or business' being carried on in houses erected on his land (p.17), but all sorts of occupations have been hidden away in these roads. One of the most notable was the prestigious publishing company founded by the Cassirer family who had been driven from Germany as refugees (p.79f). Elsie Hill married Günther Hill, Cassirer's son-in-law, in 1965.

They started up an English branch of the business, in wartime, which was done more or less from 31 Portland Road, but it was never ever on the same scale as the German business. The German business was a very big concern. My husband kept the name. When we finally closed it down in 1990, he wouldn't sell the name of the firm. He said, 'I don't want anybody to lose control of what is published in the name of Bruno Cassirer.'

Elsie speaks about the pleasures and trials of working at home, and in partnership with a spouse.

We did our work – that is the editing side of the publishing – in the bedroom upstairs. My day started when I walked upstairs. I didn't have to travel to and from work. We just went, once a week, to London, to clear up problems about the distribution. But otherwise, work was there.

I found it very congenial, but I did find I could never escape from it! People say to you, 'Oh, how wonderful to have worked together'. Well, it was wonderful working together, though if you disagreed strongly about something, it could be very difficult. One of the problems about sharing a business is that if your husband is depressed because things are going badly, you know exactly why he's depressed, and you can't say, 'Oh, there, there, dear, it'll be better tomorrow', because you know – especially if, like me, you did the financial side of the business – exactly how good or bad it is.

Elsie and Günther Hill, c.1975. (Elsie Hill)

The company published a wide range of books, some very successful.

The only novelist we published was Kazantzakis, and *Zorba the Greek* was our best seller. And then we did two cookery books by Edouard de Pomiane – our other best seller was one of his books called *Cooking in Ten Minutes*, which is still in print, but as a Faber title. The Pomiane connection came about because Bruno Cassirer himself published Pomiane in German, before the war, and Günther was friends with him. Otherwise it was mostly rather specialised – a lot of Oriental titles, because of the connection with Richard Walzer and Samuel Stern [p.80], and art books and suchlike. We did two very big projects: one was a two-volume Catalogue Raisonné of the graphic work of Goya, which was, I think, the most distinguished thing that we ever did. Then we did another book on the French painter, Chardin. Our most beautiful production was an edition of Gauguin's *NOA NOA*. Then the last 15 years of our working life were spent translating, editing and designing three volumes on French sculptures at the time of Louis XIV.

Some people continue working from home after retiring from their full-time jobs – as in a sense did Mr Cooper who lived at 57 Hamilton Road until the early 1970s. John Marsh remembers him.

He retired because of ill health. He had a greengrocery business in the covered market. He was a pretty shrewd customer. He had a heart attack or something, and then when he recovered, he used to grow quite a lot of vegetables which he took down to the market to sell, somehow or another. It was in his blood. And he was a very good gardener.

For John Herivel retirement from an academic post meant among other things the chance to get on with a particular mathematical problem.

As soon as I retired, I got on to it full time. So many times – I mean, this has been very hard on Elizabeth – I've said, 'I've got it out!' And it turned out that there was something wrong. That's the beauty of mathematics, all you need is a piece of paper and a pen. Still hoping. And for a long time I had a sort of strong feeling, 'It must come out!' And now – well, I wouldn't like to throw it away. But it will have to be thrown away if it doesn't come out!

With the revolution brought about by home computers much academic work can be done at home, even at a high level in scientific subjects which once demanded full-time attendance at a lab or hospital. The marked separation between home life and college life for (predominantly male) dons, which persisted in the 1960s and 70s, has largely broken down, as Mary Tregear notices.

The University has changed a lot, I think. It really has become very much more up-to-date. It used to be that, as far as I could see, all Fellows went in to eat in the evening, and the wives were always complaining of this business of being left in the evening, with the children, and you had your boiled egg, and that was it. The husband went into College and had a slap-up meal. I always felt very sorry for dons' wives. Now, it doesn't happen, as far as I can make out, unless it's a very special dinner in the evening. They go in for lunch, and meet people that way, and then go home after work.

A concentration of academics in these roads now can lead to useful working contacts. Lonsdale Road used to be known for having a lot of economists. More recently there seem to be a large number of medics. David Schriger came from the Faculty of Emergency Medicine at UCLA for a year's sabbatical in 2003, and found himself by chance living next door to the Petos.

Tim and I share a lot of academic interests, so we were tinkering on each other's computers and discussing statistics, and medical issues quite a bit, so that relationship really flowered. A one-year sabbatical isn't long enough Most of the work product of my sabbatical will happen in the next two years with the people here, by internet and things of that nature. The first year was sort of just a romance, and now the work begins!

Running a business from home of course is enormously easier in these days of computerised communications. Numerous people work from home here now – including the present writer – in publishing, design, the media and consultancy of all kinds, as well as psychotherapy, teaching and so on. There have also been several artists and craftworkers living and working in the roads: Kathy Clarke of Lonsdale Road for instance established a knitting business in the mid 1980s with a partner who lived opposite – an echo of the business run by Dorothy White's mother in the 1920s (p.63).

The changing world of work

The world of work in general has been transformed in the later part of the 20th century. Mary Tregear, who arrived here in the 1960s, had been born in China, and was working at a small museum in Hong Kong when she got her job at the Ashmolean with an informality which would not be found today.

> I'd never been to Oxford before. I said to the then Head of Department here, 'If there's ever a job going here, let me know, because I'd like to apply'. When I got back to Hong Kong, after nine months' leave, there was a letter saying 'The job is yours if you'd like it'. So I just walked back, in the summer of that year, in '62, and I've been here ever since! But I felt quite a foreigner, in lots of ways and it took me a long time to figure out what was going on at High Table and that sort of thing! I was elected to St Cross College, which is a post-graduate college.

It is salutary to be reminded how rapid this change has been by Martin Berry's account of the introduction of technology into Darby's solicitors, where he worked for many years, before becoming a judge in the Family Court.

> I think, 1986, for the first time, we introduced a computerised accounts system. We had at that stage got one word processor which had cost us about £7,000 in about 1981, and that was the only computer technology we had. The accounts system was extremely expensive, and several of the partners wondered whether we really needed it. A year or two later there was a considerable argument about whether a fax machine was going to be necessary, and I think, at the same time, we bought the office's first mobile telephone, which again, most of the senior partners thought was a total waste of money! Anyway, partly as a result of all this, I became the Managing Partner of the firm, and for the last four or five years when I was there, we made enormous changes with information technology, and developed a proper management structure in the firm. Whereas, previously, every time we bought a typewriter, that required a decision by all the partners, by the time I left, decisions of that sort were dealt with by those who were delegated management responsibilities. The firm is now well over a hundred people, and the number of partners has doubled, so I presume that what we did in the 1980s was along the right lines!

There is a sense of less security in work now, noticed by older people. Monica Wagstaff comments that they never had difficulty in finding work.

> We've never had the worry that young people had – there was one lot that left school really worried about whether they could get a job. [For us] you may not have been able to get a job that you really liked, but we could get a job.

Geoffrey Paine spent his working life with accountants Wenn Townsend.

> I was training as a Chartered Accountant, to go into the family business, but before I'd finished qualifying, the family business was sold, so I ended up staying with the same firm for 42 years! I started as an Articled Clerk at Wenn Townsend, which is still the same name as it was then. Everything, now, is down to one thing – money. Practically everything is money, whereas 20, 30 years ago, it wasn't. The business lunches – not that I had very many, one or two a year – some people used to go two or three times a week, almost – have gone completely. People have sand-

wiches at their desk now. And I think the pressure's on, and there isn't the security, that's the other thing.

Philippa Berry reflects the stressful feelings brought about by constant reorganisations.
I'm now working half-time in a Community Mental Health team and there's quite a lot of redeployment threatened, but we don't know anything about what's going to happen yet. So I don't want to retire just yet. I believe I can work until I'm 66, for Oxfordshire County Council – Social and Health Care Department it's called now. But we are being seconded to the Oxford Mental Health Care Trust, which is working for the NHS, which is very difficult. The NHS is a very very much more unloving employer than Social Services. So I shall probably carry on working until I'm booted, either by redeployment, or I decide I can't stand the NHS any more. It's a very stressful job.

Les Holmes, working at 45 Hamilton Road, 1982. (Philippa Berry)

With many people now working, and more prosperity in the roads, maintenance jobs have increasingly been handed over to professionals, many of whom become familiar figures in the neighbourhood (p.164). Les Holmes worked around here for about 25 years as a painter and decorator, for the Berrys among others.

The various times I worked there it was just open house, just let myself in and carry on with the job and then get called down for tea or coffee; we'd chat about different things. In the early days when she had a very young family, I, on occasions, would babysit for her, and well, we become very close friends really, rather than customers. The people I worked for, you couldn't wish for nicer people. In fact when I retired they had a collection for me which was a big surprise, almost had me in tears.

He comments on a mutually beneficial relationship.

It's a good job we've got academics, because for the likes of me, what would I do? Because they really can't do an awful lot for themselves. It works both ways. I rely on them and they rely on me!

8   Houses

They're pretty standard, Edwardian, very deep houses. You can do a lot
with them, knocking walls down.

Kate Jones Finer

*Houses are conventionally a preoccupation of people who live in suburbs. This chapter
gathers some material on how people found their houses in these roads, how they have
lived in them, and what changes they have made. As we saw in Chapter 1 the houses are
varied, built predominantly before the First World War and between the wars, with considerable infilling in more recent years. Houses in the roads can be seen to have family likenesses, but finishing details – window glazing, porches and such – are generally
varied. Suburban monotony is not something from which the roads suffer.*

Finding a house in the Seven Roads

*Chapter 3 featured a few residents who still live in the houses they grew up in. Passing
houses down families used to be very common, but since the population of the roads has
become more mobile and professional it has become rare. Helen Holland moved with her
family to Portland Road in 1997, to a house which has passed through three generations (her father gave her the house, having inherited it from his sister Elizabeth).*

> My grandmother, Frances Stewart, bought the house and came here in Novem-
> ber, 1954. She was a widow then with her only daughter, who was unmarried,
> Elizabeth Stewart. [We found the house full of] old bits and pieces – 47 saucers and
> no matching cups! Some of the kitchen equipment would have looked splendid in
> a museum of 50 years before.

*The Crows' house in Victoria Road is another to pass to the next generation, after the
death of Joan Crow in 2002, as their neighbour Mariele Kuhn reports.*

> Now her daughter, Mrs Street, has moved there with her husband, and a daugh-
> ter and a son, and now they're building on. There is an epidemic in this road,
> everybody is building!

*Many people used to have relations living in the roads: this too is rare now, though it
happened by chance to Elsie Hill.*

> By pure coincidence, Günther's grandson bought [a house in] Portland Road. They
> just wanted to be in North Oxford, because they're both academics, and they had
> looked all around, and this house turned out to be absolutely perfect for them.

*This is of course generally an area people move to on the basis of simple calculations
about amenities, house types, transport and so on, as Kate Jones Finer typifies.*

> It was the nearest we could afford. We didn't want to be out beyond the ring road,
> and we didn't want horrible town houses with the garage at the bottom. We liked
> Edwardian/Victorian sort of things, and the house we had in Lonsdale Road was

lovely. It was a south facing garden. It was the style of housing, and being near the shops, and the fact that it was quite quiet, even though it was near the shops.

However interviews also revealed particular connections of all kinds operating to bring people here. Betty Grant's father for instance taught at Summertown School, coming up on a bike from Kingston Road: when the head teacher left, Mr Grant bought his house in Hamilton Road, in 1932, where Betty and her brother still live. Beryl Phillips was part of an extended family from Wales who all found their way to this part of Summertown (p.44f). Parents have sometimes come to join children here, as did Mary Tregear's.

I had a flat in Victoria Road. Then my parents when they did finally retire, decided to come and live here. And we looked for a house, and we bought this one [in Portland Road] in '63.

Many people have circumvented estate agents. Margaret Willis, who had lived at 55 Lonsdale Road in 1954–67, moved to Bainton Road, but returned in 1983 after her remarriage. The Willises bought their house at the far end of the road direct from the Silvers (who lived in three houses in Lonsdale Road). They had been neighbours of Margaret's when she first lived there.

They had lived opposite us more or less, and at that point, Mary used to babysit for them. So we knew them from then on.

A few people first got to know the roads through renting. Philippa and Martin Berry, for instance, met as students at the University and married in 1971. They lived for two years as newly-wed house-sitters in 22 Lonsdale Road, a house belonging to an Iranian acquaintance and his wife.

We had the top floor, and they let the bottom floor. I bought a little tiny gas cooker on legs and we got a gas fitter to fit it into one of the bedrooms. But we had no water in that room, so all the water had to be carried from the bathroom to do cooking, and we had to take all the washing-up back to the bathroom!

They bought their first house in Marston but wanted to move back, and were tipped off about a house in Hamilton Road. The elderly owner liked the idea of a family moving in.

I happened to know Christine Butler [at no.13], and I said to her 'We're looking to move into Summertown again. Have you got any ideas about houses?' And she said, 'Oh yes, Mrs Loring at no.45 is leaving' to move to a flat or something, because she was an old lady, a widow. By then we had Jo, who was an extremely wriggly 10-months-old. And when Mrs Loring saw us and Jo arriving, she just, I think, fell in love with Jo, and said, 'I really want this house to go to a family'.

Dorothea Pelham first knew her house in Portland Road when she offered to help the previous owner, Miss Steward (p.77), with the garden.

She was the most amazing character. And we just hit it off right away. So I took on the end of this garden here, which was then a complete wilderness. I mean, it really is a wilderness now, it was much more of a wilderness then, because she was too old to do it.

After Miss Steward died Dorothea and her husband Richard Gombrich were able to buy the house in 1975 with the help of Richard's father, the art historian Ernst Gombrich.
  Houses in these roads have for a long time commanded a premium over similar houses in other parts of Oxford, and many people have struggled to find the money to

buy them, like John and Doris Marsh – though the sums mentioned now seem amusing.

We were married in 1954, and up until about six weeks before the marriage, we had nowhere to live. We'd spent several months looking around Oxford and various places. What we liked we couldn't afford, and what we could afford we didn't like! And we had crossed Summertown off as being too expensive.

They were told about 53 Hamilton Road by people already living in the road.

The house was being let out as bedsits to students. Inside it was pretty desperate! It was as built, all the fittings and everything. So it was a bit off-putting, those cold winter days. It was unfriendly, dark chocolate brown paint everywhere. And it was on the market, actually, at only very slightly above the average price for a three-bedroom semi around Oxford. It was a little over £2,000, the average. We put in a bid, and there was promptly a counter-bid. And we put in a second and absolute, as far as we were concerned, final bid. I think we increased it by £25! And that was trumped. I went to the estate agent, and found out who was the owner of the house, and it turned out it was a Dr Chaundy, well-known local family. He was a mathematician at Christ Church. I went along to see him, oh, only a few days before Christmas: a very nice man, and he heard the story. I said, 'We just cannot go any further. We have nowhere to live'. He said, 'What's this other chap?' And I said, 'Well, he's already got a house'. 'Well', he said, 'I'm a mathematician, not an estate agent. You can have the house on your last bid', which was wonderful. So then we're indebted to Dr Chaundy forever!

Margaret Pickles and her friend Hazel Leafe, both teachers, encountered difficulties as a pair of young women trying to buy in the early 1960s.

We didn't know one thing about property, let alone anything else! They sent a man out with us, and we said to the man, 'If you had a daughter like us, would you recommend that we bought it?' He said, 'Yes, without any doubt whatsoever.' They were very helpful. So we just managed to put enough down. Then we had the problem of getting a mortgage for two women, because this wasn't done. And my Headmaster, and Hazel's Headmaster, saw the authorities and said, 'Well, look, they both teach for the City, and if they don't get this house, they'll go elsewhere.' So they agreed to let us have the mortgage at 6 per cent, which was half a per cent more than what was currently going, and within a year it had gone up to 6 per cent, and ours remained fixed. And by the time we'd paid it, it was 13 per cent for everybody else, and we were still at 6 per cent!

Their early days of home ownership were very spartan.

We came in with just a bed board for a table, a dustbin propped underneath it, two deckchairs, two beds, and an oven that we had on hire purchase, and oddments. And we had *Oxford Mail* newspaper on the floor for two years, before we could afford anything else. Then Hazel's parents came down and were appalled at the poverty we were in! So [her mother] sent the whole of her sitting room furniture – lock, stock and barrel – down, for us to put in and use. So that started us off quite nicely.

Hilary Lloyd and her husband had been looking to move to this area for some time.

We were living in Southdale Road. We were looking for several months and had almost come to the conclusion that we couldn't afford anything down here. Then Hawkswell Gardens came up and the house was in such a terrible state, so the price was very low. When we went to see it I almost had apoplexy but my husband said 'No, this is going to be fine'. It had been lived in by someone who was a recluse and had been a hoarder. There was stuff piled to the ceiling. There were pathways through all the rooms. She was Japanese and was married to a linguistics professor, who died. She was the Avon lady round here for some years. The house was cleared for us, and then we saw what we got, only then.

Moving, down-sizing and up-sizing

It is notable how many people moving into these roads have come from areas close by, commonly the roads to the north, making an upward move when the opportunity arises. Sally Bromley, who came to Victoria Road from Carlton Road, can immediately name four other neighbours who have moved from Carlton or Southdale Roads.

There's been this slight removal from one area to another. I do remember the Headteacher at Wolvercote saying she doesn't know any other school where people move within the same locality so much!

A surprising number of people too have moved within the seven roads, to get a house that suits them better without leaving the neighbourhood. This included swapping from one side to the other of a semi-detached pair in the case of Dorothy White, who lived in 13 Hamilton Road until she moved to no.11 in 1948 (p.63). Kato Havas, the eminent violin teacher (p.94f), moved across Victoria Road to escape wrong notes.

We saw some horrors, and then we saw the house on Victoria Road, 63, and it had a lovely large garden, and it had a lovely room, and we were both not the most practical people in the world, and so that was suitable. It was sunny, it was wonderful! And we didn't even notice that it was semi-detached, because it was all in such a hurry. For three years, we lived with builders. Next door to us, lived a dear elderly lady, Mrs Moss. She had been a piano teacher, if I remember correctly. And she played the piano, and I could hear every note. She played Mozart. And she made a mistake always in the same place! It just drove me up the wall! And I tried to teach so hard, so my pupils wouldn't hear it! And we put double things on the wall, and I could still hear it! And I went over once and asked, very politely, 'Can you hear me, us? Do we make a lot of noise?' She said, 'No, I can't hear you at all'. So I couldn't say to her, 'Move the piano'. I mean, I just couldn't do it! So in this house lived a young couple, she was Polish, who were architects. And then they had a baby, and they wanted to move to London. And we had supper with them here, in the snow, and they said, 'You know, this house would suit you so well.' We said, 'To move again, we just can't face it'. And we went home, through the snow, and before we opened the door, said, 'Why not? Why not?' And we were here first thing in the morning, when they were still in pyjamas, and said, 'We will come'!

A few other examples: the Gilberts moved from one end of Portland Road to the other – though experiencing these as different neighbourhoods (p.208). John Marsh moved from Hamilton Road to Lonsdale Road in 1989 for a smaller house. The Davies family in Hamilton Road has made a habit of swapping houses: they moved to Portland Road from Islip Road by exchanging houses; then to find a smaller property themselves in 1991 swapped with the owners of a house in Hamilton Road.

Downsizing within these roads is not altogether easy as there are few smaller properties, though people are often reluctant to leave the area. Peter Clarke looked for a long time before moving from Lonsdale Road to the block of flats in Hawkswell Gardens.

I did walk the streets of Oxford, many times and oft, to see where I would like to be. I wanted to be near rivers, in part, and then I wanted convenience, and I've got it all here really. And the area's nice. I found it difficult to move, but I can't believe it, how easy it was – after the event.

A variety of roof extensions in Lonsdale Road. Planning regulations now allow only roof-light windows at the front of houses. (P. Kinchin)

A view from the rear of attic extensions in Portland Road. (P. Kinchin)

In recent decades most people have in fact upsized by upgrading and extending their houses. A majority of houses now have attic conversions, while a few had original attic rooms which have been extended. This began in the mid 1960s. Kate Jones Finer, who lived at 48 Lonsdale Road from 1977, describes some early examples.

Next door, she was a widow. She used to have a lodger in the loft conversion. And there was a loft conversion on 50 as well, and they'd said, 'Oh, we're not having central up there. You don't need central heating for children!' So these were rather makeshift! I think both of them were improved later on.

The Finers did their loft conversion a little later, in the 1980s, when Sam Finer retired.

All his books came from All Souls – tons of books – so we had to have special steel beams in to support these books, and I remember them coming back with a lorry full of tea chests, and these poor men carrying the tea chests up two flights of stairs!

Martin Berry gives an account of extensions to their semi-detached house in Hamilton Road bought in 1975, typical of changes accompanying growing prosperity.

At the side was another half plot of land on which was an old corrugated iron garage [p. 32] – there were several garages of that sort in the street at the time – but that didn't last more than about a year or two before we extended the house and had it demolished. In fact, we've extended the house several times since we've been here, so that it's now much bigger than when we originally arrived. Originally, it was a four-bedroomed house. It's now a five-bedroomed house. Certainly we turned this into a family home, and now we live here, just the two of us – but every so often the tide comes in again! Now, we wonder whether we should look for somewhere smaller to live – but we're both too busy at work, really, to get round to doing things like that.

Living in the houses

The number of Edwardian houses in anything like their original state is now very small, but we have several vivid accounts of an older unmodernised style of living from interviewees who grew up here. Dorothy Bridge (b.1907) recalls her family home, 5 Hamilton Road, where lighting was by gas, and the kitchen was the only really warm room.

We used to have a kitchen range. You cooked Yorkshire puddings and roast beef in the oven, and it was lovely and hot in the kitchen.

In many houses, like Elsie Hill's in Portland Road, the kitchen area was originally the domain of a servant, whether live-in or daily (see p.131ff on help in the house).

Bell board still in situ in the kitchen of 31 Portland Road. (P. Kinchin)

The house also has what we always, for no particular reason, called the 'breakfast room', but which would have been the maid's room, because it had the board – which is still there – with all the buttons. I could never understand how this house could have had a maid, because there was never a suitable bedroom, but then somebody said, 'Oh, this far out in North Oxford, wouldn't have been the really distinguished academics, but the ones who would just have a daily maid'.

45 Hamilton Road and its pair had housed maids in the top of the house, as Martin Berry says.

The top bedroom was a servant's bedroom originally, and was pretty cold and very small, very inferior joinery and woodwork up there. Next door even the light switch for the top bedroom was in the master bedroom downstairs – when the mistress wanted the maid to go to sleep she could turn out the light upstairs! On the side door to our house, there was a little sign where it said, 'Tradesmen's Entrance'.

When heating was by open coal fires, bedrooms were generally unheated, as Dorothy Bridge remarks.

I remember once thinking, 'If I ever have any money, I'll have an electric blanket!' I used to feel the cold so.

Betty Grant also recalls freezing bedrooms and hard winters growing up in Hamilton Road in the 1930s.

We had no heating up there at all. We had eiderdowns, and we had hot water bottles. We did have a stone one, but I think the aluminium must have come in, because we each had one of those.

Open fires created a lot of housework, and it is salutary to remember how black the buildings of Oxford were before stone cleaning and restrictions on burning coal. Betty mentions regular visits from the chimney sweep, rarely seen today.

That used to be a nice job – the sweep coming! You had to sort of cover everything up, and clear up afterwards.

The sweep, old Mr Soden from Islip Road, was a well-known character, very knowledgeable about Summertown, according to Gwynneth Twining.

I can remember running out into the garden to see the brush come out of the top. And he came to us for years. And then his son came to us eventually.

The Soden business is still operating, now run by Michael Soden and his son Gary, who is the sixth generation in the business, though they now have few chimneys to sweep.

Electricity fairly early replaced gas for lighting, but heating continued to be predominantly by solid fuel well into the 1970s. All houses had coal stores, and regular deliveries of coal were part of daily life, as Mariele Kuhn remembers.

We had a lot of open fires, we had anthracite stoves, and coal was in sacks, that came in big lumps, and we had to chop them!

Margaret Clarke, who came in 1962, did not change to gas central heating until the early 1980s.

Margaret Clarke by the original built-in dresser in the kitchen (now 'breakfast room') of 36 Hamilton Road. (P. Kinchin)

We had the coal lorry, because we had open fires and a boiler, and we built a coal bunker in the garden, to house the coal and the coke.

Edwardian and some 1920s houses had coppers built into the sculleries: Clare Wagstaff remembers the physically punishing business of doing the laundry before washing machines.

We used to have an old copper out the back we had to light every week at our peril – put a spill underneath and lit the wretched thing, and everything boiled away, and the place was full of steam, you've no idea what it was like. And then we used to have to get it out with a big pole, and it was heavy, sopping wet washing, and then get it out to the mangle in the shed and turn this wretched mangle – oh dear! Times were different, but they were hard, and the washing had to be done with elbow grease and an old mangle.

Larders were important in the days before fridges. Dorothy White recalls dealing with milk bought from the milkman in the road.

You'd take your jug out, and he'd fill it. We had quite a nice cool larder. We used to boil it so as it did keep better. It was always done before the night.

Paloma Bevir, who is Spanish, describes 11 Hamilton Road, one of the earliest houses in the road, where Dorothy White and Beryl Turner lived for many years (p.63), as it was when she and her husband bought it in 1979.

[It] was unchanged – except that the gas had been cut off. In the rooms you could see the gas fittings for the lamps. When the new gas came, the North Sea Gas, they were so frightened that the Gas Company came and they were disconnected. Nothing had been changed. There was no heating whatsoever – well, they had some storage heaters. There was ... not brown paint – purple paint, sort of lilac purple doors. They have just done the rewiring of the house, but they have put exactly the same plugs, the round plugs, so we had to put the new kind of plugs. All the fireplaces were there. All the nice features of the doors. They have a boiler in the sort of breakfast room, where they seemed to squat. We visited them, it might have been early spring, and they seemed to be always in that room, because the rest of the house was very cold. And they had bulbs in the staircase and the landing, which were 8 watts! When we removed the wallpaper in one of the rooms, I think there was a notice saying, 'This has been wallpapered 1905'.

The Finers bought 48 Lonsdale Road in 1977 in a similar unaltered condition.

It was one of these completely unimproved. It had an old lady who was crippled with rheumatism, her father had bought the house. She'd spent her life in that house. It was dark brown and – well, it was a 1910 wallpaper, most of it. What you could see was pretty gloomy!

Houses built between the wars were usually less gloomy, having better access to the garden at the rear, but were not necessarily much advanced in their amenities, as the Wagstaffs' struggles with the copper indicate above. Betty Marshall's house, new in 1925 (p.24), did not have a hot water supply to the bathroom: she remembers her mother carrying buckets upstairs, and the thrill of having piped hot water installed in the 1930s. Ted Shirley remembers lino.

The up-to-date electric kitchen of 13 Victoria Road, built for T.E. Knowles in 1939. (OPA)

No one had carpets, but lino – or oilcloth as my mother called it – with newspapers underneath.

Bill Fosdike had criticisms of the purpose-built vicarage in Lonsdale Road, erected in 1923. It replaced the Victorian vicarage (p.22) but had many of the problems of older vicarages.

It wasn't the world's most cleverly designed house. They put up something that was too big, really, and lots of little rooms. There wasn't a decent-sized room. We loved it, in many ways, but it was a wasteful house – a house could have been built with much less ground around it, and a much more practical house.

Professor Kolakowski lives in an unusual house in Hamilton Road built in the later 1920s, when bungalows were fashionable: they are now common targets for developers.

It's all on the one level. And I have problems in walking up and down the steps, so it was most convenient to me. It has, in fact, four bedrooms, this drawing room and a dining room, which we use only occasionally. There is one more small room behind the kitchen. So it is quite large for us. We lived with our daughter first. For some time the mother of my wife came here from Poland. And we are very pleased with this house. It is, of course, full of books. This entire house is full of shelves, bookshelves!

Houses of post-war date are generally not highly esteemed today for their architectural qualities, and do sometimes suffer from the use of cheap standardised materials. However they are often pleasant to live in – as Holly Kilpatrick says of her house, originally built in 1957 on a river garden plot in Lucerne Road, but greatly extended since.

A house like this is considered 'untrendy' around here. In fact, that is an interesting aspect of North Oxford, that a lot of people would rather live in a period house, whatever the disadvantages, than in something modern and of no architectural interest whatsoever. Personally I was more attracted to an older house but my first husband loved gardening and fiddling about with cars so we had to have a big garden and a garage (now a table tennis room)! I'm really glad that we bought this as generations of children have so adored the garden and river.

The houses in Hawkswell Gardens were built in the early 1960s, in contemporary style. Alan Knowles remembers their construction (p.29f) and the attention paid to heating.

They were considered to be fairly forward-thinking. They were all electric which was the big thing at the time. They all had electric underfloor heating. They all had individual staircases, so there was a whole series of staircases that people could choose.

Hilary Lloyd has lived for some time in one of them.

My friends thought we were mad to be buying a 1960s house. But we got what we wanted – a bigger house, four bedrooms, and detached, and we got this most beautiful setting, with the lawn and the beautiful willow tree. I cannot believe we are living in Summertown.

Hilary Lloyd outside her house in Hawkswell Gardens, 2006. (P. Berry)

Changing the houses

At the beginning of the 21st century few of the older houses in the roads have not been altered now. Even houses built to the same plan – two pairs of houses erected by the same builder for instance – have over the years evolved into different forms through additions and changes, as Elsie Hill of Portland Road points out.

No.19 began its life as [an] exact replica of this [no.31]. And then no.29 was the same as no.17. But they're now totally different, because they've all been adapted differently.

The new wave of younger people moving into the roads from the 1960s generally found unmodernised houses which they wanted to alter to suit different, more informal living patterns. Christine Butler came to 13 Hamilton Road (the other side of the Edwardian house described on p.157f), in 1964, and found it rather dismal and inconvenient.

It seemed to me a tall gloomy house with a narrow passage way between ourselves and 15. It was painted an extremely ugly deep dark maroony red paintwork. [It was] an awkward house because of its corridor. I wasn't fond of it, because it wasn't sociable. It was OK for formal do's when you sat and had drinks in the front room, then walked down the corridor and sat down at a table; but it wasn't good for mixing-about parties.

Kitchens, as we have seen, were originally regarded purely as service areas in 'better' houses. Helen Holland remembers visiting her grandmother in Portland Road after 1954.

There was actually, literally, a green baize door, and my grandmother, when I first came here, had a maid called Mabel, who lived in the tiny bedroom upstairs, but had her own little cloakroom beyond, at the end of what was the scullery kitchen.

On the whole, however, servants of this kind for the middle classes disappeared after the Second World War. As the warmest part of the house kitchens in Edwardian houses had often been used as living areas. Later they were rebranded 'breakfast rooms', and people found it increasingly convenient to eat at least some meals there. The advent of fridges and fitted storage cupboards did away with the need for larders; small electric and gas cookers, and central heating, rendered obsolete the solid fuel ranges which had domi-nated the kitchen and the coal stores necessary to feed the fires; washing machines dis-placed coppers and the need for a separate scullery. Margaret Clarke made typical altera-tions in Hamilton Road in 1962 before they moved into the house.

The kitchen was two rooms. We enlarged the kitchen by incorporating three small rooms leading off it – a larder, coal store, and a dark room – and made a window onto the garden.

Left: The rear of 36 Hamilton Road in 1962.
Right: The house in 1972 after alterations to include the old larder and coal store in the kitchen area. (Margaret Clarke)

Most of these Edwardian houses had a lavatory for servants' use at the back, and Elsie Hill describes another common alteration of the 1960s and 70s.

When I first moved here, it had a downstairs lavatory, approached via an outside door, and there was a tradesman's door in the kitchen, and all that's been blocked off, and it has one big open window now. But I have had a shower room and lavatory built at the back, so I've got a downstairs shower and an upstairs bathroom.

Extensions done later have often removed the old lean-to storage areas at the back of the kitchen and scullery altogether to open up an additional eating/living room with views

A new kitchen installed in the Petos' Edwardian house, 79 Lonsdale Road: an extension replaced the old larder, coal store and toilet, giving full access to the garden. (H. Clarke)

to the garden – something which Edwardian houses did not allow – while a lavatory is squeezed into what was the cupboard under the stairs. Many people now live most of the time in the back of their houses, as Martin Berry describes.

It was virtually unchanged from when it had been built. [There was] a very small scullery, and there had been a sort of downstairs larder which had already been turned into a downstairs lavatory. The kitchen, itself, was a minute little room, with a very small window. So we've opened all that up and built an extension, so that the kitchen is now by far the biggest room in the house, and it's where we have spent most of our time for most of the last 25 years, where the children have grown up, and we've had many meals with friends and neighbours. The previous owners would have used the back reception room as a dining room, but we've always found it easier to eat in the kitchen.

Separate 'front room' and dining room were fundamental to respectable middle-class life in the earlier part of the century. Elsie Hill's account of knocking them into one in Port-

land Road, after she married Günther Hill in 1965, describes what has happened in many houses in the roads, reflecting a general desire for larger, flexible spaces.

> We turned this into one long room. There was a dining room at the back, which never ever got a ray of sunlight. And then this was not really a very big sitting room, and as you walked straight into it, there, bang, was the grand piano. I just hated it! And the only way I was persuaded to stay here was having that change made.

The installation of gas-fired central heating seemed a crucial improvement to younger people moving in, as Philippa Berry says of their arrival in 1975.

> We had a huge amount of work on our hands, but we didn't have a lot of money. But we did get the plumbers in to put the heating in the following summer. It was very very cold that first winter. We had a coal fire and logs and so on, and we huddled around it.

Renovation and restoration

The impulse to alter houses is not a new one. Martin Berry describes modernisations of the late 1930s or 1950s which were not to their taste in 1975.

> Most of the doors in the house had been covered over with hardboard, which was the sort of style in the early 1950s, to get rid of the traditional Victorian and Edwardian joinery, so that you had nice smooth doors.

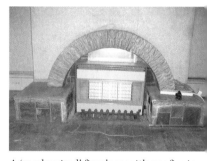

A 'modernised' fireplace with gas fire in 45 Portland Road, an Edwardian house, 2005. (P. Kinchin)

> The fireplaces had been covered over, with a rather horrid little gas fire in the front sitting room. A nasty sort of brick, or tiled brick, fireplace had probably been put in as an improvement. It was a great relief to get rid of it fairly soon after we moved in, because it was so hideously unattractive! The only fitted carpet in the house was in the hall and stairs, and that was pretty repulsive, but all the other carpets, as would have been the case 30, 40, 50 years ago, were square carpets with stained boards around them.

In the 1950s and 1960s things seen as 'Victorian' were not in favour, and there was a tendency to rather casual destruction of original features like fireplaces. Christine Butler admits to having done this when they moved into 13 Hamilton Road in 1964.

> We did something which people now would think was vandalism. We took out the old pseudomarble fireplaces and the little metal ones in some of the upstairs rooms. But they were huge and ugly and dark and nasty, and we wanted to have some form of continuous heating.

Much of the work done on houses in these roads in the 1960s and 70s was of poor quality. Bertram Mandelbrote, who bought 76 Lonsdale Road in 1980, speaks of the previous owner's efforts.

> He was very much a DIY exponent, and the bathroom was in an appalling state

and the kitchen not much better. The garden was almost entirely vegetable patch. We had quite a lot of renovating to do. And so we had Knowles & Company in because I know Alan Knowles very well, he's a Rotarian friend of mine.

Now that the area has become more prosperous more value is placed on original architectural details. While internal arrangements have almost always been changed to make more or bigger rooms, more livable kitchens and so on, there is also a tendency to restore features like fireplaces, even if they are fitted with fake-coal gas fires. Verity Peto of 79 Lonsdale Road salvaged fireplaces which were being ripped out of neighbouring houses at the point when the tide of taste was turning in the late 1970s.

When we came in 1978 there were lots of skips in the road, and I took out a couple of fireplaces and kept them until we had the money to put them in here – because someone had taken out the ones here.

Peter Clarke admits to later replacing a fireplace that he and his wife had destroyed when they first came to the house in 1975. Many 'period' fireplaces in these roads are not the originals. In some major renovations however chimney breasts have been removed altogether to make more space in rooms.

Several houses that were broken into flats and rather run down have by now been restored as family homes. In 1980 the Thompsons bought a house that had been split into two flats by the elderly lady who owned it, who had lived there from her childhood.

The front room of 79 Lonsdale Road, with a fireplace thrown out of no.70 installed to replace the one earlier destroyed in this house. (Henry Clarke)

She lived on the first floor. I guess she had arranged for it to be divided into two flats probably 1965 to 70-ish, and probably because she was somewhat impoverished when her parents died. It was split horizontally, with a partition across the front entrance hall, so that the upstairs flat used the front door, and the downstairs flat used a door out into the garden, where the conservatory now is. A bathroom had been created downstairs, rather crudely, in what had originally been the lobby inside the back door. Basically we just restored it to the geography that it had originally.

While many windows, and even doors, have been replaced with rather crude UPVC double-glazed units in the home improvements common in the 1980s and 90s, some people are now replacing with more expensive wooden windows, though the building regulations' requirement for double glazing makes it difficult to reproduce the slender glazing bars of the old windows. Certain people have even started to remove UPVC replacements. A few houses survive with a full set of the original Critall metal windows

1920s houses in Hamilton Road: original Critall windows on the right, replacements on the left. Front gardens have been surrendered to cars. (P. Kinchin)

installed in houses of the 1920s and 30s – these are the ones most likely to have been replaced with UPVC, and the loss of the original glazing detail has often spoiled the appearance of houses of this date.

Few people have so far taken the expensive step of restoring the iron railings stipulated by Francis Twining (p.17) but stripped from front walls during the Second World War – indeed the walls themselves have often gone to make parking space. Some of Lady Gurden's in Portland Road were hidden and thus survived.

There are iron railings between the houses, there's good old dark black iron railings underneath the hedge.

Skips and vans in the streets testify to the continuing investment of residents in the maintenance and improvement of their homes, and some tradesmen have a long and happy association with the roads, passing from house to house by recommendation (p.150). As the Biddles say:

Once a good workman gets into Hamilton Road, he never escapes!

Paloma Bevir comments that Mr Harris all but lived in Hamilton Road.

There's somebody in the street, who doesn't live in the street, but seems to spend most time in the street, who is Mr Harris, the builder, with his red van! A long time ago, he was the milkman in the area as well. Hamilton Road residents give him enough work not to have to move his equipment, that he keeps in one of the sheds in the street.

Gardens – and the motor car

Front gardens have suffered badly from the pressure of the motor car. Mariele Kuhn remarks on a car-free environment when she arrived in Victoria Road in 1938.

There were hardly any cars. Then finally we bought, I think it was fourth-hand, a little Austin, so it was quite useful to go out into the countryside. Of course, many people had no drives, they had the front gardens, there were no cars standing around.

In the early days of increasing car ownership in the 1950s unlit vehicles were not supposed to be left on the public highway overnight. Margaret Clarke and her husband coming to Hamilton Road in 1962 were typical in arranging to have the car off the road.

It had a big tree in the front, which we had to get down, because we had to have somewhere to put the car. So we had a run-in, and it was some time later that we actually had it properly paved. People either had garages, or [cars] were off the road, or they just hadn't got cars.

Lonsdale Road was mainly densely developed with Edwardian houses which were not built for people who aspired to private transport – Gilbert Twining at no.76 was the only early resident to have a carriage house. Peter Clarke moved in in the 1970s.

People would remark, 'Oh, it's a nice road, because it's got lots of trees'. I think that's changed. Lots more people have chopped trees down. And these drive-ins, that's all new. The road is much more crowded with cars.

The Finers were anxious to buy one of the few garages in Lonsdale Road, near the top of the road, when they were told of it by Kate's sister, also a resident of the road.

'There's a garage for sale', and we said, 'What!? Put the money down for us!' It was quite difficult from Hong Kong! It saved us having to spoil the front garden.

Victoria Road from the front garden of no.45 in the 1960s, showing one of the old gas-lamp street lights surviving in the roads. (Betty Marshall)

Lady Gurden of Portland Road shows that people have long felt proprietorial about the bit of road outside their house.

I've still got a beautiful old iron notice that my opposite neighbour put up – he had it specially made. In front of his wall . It says, 'No Parking'.

When there began to be pressure on street parking some people would leave out cones and wheelbarrows to guard 'their' places.

In Victoria Road some up-to-date houses of the 1930s

Lonsdale Road overwhelmed by vehicles, 1988. Two men are trying to move the car on the corner to enable the lorry to turn into King's Cross Road. (Peter Thompson)

had integral garages, but being rather small these have mostly been converted to rooms. Similarly the free-standing garages of many interwar houses have been replaced by extensions or complete new houses, leading people to sacrifice their front gardens for rather unattractive parking space. Street parking had come under intense pressure by the 1990s. This project was running during the long-winded consultation over the permit parking scheme finally introduced at the end of 2004. Martin Berry reflected common anxieties about the scheme.

The object is to prevent commuters into town parking in this street. But because of the relatively limited parking, which will be permitted to residents, we fear that even more people will start to pave over their present gardens, and rather change the character of the street.

Now that the scheme is running, pressure on parking for residents is actually much relieved, at the cost of some visual clutter of parking signs and lines in the road. There is perhaps now the hope that some people might restore the front gardens that contribute very much to the pleasant appearance of the streets.

In the hidden areas behind the houses back gardens vary greatly in size and and style. Paloma Bevir inherited the garden of Miss White and Beryl Turner in Hamilton Road.

They were very keen gardeners. In fact, it seemed to us that they spent more time in the garden than they did in the house! I think they still were doing it as a war effort, because they had a lot of the garden consecrated to vegetables.

Dorothea Pelham in Portland Road created an unorthodox suburban garden.

I put two beehives in there. I went and bought four big trees – an oak tree, a birch tree, an alder tree and a hazel tree. I think that was in '84. Obviously I then was getting sort of less formal.

She was further influenced by a part-time job she had with the regional wildlife trust BBONT (now BBOWT). She was interviewed in 2000.

I started putting this hedge in, to make a natural hedge. Then I put a pond in for frogs. And then I put this rock wall for toads. I got the whole thing sort of going in the early 90s, and about '96 or '97, I thought, 'This is good now'. I had the toads, I had the thrushes. But in the past year or so, I've noticed a great falling away. Although it looks like a mess, in fact it's designer mess! The idea is not to have everything cut back and exposed. Whenever I put something in, I try to make it be a native plant, simply because native plants encourage the insects that are here, and the insects are the ones the birds are used to having. Again, butterflies have totally fallen away. It's frightening. We used to have lots of holly blues, for example, in that holly out there. Used to have lots of speckled woods, orange-tips. Last year, there was just nothing.

Old trees in some gardens go back a long way. Martin Berry is a keen gardener.

One of the problems with our garden is that our neighbour has huge self-seeded trees, so we have quite a lot of shade. The garden was full of old fruit trees. We met a man, a year or two after we moved in, who had known the street before there were any houses on it, and he told us there was an orchard here. And one of those trees is still left. The apple trees were extremely old so after several years of struggling with our conscience, we decided to get rid of those trees. One of them had a tree house in it for many years, whilst the children grew up.

Over the years gardens, like the insides of houses, change their style and the way they are used.

Originally it was a garden full of swings and roundabouts and toys for the children, but now it's a flower garden, where we eat, whenever we can, in the summer. We try and treat it as an extra room to the house, really. We can see it easily from the kitchen ... and we think it's very nice.

9   *Summertown and Its Shops*

This area is now first class for shopping. And to me, it's an absolute boon.

Elsie Hill

The wider community of Summertown has changed greatly over the 20th century, reflecting the social changes seen in the seven roads. From a 'village' offering basic local essentials – churches, small schools, bakeries, butchers, grocers and so on – it has become a sophisticated office and shopping centre, with supermarkets, delicatessens, numerous cafés and restaurants, and frills like art galleries and designer clothes shops. The proximity of our roads to a good shopping centre and facilities like library and swimming pool is one of the things that makes them exceptionally desirable today.

Early shops: Twining's and the Co-op

Early shops were concentrated in the original centre of Summertown village, between the Banbury and Woodstock Roads: a Co-op was established at 10 George Street (Middle Way) by 1890, along with other shops on South Parade. The Co-op moved to purpose-built premises at 4 South Parade in 1899, serving the village at large. Aiming for the higher class of customer moving to the new middle-class housing in the area,

Francis Twining established a Summertown branch of his grocery business, opened in 1902 at 294 Banbury Road, next to the Congregational Church. The frontage, designed like the Co-op by J.R. Wilkins, was restored by its owner Sydney Denton in 1989 and the buildings make a pleasing landmark in the approach to Summertown today, as Sally Bromley comments.

> It really is a beautiful frontage to that building. It's got the initials entwined [FT for Francis Twining], and it's got the wonderful cornucopia, and it balances well with the United Reformed Church next door.

The shop was managed by Margaret and Gwynneth Twining's father: Gwynneth ran errands there for her mother in the 1920s.

> I quite liked that, because in front of the counter, there was these biscuit tins, big ones with see-through tops, and I used to be given a chocolate biscuit!

294 Banbury Road, opened as Twining's grocery shop in 1902, owned by Sydney Denton from 1978, photographed c.1990. (S. Denton)

It was a traditional high quality grocer's shop, as Betty Grant describes.

Really old-fashioned but very nice inside. We used to go there for all our shopping. The sugar was all measured out and put in blue bags. One side was wine and things like that, and the other side was ordinary provisions.

John Rowe remembers it too.

You'd get a round of bacon, and they'd slice it, no.1, or no.2 or whatever. You chose to your taste. It was high class.

Beryl Phillips knew it a bit later. The shop sold the well-known Twining's tea, though the family had no close connection with the tea Twinings.

It was just a lovely shop. They had big tins of coffee beans, and tea, all different teas. Everything seemed so beautifully set out. Expensive looking things, and things smelt nice. It was a little bit upmarket sort of shop.

A similar shop was the purpose-built branch of Grimbly Hughes opened in 1911 at the other end of Summertown, 203 Banbury Road, but this became Lloyd's Bank in 1933. Twining's was still going after the Second World War. Margaret Willis remembers it from the late 1950s.

It had old-fashioned sort of people in it. They wore big white aprons round them! And, of course, they delivered. You could take an order in, and it would all be brought up.

The Co-op, an important institution from the 19th century, especially among the respectable working classes, remained at its premises in South Parade (now a restaurant and yoga room) for about a century until it moved to its present place in the Banbury Road, where it flourishes still with loyal customers. Beryl Phillips came to Summertown from Wales during the war: her uncle had come here as a railwayman. She describes a cash system that survived in larger shops until the 1950s to obviate multiple tills.

My Aunt and Uncle were big Co-op people: they bought everything in the Co-op. You had your dividend twice a year. There was a little office, a little cubby hole where a lady sat, and at the counter, they put your money, and your ticket, how much it was, in this little thing and they pulled the pulley and then it shot along to this little cubby hole. Then she put the change in and whizzed it back along again.

The Co-op at 4 South Parade, 1937. Next to it is the entrance to the businesses of J.H. Bruce, plumber, and A.W. Bruce, funeral director. The fine house, no.6, belonged to the Horns from 1901 – first as cab proprietors, but by this point 'wireless engineers', a very long-running business. (OPA)

John Rowe's family was one which had its bread deliveries from the Co-op.

The Co-op brought bread round. You'd take a book into the Co-op in South Parade. The Co-op was the biggest general grocery.

Bakeries and dairies

A favourite place in South Parade was Paine's Bakery, which had begun at 25 Islip Road around 1896, but transferred to 1&2 South Parade by 1902. Dorothy Bridge (b.1907) recalls a service offered in days before reliable and easy domestic ovens.

> You could take a cake round there, and they'd bake it for you. My mother made lovely cakes.

Sally Bromley's memories of Paine's are from the 1950s.

> We used to get what my mother called 'fatty cake', but it's now generally called 'lardy cake'. She used to go in there, and say, 'Oh, it looks really good today, Sally, we'll have some fatty cake'. We used to buy our bread from there. I do remember that, and the room behind, and the oven.

The smell of baking permeates Beryl Phillips' memories of Summertown.

Paine's Bakery, 1–2 South Parade, c.1932. (D. Paine)

> The Old Bakery in South Parade, they baked the bread at the back, so it was lovely and fresh, you could smell the bread. And then we had Oliver & Gurden, the cake factory. They had a little factory shop where you could buy – course it was wartime – pieces like the ends of cakes they'd cut off, or things that were not perfect, you bought them cheaper. So we used to go over to the shop and get a bag of misshapen cakes, and biscuits and things like that. There was always a nice smell in Summertown, you could smell the cakes cooking, in Oliver & Gurden.

Oliver & Gurden, established by two Keble chefs in 1919 (William Oliver lived in Portland Road, then at 103 Lonsdale Road), made its 'Famous Oxford Cakes' in Middle Way in Summertown until it was sold to J. Lyons in 1969 and closed in 1975. Lady Gurden (no relation) has warm memories of it.

> We used to love that shop. 'Shall I go to the bent cake shop, Ma, and see what we can get?' – because they were very cheap. For about a shilling, you could get a jolly nice cake, because something had happened to it slightly. It was very sad when that closed. There was a nice cakey smell, all round there.

Paine's bakery was sold in 1958 in the face of the economic changes beginning to sweep through manufacturing and retailing, as Geoffrey Paine explains.

> That was sold simply because you either sold out or you got squeezed out. That's when the big boys were coming along, and Spiller's offered a stupid price, and we accepted. Otherwise, if you held on for another ten years, you got nothing.

Dairies in Summertown included Walter Edmonds' at 34 South Parade, there from the beginning of the century. Gwynneth Twining remembers the Paternoster Dairy being built opposite them at the top of Victoria Road in 1925 (364 Banbury Road, now a

mobile phone shop). She was friends with Mary Stanley, whose parents ran the dairy.
They had a little shop in the front. Her mother used to make wonderful ice cream. Real, proper ice cream. They had a farm out at Yarnton, where their milk came from.

Alfred Stanley delivering milk, 1920s. (Mary Shurmur)

This was College Farm: the Stanley's grandaughter Rosemary Smith remembers herding cows down the A44 for their 'summer holiday' in new fields. She too re-members the ice cream.

My granny used make ice cream with fresh strawberries. She was a real businesswoman, my granny; she used to have someone come to look after the twins.

Mary Stanley's twin Jack (p.173) had worked in the dairy since 1938 after an abortive apprenticeship at Elliston & Cavell, and took over running the dairy in the 1950s, when his parents moved to the farm, until his retirement in 1989. The shop also sold general provisions and was widely used by inhabitants of the more northerly roads. In days when shops ran accounts for regular customers, children – even young ones like John Rowe – were often sent to get things.

The dairy was where they've built the new houses. There were milk churns and freezers in the back. I used to be sent up to the dairy, the little shop, with a list. They sold butter, veg, and so on. Then it was delivered. Mrs Stanley was behind the counter. I used to be down below the counter and they didn't see me!

Banbury Road and South Parade before the war

Summertown's shops in the early 20th century were mostly converted from houses to meet demand as the population grew. On the eastern side, the right coming from Oxford, were 19th-century terraces and cottages. A few small businesses were established on this side in the older buildings still extant to the south (see Appendix 2, p.226ff): for example there was a chemist's at 194 from early in the century to the 1960s (it was later a hairdresser and from 1970–8 Denton's bicycles). Demolished in the 1960s was Harry Simmonds' long-running greengrocer (no.204), which had begun in 1908. At 220 the Misses Atkinson were hardware and wallpaper dealers for many years.

In response to the continuing shortage of commercial premises the ground floors of Edwardian houses on the other side of the road, on the left coming from Oxford, soon began to be converted into shops. A few premises, 207–13 at the Oakthorpe Road end of the parade, included shops from the beginning: in 1905 are listed the Misses Kimber, stationers; a fruiterer; Alden's the butcher; and a hairdresser and stationer – but the rest were private houses. At 265 was the spacious Vicarage on the corner of South Parade, demolished to make way for Hartwell's garage in the mid 1930s, and then in 1968 the shops of 'Suffolk House'. The process of conversion of houses to shops with flats above began before the First World War and proceeded steadily after it.

On this western side grew up a substantial range of basic shops, normally run by their owners. Betty Grant, who came to Hamilton Road in 1932, has a remarkable recall of the Summertown shops from early days.

From the bottom [Oakthorpe Road], there was Alden's, that was another provisions shop, then there was Bird's the newsagents, then there was Morris's the greengrocers, and there was a hairdresser's. Goundrey's, the ironmongers. Then next door Geoff Smith owned Swann's, hosiery and ladies' wear. Then there was Marshall's, another newsagent's. Then there was Bond's, the bicycle shop. Then there were Cooper & Boffins the bakery. I can't remember what came after. Maybe it was one of the houses, because I think the Trustees Savings Bank came there, and, of course, they did away with the garden. Then there was Wallington's, an-

Older 19th-century houses on the eastern side of Banbury Road, nos 214–18, photographed in 1992. (S. Khawaja)

Edwardian houses on the west side of Banbury Road, 239–41. The shop on the left was the site of Argyle's fishmonger. Photographed in 1992. (S. Khawaja)

other greengrocer's. Argyle's, the fish place, he had a lovely fish shop down there, a beautiful one. And next door to him was Butler's, that's another provision shop, corn merchants and all sorts, and they had a big shop up on the Cowley Road. Then there was a sweet shop. And, of course, there were quite a few houses with the front gardens. There was a gentleman's hairdressers – it was called Tommy Hutt's – and then on the corner ... Hartwell's garage, that was all round the corner, that whole block.

There was a dairy in South Parade – Edmonds', right down on the left-hand side, where the estate agent is. And on the corner of Stratfield Road was a second-hand shop. Then there was a butcher's shop, Edwards's. Next door to that was Mr Burbank's, the chemist: later on Mr Footner, he lived in Hamilton Road, he was the head man there. Then opposite, where the library is, there was a garden shop, Mr Horn, he lived in Victoria Road. He did all garden implements and things like that. And next door to that was a sweetshop. Before Mrs Church, I thought it was

Mrs Chapman, it was an old sweetshop, very old-fashioned. You'd go in, and little kids had to climb up on a form to look over and see what was in. And on the corner was the Post Office. It always was there.

There was another little sweetshop down in Middle Way, opposite the Spiritual Church. And, of course, there was Oliver and Gurden's factory. That was lovely. We always used to go there at least every week, and get some cakes. During the war, we used to go over early, eight o'clock in the morning, and join the queue to get some cakes, and he'd make so many, and then when they'd finished, you couldn't have any more. There was another sweetshop in Rogers Street, Ma Stroudley. That was another little shop we used to go into with your pennies.

Childhood memory emphasises the numerous little sweetshops, often run by widows or spinsters. Dorothy Bridge remembers other modest shops.

Haberdashers – there was a Mrs Hall, this old lady. There was a nice draper's shop in South Parade [Wright's, no.9]. Of course, the Post Office was in South Parade all my life – till now.

This Post Office at 13–14 South Parade was run for many years by Betty Marshall's uncle, George Howes, who sold groceries, and later by Hugh Erlund (the Erlunds lived in Hamilton Road) from 1948 to the 1970s – he sold china and garden implements. In reduced premises it was taken over by a Kenyan Asian couple, Mr and Mrs Shah, in 1995 but finally closed at the turn of the century.

As Betty Grant reminds us, shops were open on Saturday mornings, but had a half day closing during the week.

They never opened on Thursday afternoons, and never opened on a Sunday.

Mariele Kuhn, living here from 1938, also evokes these days.

Well, there were no supermarkets. They were just ordinary shops. I remember Mr Brown, he had a kind of grocery shop where the cat was lying on the counter!

John Rowe remembers from childhood in the 1930s the greeengrocer's at 209 Banbury Road run by the Morrises, of Hamilton Road, until the 1950s.

The fruit and veg shop – there was ever such a nice, kindly old boy in there, Mr Morris, and he used to give me an apple.

Denton's fruiterers at no.207 took over the niche for many years but like other traditional shops this recently closed

In earlier days fishmongers were important when menus standardly included fresh fish on Fridays. Dorothy Bridge remembers Turrill's fishmongers at 245 between the wars, as well as Argyle's at 239. This long-running business was founded by Keith Argyle's grandfather Dan in 1895 with a shop in Little Clarendon Street. A Summertown shop was opened in 1913 but closed during the First World War, to be reopened by Keith's father in 1919. (The Argyles lived at 2 Portland Road from 1924.) For Dorothy White the wide range of basic shops offered everything one needed.

There were plenty of shops, and you could get anything you wanted up there – not like now. I mean, there were electricians, hardware shops, paint shops, materials – anything you could get. We used to make our own clothes. There were plenty of fruit shops and greengrocers and butchers and so forth.

Betty Marshall remembers 'Elizabeth's' as one of these typically useful shops.

> If you made your own clothes, you could take your dress or blouse in there to have the buttonholes done, if you didn't want to do them yourself. We had another shop, similar sort of thing, called Wright's, in South Parade.

Deliveries

Deliveries and house-to-house services were a feature of middle-class life in earlier days which died away in the later part of the century. Horse and cart were remembered by several interviewees, like Betty Grant.

> The railways, they had a horse and cart, the big horses, to bring the luggage and all the parcels up from the railway.

The last such vehicle to visit the streets was the 'recycler' remembered by Verity Peto, who moved into Lonsdale Road in 1978.

> There was a rag and bone man who used to go round the roads on his horse-drawn cart, shouting out the rag and bone man's message, which was quite difficult to understand, unless you actually looked out of the window and saw what it was he had in his cart!

Gwynneth Twining and her sister Margaret can remember the milkman coming with a horse-drawn van between the wars.

> I can remember the milkman coming, when Edmonds' brought the milk in the pail. He kept [the pony] up the bottom of Hernes Road.

Joseph Shirley of Hamilton Road, known as 'Old Joe the Whistler', was for a long time the milkman for Walter Edmonds (p. 38).

Jack Stanley at the family dairy in Victoria Road c.1932. (Mary Shurmur, née Stanley)

> *Bread was the other staple regularly delivered, as Dorothy White remembers of the 1920s.*

> The baker used to come round. Morgan's, from Friar's Entry in the town. That used to be a horse and cart always. It was about twice a week, I think.

Mariele Kuhn recalls a later van-borne baker.

> We called him 'Bakey', he was very friendly. Well, he came by a little green van and brought the loaves. All the sparrows came to eat his crumbs! There are no sparrows now.

Sydney Denton sometimes did the bread delivery when he was an apprentice at Paine's Bakery around 1950.

> The horse and carts had gone, and everybody was using vans now. They were only small little vans, and they taught me to drive, because I was an apprentice baker/confectioner, but if a delivery man didn't turn in, then Roger [Paine], who didn't like doing the deliveries, if he could teach me to drive, he could send me out. Of

course, I was desperate to learn to drive, and, in fact, I eventually took my driving test. But then I had to do the rounds occasionally, but that was all right, it was a change. Every other day we went round. And you'd knock on the door, you'd have your big basket on your arm. You basically knew what the customers wanted, and often the bread tin was left outside with a little note in, and you'd just drop it in, and then you would pick up the money at the weekends, or whenever. You used to try not to pick everything up at the weekends, because that was a pain, that meant a lot of work taking all the monies in, so you used to calculate it on your books. Before I became an apprentice I worked on a bread delivery round [in Marston]. There was two of us on this round, and one of the chaps used to drop off for a while, right? He had two ports of call! He had one on each round! I don't know what he got up to, but it took a little while!

These regular door-to-door traders, who always of course called at the back 'trades-man's' door, are often fondly remembered as individuals, as by Dorothy White.

We used to have a greengrocer come in from Wootton, near Woodstock. We used to get rabbits from him, and chicken and vegetables. Dear old thing he was! Mr Wooding.

Monica Wagstaff notes the simplicity of shopping before the Second World War.

All your shopping could be delivered, and not only that, but a boy used to come round and take the order, so you really didn't go shopping that much. It was a fairly good system: meat was all delivered, bread, milk, veg – you'd just put the order in. Actually, there wasn't the choice in shops, particularly in fruit and vegetables, nothing like the choice you have today. Fish was always delivered – Argyle's delivered, they had a big fish shop on the front. There was much more of a service provided by shops.

A milk float still trundles round the streets but this is a service whose days seem numbered, with supermarkets so close. However competition has led supermarkets themselves to introduce home deliveries in recent years.

Old-style shops after the war

Change after the economic destructiveness of the Second World War was slow, and Summertown remained much as it had been through the 1950s. Yvonne Hands remembers with affection some of the old shops which persisted, and the last surviving private houses on the parade.

They were dear little shops – haberdasheries and all sorts of little shops. I remember a grey-haired lady, very neatly bunned, right in the middle, would be watering her plants. They all had little gardens. And gradually, they disappeared, and then the last one disappeared.

Sally Bromley clearly recalls this last one.

There was one house still there, and it had a garden out the front, so it was really weird: you'd be walking along, looking at the shops, and then you had to walk all the way outside of this garden, and all the way back in again to the pavement.

Sally has a series of vivid small child's memories of the parade in the 1950s, before changes set in. 'Elizabeth Swann', continuing at 217 Banbury Road, was a favourite.

I clearly remember the front, because it had two entrances that you went in, to a door in the middle. At this front, there was a glass display cabinet of various things that they had for sale, as well as all the displays at the side, so you had these two entrances that met and went inside. I remember going inside and seeing just wood, wood everywhere, because all the shop counters were made of wood. I can remember having to hold the top to peep over the work surfaces to see the fabrics, which I always loved looking at. They had bales of fabrics in these wooden shelves behind. I can remember the feel of the wood, and I can remember sliding my coat along the wood, because it was very smooth, and it's a very warm recollection. I remember having that exact same feeling when I was in town with Grimbly Hughes [in the Cornmarket] – which has long since gone.

Swann's was sold by its owners Geoff and Grace Smith to the gents' outfitters Jackson's in the 1960s. Another well-used shop of this kind was the Wool Shop on the corner of Oakthorpe Road. With the near death of home sewing even the centre of Oxford scarcely offers such resources now. Sally's memories of the 1950s continue with the Home and Colonial, no.231 (later Shergold's), and the shoe shop next door, no.233.

The Home and Colonial had all the foods from Britain and from abroad. That was when you bought your biscuits loose. And loose sugar. I can remember once there was a queue of people, and I must have just left my mum, and I walked across to look in these glass fronts and things, because it was Christmas! It was just glorious, looking at these wonderful meats and cheeses and things! And I walked back, and I wasn't looking, and I put my hand ... and it didn't feel right – I'd picked up the hand of some other lady, and it wasn't my mum! I can remember this feeling of fear, that my mum's hand didn't feel the same! I grew up buying my shoes at Jack Venn, which is now Michael Greenwood [now Clark's], so that has as far as I can remember, always been a shoe shop. I can always remember having my foot X-rayed on the machines there.

Argyle's fish shop continued prominent at no.239. (When his mother sold up in 1975 Keith Argyle opened a small fish shop in Rogers Street, which was still running at the time of Sally's interview in the hands of John Toop, who took over the business in 1990. Sadly it closed in August 2006.)

I vividly remember it being cold in there, and this big leaning marble slab all covered in fish, filleted or not filleted. There was a little lip at the bottom, and as this ice was melting, I can remember the water dripping off each corner, and having to avoid this little puddly area. And Mr Argyle, who was serving in there, actually served me my fish about three weeks ago, in Argyle's, just behind the butcher's here now.

Staff of Argyle's fishmongers and Coulling's butchers in Rogers Street, c.1982. Front, left to right: John Toop, Bert Coulling, Fred Coulling (the butcher). Centre back: Keith Argyle. (Keith Argyle)

There were several butchers still – Alden's was at 211 Banbury Road from the earliest days of the parade but moved into the new building at the end, no.205, by the 1930s, then to no.209 in 1960. Another long-running butcher's business is remembered by Christine Butler at 37 South Parade.

> Mr Edwards the butcher used to buy prize carcasses at Christmas and give Joseph the rosettes.

Nick and Kathleen Burgess, who ran Bonner's, also remember the Edwards brothers.

> Ralph and Phil Edwards they were real characters, very old-fashioned butchers. They would cut it off the beast as you went to buy it. It was all very very old-fashioned – where the launderette is.

Bonner's, a grocery in South Parade on the corner of Stratfield Road, was run by the Burgesses from 1968 to 1983 in very much the old way. Their employees included Bert, who had been 'the noisiest milkman ever', as a part-time driver, and Sam Busby as casual help.

Bonner's, South Parade, c.1974, featuring in a publicity shot for British Leyland vans. (N. & K. Burgess)

> It was busy, we used to have a lot of good customers – families, good class families. Most of our trade was an order trade, we used to do 40 or 50 – not every day, but at the weekend we were busy. We used to line them up in the shop. Bert would come in – 'Out the way Misssis'. He was very very rude! Sam just appeared one day. We had a yard at the back of the shop, and for some unknown reason he started tidying up. If you asked him to come he would never come. He used to come about four times a week and we used to pay him in food on a Saturday. I bought him some boots once.

Mary Tregear, who came here in 1962, remembers a good range of old-style shops, including Bonner's; and she appreciated the people who worked in them.

> Two or three butchers, and very big greengroceries. Then there was Bonner's, the general greengrocer-cum-grocer, round in South Parade, which was a very good shop too, for everyday. I get the impression that there was a workforce that worked in Summertown, and they moved from shop to shop, so that you'd see somebody in the hairdresser's, then turned up selling things in the shoe shop or something. They sort of formed a general population of the shop area. And that was quite good. And some quite elderly people who worked in shops too. Great characters, ticked you off for things!

The biggest greengrocer was Durham's at 257–9 Banbury Road, which had opened just before the war. Here produce was mostly seasonal and locally produced, as Sally Bromley recalls.

> That was a big walk-in shop, and you bought everything by the pound, and the potatoes were weighed on these huge great big scales, and I can remember think-

ing, 'I wouldn't like to handle dirty potatoes all the time', because nothing was washed in those days! You now have sort of ready-washed potatoes, or ready-washed celery: everything was as it came out of the ground.

This is the greengrocer's that Yvonne Hands remembers.

[It was] there for years, run by a Pole and his wife. It was a big greengrocer's. But the Pole went off with one of the women in the shop, to the great distress of the woman who owned it. It was owned by a woman, and the Pole married her. A handsome Pole. He died choking on rice.

Sydney Denton mentions several other family-owned shops after the war, including Shergold's, a hardware store which has left a gap behind it.

There was a lot of personal little shops. Shergold's were there [no.215, then 231]. Shergold was a man who, when he come out of the RAF, I think, he started a business at Green Road roundabout, and his first expansion shop was Summertown. He started that on the strength of his gratuity when he came out of the Forces. Of course, it turned out to be a big combine. Burton's Dairies [no.223], they were a general grocers, but with a dairy background, and they had a number of shops in the areas, and, in fact, I think the Oxfam Shop still belongs to the family. Rising's was a sort of bit of everything shop – toys, clothing. There was a Mr Bush had a sweet shop, which is now where the Curtain Shop is – Curtain Bob as we call him: he's now just handed all that over to his daughter. There was a gent's outfitters, which was called Jackson's, down South Parade, which I think is now the Guitar Shop [no.8], which was formerly the Paint Pot.

There was also a surprising number of garages in Summertown, all of them now gone. On the east side Organ's Garage expanded from a garage and taxi cab business at 250 to cover 242–54. It was later rebuilt as Barclay's, as Sydney Denton describes.

What was Allied Carpets was formerly Barclay, the Rolls Royce agent, so that big palatial building, before Allied Carpets went in there, sold Rolls Royces, of all things! And obviously there must have been enough demand – you can't think of that in Oxford, can you, but that's what it was.

Betty Marshall mentions the garage at 278–90 Banbury Road, next to Twining's shop.

The North Oxford Garage, that had petrol pumps at one point.

This survived as a car salesroom until very recently. On the opposite side was Hartwell's Garage on the corner of South Parade, and further up the Banbury Road a large garage, Bristol Street Motors. Between them was Salter's Garage on the corner of Grove Street, adjacent to the King's Arms Public House, which was run by the family from well before the seven roads appeared. Now rebuilt as flats, it is remembered by Mary Tregear.

They were very helpful, particularly for people all round here, because you knew the man who ran it, and he was the old father, and was very good to me because I couldn't get around without a car. The pub next door was theirs too. The Salters were a notable family, and they were really quite a power in the land. The old man, Salter, died, and that closed up. And then very quickly, actually, all the filling stations closed, and I suppose that was a general thing that happened, and suddenly, there were no filling stations anywhere in Oxford.

Change in the 1960s and 1970s

It was in the 1960s and early 70s that the economic changes fermenting in the 1950s broke through to have a marked effect on Summertown. It was most obvious in a spate of demolition and rebuilding (p. 31). Almost all the old houses on the east side of the Banbury Road disappeared to make way for office blocks with shops beneath. First came Oxfam House (264–74), then Mayfield House (256), and finally Barclay House on Organ's site (242–54). Only the old Dewdrop Inn survives, crouching between its unattractive neighbours. The Windsor Fish and Chip shop at 264, opened in 1954, had to be demolished and reincorporated into one of the blocks. Sydney Denton is not a fan of the architecture but sees that it has brought economic activity to the area.

The Oxfam building, Banbury Road, 1992. (S. Khawaja)

Oxfam built that great big building, and it's a horrible building, but at the time, we had so many restrictions on building materials, and everything was flat roof. It was very mundane, and it still looks very mundane. But they brought a tremendous amount of work to the area.

The wide pavement left by the cottage gardens is increasingly used now for café service, and for occasional events and sales and is an asset that could well be more attractively developed.

While Twining's stayed in business until 1968 it suffered from competition towards the end from the first supermarkets. Yvonne Hands remembers it as rather expensive at a time when people's habits were still marked by post-war austerity.

Prama House, built in 1962 on the site of 'Southlawn', 267 Banbury Road, with a top floor added later. Photographed in 1992. (S. Khawaja)

We all had this thing about buying cheaply, when, in actual fact, I could have afforded to have gone in, but we all bought cheaply, it was the thing you did.

Sydney Denton evokes the old style of service which became uneconomic: it survives now only in the delicatessen.

There would be lines and lines of people behind the counters. 'What would you like, Mrs Jones?' And they would put a piece of paper in their hand, and you would say, 'Oh, I'd like a pound of butter, please', and they'd do the wrapping, and they'd price it and put it down. 'And you would like some cheese?' 'Yes'. 'Your usual?' 'And how much would you like?' 'Oh, I think I'll have eight ounces', and he'd get his board and cut his eight ounces of cheese. 'Oh, it's just a little over' – it was always a little over! Well, of course, all those things have gone, it's all pre-packed, it's all much more hygienic. But you lose all that personal service. But if you want low prices, you've got to pay – you can't have it all. You can't have service and low prices.

The first supermarket was built into Prama House, the earliest of the office development buildings in Summertown, at the beginning of the 1960s. Paloma Bevir recalls this time of transition and the early Summertown supermarkets.

There was Budgen's, and Spar, and Fine Fare, which was where Laura Ashley is now. Then we have what is called now 'Somerfield', which was then 'Gateway'. But there were at least three butchers.

When Philippa Berry first lived here in the early 1970s she remembers shopping cheaply and cooking simply.

I have memories of going to shop in something called 'Fine Fare', which was then a rather grotty supermarket, underneath Prama House. It was the cheapest supermarket, and we really were living on a small amount of money, because Martin, when he was an articled clerk, I think he was paid £8 a week, and I was working as a social worker, but I can't remember that I was earning very much. So we just never ate out. We cooked. I can remember buying a leg of lamb and it lasted three or more days, because you made a shepherd's pie, and you had cold meat. So we were quite frugal in our shopping. And we certainly didn't have yoghurts and corn on the cob and avocados, and all the things that we eat now. It was very much meat and two veg.

Paloma identifies the old type of 'useful' shop that began to be lost – first Elizabeth's haberdashery.

The assistants were very nice ladies, very welcoming. I must say it, with big moustaches! But they had absolutely everything you needed or wanted. We had an ironmonger as well, which then was Shergold's, and then it was something else [Carpenter Shergold, then Cargo, a lifestyle shop] which has nothing to do with an ironmonger. These are the two shops, really, which gave more character, because after that, there have been loads of cards, estate agents galore!

There was still a community among traders, which could be valuable, as Nick Burgess of Bonner's narrates.

Mr Erlund kept the post office and hardware shop. He was like the old school, very military sort of a man. One afternoon I saw a lady coming out with some saucepans under her arm. Later that day I saw Mr Erlund and said to him 'Things must be bad if you can't wrap up any saucepans'. He said, 'I haven't sold any saucepans today.' I said Mrs So-and-So went out with two or three saucepans under her arm.' He was a special constable. So off he trots, and she's got a house full of Shergold's goods and Mr Erlund's goods!

Sydney Denton also had stories to tell of shoplifters in his cycle shop at 294 Banbury Road, which had rear access onto Lonsdale Road.

One of the things we came up against was 'dippers' – these are people who steal from you. You have to read the signs. They come into the shop, and they move around, and they home in to what they want. So there are always these head movements, looking around trying to see where the staff are. Either myself or my manager would go out the back door, walk all the way round, up Lonsdale Road, come in from the front and then we would just give a little nod that we were out in the right location. Then the staff would say, 'Tea up!' or something, and move out – give them the opportunity to steal what they wanted; they would take it, run out the shop, and you just stuck your foot out, and they fell over it! And you've caught another one!

Sydney Denton's wife Lilian and son Shaun outside his first Summertown shop at 194 Banbury Road in 1978. (Sydney Denton)

207–9 Banbury Road, two of the old style shops now gone: a fruiterer's run by Sydney Denton's brother Rodney, and butcher's premises (previously Alden's), photographed in 1992. (S. Khawaja)

Despite changes Mary Tregear feels that Summertown in the 1960s and 70s was good for basics. There were many people living here who didn't have transport, and met their needs locally.

My general impression is that there were lots more different kinds of shops, of wool shops and shops where they sold needles and cotton, and it was a very easy place to survive in. You didn't have to go anywhere else much for anything. I think there were very good food shops, very good everyday shops here. I don't think there's anything tremendously smart, but it was a very friendly, easy place to live in.

People with different demands saw it as ordinary and dull, like Peter Clarke, living here from the later 1970s.

It wasn't so convenient in the early days, because there were very few shops in Summertown, very few restaurants, very few facilities. I can't remember a sandwich bar or anything like that. There were more local butchers and greengrocers and things like that, but you had to go into town for most things. Summertown wasn't that busy in those days. I would describe it as being rather dreary. It's now crowded, of course. I didn't find it crowded in those days.

One of the few restaurants Summertown did have at that stage was however the early incarnation of Raymond Blanc's famous Manoir aux Quat' Saisons, in a rather unprepossessing location at 272 Banbury Road (previously the Landau Restaurant, currently the Greek Taverna). Christine Butler remembers going there.

> We did once go to the Quatre Saisons for Joseph's 14th birthday, and Raymond Blanc came along and interviewed everybody at the tables.

Summertown at the turn of the century

The number of restaurants in Summertown at the beginning of the 21st century will strike anyone, and amaze those who wonder how people afford to eat out so much. Chinese, Indian, Italian, Greek, Thai, pizzas, bistros, cafés, delicatessens, sandwich shops – Summertown offers a full range of eating places (though in another significant change the fish and chip shop here for many years closed early in 2006). Eating patterns have altered enormously over the last 30 years or so, and the proliferation of restaurants is another thing which draws people here from outside the area.

Among older people there is a strong sense of loss of the personally run shops, as Mary Tregear, interviewed in 2000, says.

> It's really changed its persona quite a lot. There really isn't anything very special about things now. What's lost is the choice between shops, different sorts of shops, and different personnel. Just recently, we've lost that Paint Pot, and that was one of the old style shops, where the man in the shop knew who you were, and could help quite a lot, and he belonged in this area, and knew people. And there were craftsmen around the place, who could do things. We've just finally lost the little shoe-mender [in Grove Street].

Sydney Denton comments on the changes in the shoe shop at 233 Banbury Road, which has existed since earliest days, and is now corporately owned.

> Jack Venn, the shoe people, he sold shoes, and did repairs. That got taken over by Michael Greenwood, he's now sold out and it's Clark's Shoes now, it's a combine.

Of course family-run businesses come to a natural close when the proprietor wants to retire or trading conditions change. Twining's had become a wine shop when Sydney Denton acquired the freehold in 1978 and moved into it the bicycle business which he had been operating at 194 Banbury Road from 1970. Sally Bromley shared the community's general distress when 'Mr D' too decided to retire and close the business in 2000.

> I don't know how many bikes I must have bought from there, or how many puncture kits I got from there, or how many punctures I had mended there! But I do recall they were closing, just a few years ago, somebody coming in and saying, 'What do you mean, you're closing?' Mr Denton said, 'Well, I'm closing. I can get more money by renting it than I can by selling things in it. Yes, I'm closing.' He said, 'But you can't close! I've been bringing my bicycle here for 26 years!' And I was thinking, 'Yes, I've probably been bringing mine for even longer!'

Fortunately the uncomfortable gap left by the closing of the shop has recently been filled by the opening of a new 'Summertown Cycles' at 200–2 Banbury Road, first sharing, then taking over, the premises of the garden shop which is another sad loss in 2006.

All butchers have now gone from the parade, but one survives in a small shop on the corner of Rogers Street, once Howard's butchers, then Coulling's (p.175). Here Alcock's maintains a niche by selling organic meat and vegetables. Philip Gilbert, who for many years ran a bookshop in the covered market, commented in 2001 on changes which are hard for small businesses to withstand.

Alcock's butchers with Argyle's small fish shop behind, 2006. The Radio Oxford building on the left replaced one of Summertown's large houses, Uplands, 269 Banbury Road. (P. Kinchin)

The high rents of shops, it forces people to push for sales and targets etc. That's one of the reasons why there's a change of shops and ownership. You see it here in Summertown, owners have just been forced out because of high rents and high rates. In the covered market, we've been battling over our rents for the past two years.

Paloma Bevir points to the proliferation here of charity shops, which are viable because of reduced rates and low overheads.

We used to have Jumble Sales, they were quite common, but we had to wait until there was a Jumble Sale to donate all our junk, you had to store it and it wasn't very convenient. That has been replaced by charity shops. Anything you gather, you instantly take to the charity shop. You recycle through charity shops.

Altogether there is a clear perception of change, as Philippa Berry remarks.

Obviously Summertown has changed a great deal since we were first shopping there, because it is very much busier, and many more cars parked along the front, and lots more people. It's packed!

Increased traffic and parking difficulties are noticeable. In earlier days Mary Tregear found no problems.

Everything was a two-way street, and you could park your car anywhere and it was all easy-going, and there were no humps! Summertown had marvellous garages, and you could pick up petrol anywhere along the road, it seemed! It's really gone now.

Garage businesses have mostly moved to peripheral sites where parking is not a problem. The car has of course been responsible for radical changes in the way people live. Geoffrey Paine, in Lucerne Road, is typical of those who now go out of town to big supermarkets.

Now, I'm afraid, we, probably like everybody else, do most of our shopping at supermarkets – a certain amount in Summertown, but it's really only the odds and ends.

However, perhaps increasingly, the proximity of a good range of food shops – at time of writing Somerfield, the Co-op, and Marks & Spencer as supermarkets; a specialist butcher, and a bakery; and a French pâtisserie, Taylor's delicatessen, and a Lebanese delicatessen as extras – is key to the quality of life experienced by people living in the roads. David Schriger, a visiting American living in Lonsdale Road, really appreciated this.

> You would walk to the shops, for the most part. My sense is that Oxford has so many different sort of micro-cultures – that you could live, you know, on Upland Park or Squitchey, and you probably wouldn't walk to the Co-op very often. My suspicion is that a lot of people would then drive, up to Sainsbury's [at Kidlington], or something like that, because it's just that extra five or ten minutes; so that being right here, in a way, is a different experience.

This has great appeal for older people who have smaller needs. It was certainly a factor in the Herivels' decision to retire here.

> One of the things that attracted us about Lonsdale Road, I remember, was the convenience of the shops, certainly. I suppose I was thinking of being ancient!

Elsie Hill of Portland Road, interviewed in 2004, underlines this convenience.

> To me, it's an absolute boon, because I can't carry things, and I can't drive any more, so I just go shopping with my trolley, and really there's very little that you can't buy in North Oxford. We have the 'Real Meat Butcher', and a fresh greengrocer's that I understand are going to close down, which is very sad. And also, of course, we must have the best bus service in Oxford.

An increasing number of residents concerned to be more 'green' in their shopping now eschew big supermarkets in favour of shopping locally, like Philippa Berry.

> I must say I'm very happy with the shops in Summertown these days and I hardly ever drive to an out of town supermarket. I go to the Farmer's Market at Wolvercote every Sunday – on my bike or on foot of course! Alcock's is still a wonderful old-fashioned shop. I was cycling past one day recently when I heard several of the guys who work there shout out 'Mrs Be–rry!' I slithered to a stop and I went in and they said 'Do you want an oxtail?' 'Yes please!'

During this project, between 2000 and 2006, there have been many changes which exemplify the quite rapidly changing social and economic character of this area. Home deliveries by supermarkets have recently appeared, together with deliveries of organic

A Post Office still operating in premises it occupied throughout the 20th century in South Parade: a charity shop occupies the front shop, 1992. (S. Khawaja)

The same building in 2006: a designer clothes shop in the front shop, an African crafts shop in the rear (now closed). (P. Kinchin) veg boxes and goods ordered on the internet – all restoring some of the convenience described earlier in this chapter, with of course a far greater range of choice than could have been dreamed of by older residents.

South Parade since 2000 has become much more obviously chic, led by an art gallery which arrived in 1998. 'Vanilla', selling designer clothes and accessories to people with substantial disposable incomes, is the kind of shop which attracts people from a wider area. A lingerie shop has just opened next door, while a shop selling African art goods has until the end of 2006 occupied the premises last used by the old Post Office. A guitar shop serving Oxford at large has replaced what had been a good specialist paint shop. Restaurants have increased, including now an Italian restaurant in the old Co-op building, and an elegant 'wine café' in what was Buckell & Ballard surveyors (before that a hairdresser's and a junk shop and auction house). Restaurants also are making more play of eating outside. The local bookshop survives; the pet shop, one of the 'useful' shops that disappeared, was after a gap replaced with 'Smart Pet' at 35 South Parade, but this too closed in 2006 to be replaced by an upmarket flower shop.

The Co-op building transformed into one of several restaurants in South Parade, with Bang & Olufsen in the old Horn's premises (compare p.168), 2006. (P. Kinchin)

On Banbury Road a major departure is that of the Oxfam HQ, which left in the autumn of 2005. While its developments degraded the architectural attractiveness of Summertown it was a worthy organisation to have here and its office workers have supported the shops. Allied Carpets, in what had been a car salesroom, was not lamented when it gave way to a food Marks & Spencer, popular with the kind of people now living in the roads, and drawing shoppers from other areas, like Headington. A small independent flower shop opposite was one of the casualties of its arrival, though a pavement flower pavilion appeared briefly, a pleasant use of the wide paving area, which has been increasingly colonised by tables and chairs from eating places. Rising rents in 2006 closed 'The Shop', an idiosyncratic 'useful' shop. A branch of Laura Ashley furnishing in Prama House was a significant successor to an auto accessories shop. Two remaining garages – Toyota on Banbury Road and Kernahan's on King's Cross Road – have been demolished for the erection of flats, and the last operating car salesroom premises on Banbury Road have closed at the time of writing.

Things then continue to change, but as Mary Tregear comments:

It's always the cry of people who have lived in a place for a long time, that it isn't quite the same. It isn't quite the same, but nor are the people who live here, and there's a quite different demand on things now.

10 Organisations, Activities and Events

It was a real huge piece of work, to get that street party up and running. But it was absolutely brilliantly done!

Philippa Berry

Here we look at some of the institutions, groups and events which have drawn the community together over the years.

The churches

In first place come the churches, which have remained an important part of the neighbourhood even if regular church-going has declined. In the earlier 20th century the church was central to people's lives: Dorothy Bridge carries us back to the period around the First World War, when people had varied religious allegiances.

> You didn't judge people, in those days, by their cars, you judged them by what church they went to. My father went to the Congregational, and my mother went to Summertown, because she was an Anglican. As soon as I could walk, she took me, and I loved it. The Turners went to the Wesley Memorial. Mrs Turner used to go up the road at quarter past two every Monday, going to the Wesley Memorial Church. The family opposite, Eldred, they were Baptists, went to New Road Baptist Church, and I didn't know anything about them. But lots of people, especially the Colgrove family, went to the Congregational Church.

The new Congregational Church attended by Dorothy's father, which replaced the original chapel in what is now Middle Way, was built on the Banbury Road in 1893, as Summertown started to expand. The Thorntons and the Lindseys of Victoria Road were other 'founding families' of this church. Francis Twining's shop at 294 Banbury Road was later built adjacent to it but turned slightly away – perhaps because he was an Anglican. Gwynneth Twining recalls his part in creating a church in Lonsdale Road commensurate with the new status of the suburb he was helping to develop. This was to replace the original Summertown church, built in 1832.

> Grandfather, of course, was very anxious for the church to be built in Summertown. There was a church in what is now Rogers Street, where Dudley Court is, St John the Baptist. But further down the road there was St Andrew's, and St Phil and Jim, and St Margaret's, all big grand churches, and he thought that they should have a big grand church in Summertown. So he gave the land for the church in Lonsdale Road. But, of course, it's a bit big these days, isn't it!

The plot of land was very large, as was the church designed by Alfred Mardon Mowbray (who lived at 277 Banbury Road) and started after four years of fund-raising. 'St Michael and All Angels' was quickly built and opened in 1909 with a 'temporary' west wall to save costs. It was never completed. St John the Baptist fell out of use and was

Architect's sketch of the proposed church in Lonsdale Road, 1906. The west end was never built. (OCS)

finally demolished in 1924, its stones and roof timbers being used to build the Church Hall in Portland Road. A new vicarage was built in Lonsdale Road in 1923 for Canon Burrough, vicar from 1923 to 1956.

Much social life revolved around church, as Dorothy Bridge remembers.

We always kept open house at my house, especially on Sundays. After some years, I left Summertown Church and went to St Aldate's. They had a Youth Fellowship, and there were lots of homeless people, and one especially loved the piano, and she hadn't got a piano in her lodgings, so she used to come to our house every week and play our piano.

Helen Holland's grandmother Frances Stewart lived in Portland Road, with her unmarried daughter, from 1954: the church was the centre of their lives.

Their little diaries, which contained very little, except odd references to people coming to visit, mostly are filled up with, 'Church and chores', as regular items. That seemed to be the pattern of their days. My grandmother was certainly very devout, in a practical way as well. Good works, in terms of giving to Societies, and baking cakes for bazaars and things like that, and being kind to neighbours.

Dorothy White switched churches when the style of service changed.

St Michael's went very high church, so we didn't bother to attend there. We used to go down to the one in Linton Road – St Andrew's.

When Margaret Clarke and her husband, regular church-goers, moved to Hamilton Road in 1962 they went along to St Michael's.

We went there straightaway, of course, because we thought we should go to our Parish Church, although it was a very high church then, and not at all what we'd been used to.

The vicar at the time was Kenneth Martin.

He followed Canon Burrough, who was still living here, in fact, visited us. I gather that was one of his things – he reckoned to visit every house in the Parish – and he'd been there for years. Kenneth Martin was here just for another two years. I've since heard that he was very inhibited by Canon Burrough still living in Portland Road [at no.10], on his doorstep, still with a gate through to the church.

The next incumbent (1964–89) was the much-loved Bill Fosdike: he also retired locally, to Osberton Road, but according to Margaret 'he never ever interferes'. Bill gave a long and thoughtful interview in 2000. He spoke of changes in lifestyles which affected traditional pastoral visiting.

The timings of meals changed: a bit back, 7.30 was quite a common mealtime, in the evening. Over the years, [it became] earlier, sort of 6.00, 6.30, when the husband got back from work. So you didn't go at 6.00, before people's supper. And later on in the evening, you had to make sure you worked out the television programmes. By and large, off-the-cuff visiting, I found, became less and less pointful. You used opportunities that grew up in this way and that way, whether it be the occasional services – baptism, marriages – or meetings through Ferry Centre, or a meeting in the community about the roadworks, or whatever. You'd sit and talk with people, and very often out of that, they'd say, 'Oh, come round and meet my husband'. So a lot of visiting was focused and pre-arranged, rather than the old system of knocking on the door, which – I suppose that was a generational thing as well – I've found extremely difficult. 'Oh, I've come to see you'. 'Oh!' It always struck me as rather impertinent.

A nativity play at St Michael & All Angels, late 1960s. Bill Fosdike is on the right, John Helsby is next to him. (Margaret Willis)

He also describes difficulties in organising meetings.

If you had afternoon, young mothers could come, but they'd have to dive out to get the children from school, and evening meetings, the elderly said, 'We don't like coming out in the evening too much', and the young ones said, 'Well, my husband's got home now, and the children ...' Women's groups are always extremely difficult to organise, because of those pressures upon women, in a way that men haven't got the pressures. People were going out much more, people weren't available in the evening, and also, of course, television had an influence.

Bill spoke about fruitful moves in the early 1970s for greater ecumenical contacts – particularly the drawing together of St Michael's and the Congregational Church on Banbury Road, known as the United Reformed Church after 1974.

Partly for theoretical, theological reasons, because the Gospel, to me, talks about unity, and we seem to be much better at splitting things up; and secondly, the front gate on Lonsdale Road, of St Michael's, and the back gate of the URC, are slap opposite each other, which said something to me. And then Tony Tucker, who was

The Rev. Donald Norwood outside the United Reformed Church, earlier the Congregational Church, in 1977. (Donald Norwood)

Bill Fosdike came out of retirement to officate at the wedding of the conductor Daniel Harding in St Michael's in 2000. (© Paul Freestone)

the Minister here, we got to know each other pretty well, we're of an age, of a background, and we were both graduates of this University. With the exception of denominational discipline, we were very of a mind. And there was a big movement, that by 1980, the Churches ought to have got together. And I remember Tony coming in one day, because we wandered into each other's place. And he said, 'Look, the likelihood is that we'll both be in post' – in fact, he wasn't – 'in 1980. So we'd better start doing something about it!'

Our church boiler failed, and so for one winter, at least, they warmly offered us shelter, and we had our services there. They changed their times a bit, and we both had our services, and that was the beginning of it. We gradually learnt to recognise that a Congregationalist, as they were then, was probably a better Christian than half the Anglicans. Your denomination was important, but there was more. That's gradually how we built together. One of the valuable stages was when, right at the beginning, we started saying 'We'll come to your services Sunday, you'll come to ours another Sunday, and each of our services will be our normal.' At first, it was a bit odd. But as time went on, people were saying, 'Well, it's not the style I would choose, but I'm finding it's real, and it means something'. We did a lot of study together, and it would be interesting that when there was any sort of division into outlooks, it was never denominational, it was invariably for some other reason, very often age. The other healthy thing was that you'd say something, and Donald Norwood, or one of the URC, [would] say, 'Why?' 'Oh, well, you know ... yes, well, why?' It was part of your baggage, your inheritance, and you would cease to question it. Sometimes you thought it through and stood by, sometimes you felt, 'Well, that's not really very solid'. So that was really quite a hard business, but a very valuable business.

Donald Norwood, an Oxford graduate himself, was the URC minister from 1974 to

1995, living at 100 Victoria Road. He speaks of the growing friendships which led to the formation of the Ecumenical Parish of Wolvercote with Summertown in 1982.

At the time of our coming together people could still remember in the old Congregational Church being told that their ministers were not proper ministers, their sacraments were not valid etc., by the then Vicar at St Michael's, Canon Burrough. The changed attitude was for them nothing short of a miracle of God's grace!

St Michael's was built in the last days of the prosperity and secure assumptions which were shattered by the First World War. Practicality has been a headache ever since. Bill Fosdike was one of those prepared to contemplate its demolition to rationalise multiple buildings on valuable land.

In terms of running costs, heating particularly is a horrendous problem. We came to the conclusion that, for practical reasons, it would be far better to rationalise. We didn't really need two worship places, and we didn't need two sets of halls. None of the buildings was particularly practical in everyday use. So there would be quite a case for building something new that was much more appropriate, and much more adaptable, so that in 20 years' time when the requirements are different, you can pull down the inside walls, and have something that is flexible. We got the Church Commissioners' Committee to send down some people, and their view was that it was a magnificent example of its period and deserved to be retained. Which I didn't entirely agree with! I've grown very fond of the building, but nobody can suggest that it has any particular architectural or other merits!

St Michael's survived this crisis, and later proposals for alterations. Now its current vicar, Jan Rushton, has spent time and money on re-furbishing the interior, transforming its attractive-ness, and is actively encouraging community use of the building. The garden is well maintained and often used by young people for general hanging out – though Dorothea Pelham, whose garden backed onto the church grounds, was attached to its earlier over-grown state for its wildlife value.

This churchyard was really rough, and since then, unfortunately, it's all been cut down. There was a gardener who let it all grow, and there was a lovely lot of high bushes, and there were some thrushes and things, and the grass was left to grow long.

The lych gate of St Michael's with the garden beyond, 2006. (P. Kinchin)

Various houses in the roads have been used to house clergymen. Monica Wagstaff remembers the Lutheran minister, Pastor Adolph Kurtz, living at 24 Hamilton Road in the 1950s.

The big detached house, just after the war we had the Lutheran minister live there. At Christmas, they used to have the carol practice at their house, it was lovely to listen to.

Pam Robinson, who bought the house, was told about this.

It was decorated beautifully at Christmas, apparently, they did the outside and the inside, everybody used to go to look at it.

Sunday School was a widespread part of young lives in earlier days, as Sydney Denton says.

The churches were still very strong in those days, Sunday School, and lots of meetings. There are numerous churches here, as you know.

Attendance at weekly services has declined steeply since the 1960s. Peter Clarke's experience of a widening and loosening of his beliefs since his Catholic upbringing after the war is probably a common one. He went on to study Islam as an historian and sociologist.

Local angels: St Michael's Sunday School Nativity play, 1994. (Holly Kilpatrick)

When you encounter other cultures – which I've been fortunate enough to do in Africa, Latin America, Japan – and other systems of thought and belief, it relativises your own, so you lose that certainty, or that conviction that the truth resides within your tradition, and you become much more open to the suggestion that, perhaps there are truths embedded in all traditions. In a way, my Catholicism is there, but it probably wouldn't be understood very well by an official Catholic. I can't remember the last time I ever thought it was important to follow Papal guidance on issues. But it's part of my culture. So it's more or less that identity thing, belonging to a culture, as much as it is belonging to a set of beliefs.

Performing

The church halls of course have continued in use for a wide variety of community activities, not connected specifically with the church. Sally Bromley performed at a tender age in the Church Hall on the corner of Portland Road.

Betty Howes (Marshall), c. 1931. (B. Marshall)

My mother was a keen member of the Townswomen's Guild that would meet in Summertown Church Hall, and I can remember seeing some plays there. As a little girl, I belonged to a drama group that was run there, run by Lady Bonham-Carter. My mother told me that when I was three, I was on the stage, dressed in a nightie, and I had to carry a little candle, and I had to say, 'Night, night, Mr Moon. Night, night.' And it brought the house down, because everyone went, 'Aaah!' I have no recollection of it. But in my own later life, I joined the North Oxford Junior Dramatic Society, where a lot of our youngsters, around here today, belong.

Joe Butler was one of those hooked by a play here, as his mother Christine remembers.

The first time he ever saw a staged play it was in

Summertown Church Hall and it was magic as far as he was concerned.

Joe likewise went on to join the North Oxford Junior Dramatic Society. Run for many years by Peter Bridges, based at Wolvercote and particularly encouraging boys, this still flourishes as the North Oxford Youth Theatre.

Standing out in many memories is the remarkable Children's Panto-mime Society run by Mrs Corden of 74 Lonsdale Road (p.76). Joan Crow's children were enthusiastic participants.

A play in the Portland Road Church Hall, 1948. Betty Howes (Marshall) is second from the right. (B. Marshall)

She started these little pantomime playlets during the war with her own children to entertain friends. After the war it grew. She wrote her own scripts. Her husband looked after the finances of the show and gradually it became a much more ambitious enterprise which took place in the church hall at the end of Portland Road. We heard about it in the early 60s. By then its fame was growing and Mrs Corden organized auditions every year, and the pantomime took place after Christmas. It meant effectively that her troop of children were all organized in military fashion and occupied very happily and very fully during the Christmas vacations, which of course was a godsend to parents. She had considerable success and her own son [Kenneth Corden], who obviously had a great dramatic gift ,went into the BBC and became a rather distinguished administrator there. He used to organize the Proms at one time.

Margaret Willis, then Margaret Helsby, was a resident of Lonsdale Road: two of her children took part, and she too saw it enthusiastically as a 'godsend'.

The rest of us used to back it up, you know, we had to make the costumes, and my contribution, because I was worried about Mrs Corden, that she and her husband didn't get a proper meal, I used to make them a meal and put it in the oven for when they came back from the evening performance. [The children] did everything. Absolutely the lot. The parents did the keeping order behind the scenes. It was an absolute godsend, because it occupied them for the entire Christmas holidays!

Josie Patterson also wanted to testify to Mrs Corden's contribution.

The children adored them. I phoned both my boys and I asked them about it, and the minute I said, 'Mrs Corden's North Oxford Pantomime Society', they just replied by singing some of the catchy tunes that were part of each of the productions! So it's fair to say that it's lasted, and lasted a long long time, with great pleasure. The roles were divided out, rehearsals began, and they were usually in the Old Bakery, in Summertown. We weren't very good at time-keeping, but we never were late for rehearsals, because the boys insisted they didn't want to miss a minute. It really influenced our lives – in the best possible way. Then I started to study to become a teacher, and I organised my life so that I could do my college work, and they'd go to rehearsals. And they loved it! They really did.

Everything was extremely well organised.

We turned up to her house and her front room was devoid of furniture, but from floor to ceiling were racks upon racks of costumes! I was absolutely amazed! It was run for three days. Saturday night was mums and dads night. And, of course, it was such a wonderful audience, willing these children to do well – which they did. We brought the house down with applause and cheers.

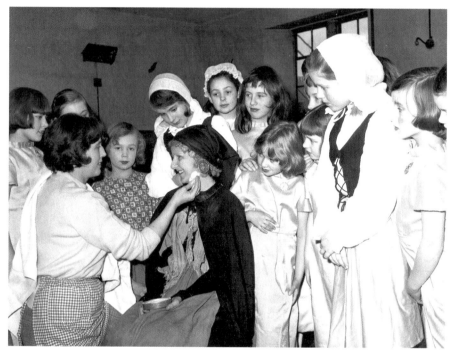

Preparing for Mrs Corden's production of *Twelve Dancing Princesses*, c.1964. Susan Crow is centre right at the front. (Susan Crow)

Joan Crow underlines the importance of Mrs Corden's exacting standards.

Mrs Corden really could be said to have given wonderful opportunities to young people and children who are interested in the theatre to exercise their talents and to see what it was like to take part in a real professional production. It was a great experience: she did it superbly well, she took endless trouble.

A number of children involved went on to careers in the arts – like both Joan's children.

John played Rip Van Winkle, quite a starring role. He loved the theatre and was very good at it and went on to become a theatre administrator. [Susan] went to the Royal Ballet School and was taken into the company and was very good. Then she went to Sadlers Wells Royal Ballet. The other person who can be said to owe something to her is Humphrey Carpenter, who was also a star of the children's pantomime. I remember him taking the role of Rumpelstiltskin, and he was very good at it.

Several children who became too old to act continued to be involved in various ways: Humphrey Carpenter helped with the lighting (in later life he became a writer and broadcaster, but also ran his own drama group, The Mushy Pea Theatre, in which various children from the roads were involved). Josie Patterson's son Dan changed to media studies at university and went into the BBC. Verity Peto adds some other names.

Jeanetta Bumpus, now Jeanetta Lawrence, became Sadlers Wells Royal Ballet Assistant Director. Judith Vickers went to the Royal Opera House. Andrew Vernede is a theatre director. And, of course, Hugh Laurie, who's now very well known for television and cinema, was another of the children who took part.

Among musical activities in which many residents have shared is the Summertown Choral Society, running since 1961. It meets in the United Reformed Church and has often performed in St Michael's Church. Sally Bromley met her present husband there when she was a single mother and teacher.

I wanted to be known as me, and I joined Summertown Choral Society, so there was a place that I felt I was just me. So on a Thursday evening, my parents looked after the children overnight. I loved the singing, and I really enjoyed it. And that is where I met Jonathan.

Other activities

Sydney Denton remembers a wide variety of activities for all ages in the area after the war, at a time when there was little private entertainment beyond the radio.

There was much more of a community spirit, because you didn't have television. There was Guides and Scouts and Youth Clubs, and there's the Grove Street Club in Grove Street, the Conservative Club, and all. There were lots and lots of local football teams. There was no television, so you had to make your own sport, and there were cricket teams here, there, and everywhere. The Radiators, the entertainment that they put on was brilliant! They would have Sports Days, they would have cricket matches, they would have football matches, so all this was going on all in this community – because, you know, we couldn't afford to go and do anything else. Today, you decide, 'What shall we do this weekend?' It might be to go to Paris to do some shopping! It's that simple! And people can afford to do this.

A fondly remembered but long extinct annual community event was the Summertown Flower Show, held on Summer Fields School grounds before the war. Margaret Twining recalls it for its amusements, which were important in days when entertainments were scarce.

There were things like bowling for the pig, and knocking down the coconuts, and all that sort of thing. And a little roundabout, and swings. There were lots of competitions. I used to pick wild flowers, and make a bunch of wild flowers, or paint a picture.

Her sister Gwynneth describes the central displays.

A lot of Summertown people went to it. A lot of people showed their onions, enormous onions and things. I can remember the long tables where all these things were spread out.

Many people in the roads have been keen gardeners, and there have always been allotments in the area. John Rowe from Victoria Road used to help his father.

My father always grew veg, it was a standard thing to grow veg. He had an allotment down behind the cottages on Banbury Road, where there's now a carpark, it was an open field. The allotment was full, particularly during the war. There was

a mix of people – Mr Hobbs, down Victoria Road, who was a bank manager, quite a mix. More the professor types or lower grade jobs. People's gardens were for flowers, particularly along Victoria Road, because of the heavy ground. I worked down there with him, in the summer after work, I got pocket money for digging it over. There was an old gent down there, Mr Truby. He had an immaculate allotment. He wore a suit, shirt, and a black homburg hat. He used to tell me 'You don't need to throw that earth around'.

John Rowe among the beans on his allotment, 2006. (P. Kinchin)

In the 1990s John went to the allotments off Marston Ferry Road where several people from the roads have plots, often handed on through personal contacts. He comments on social change on the allotments, particularly the arrival of many women in what was traditionally an all-male world.

Tom Stross in Victoria Road mentioned it – said it was lovely soil down there. Today it's all middle class. I never saw a lady on the allotment [earlier]. Sometimes they'd go to collect veg, but it was very unusual.

It is a sociable and productive activity.

I do my best, it's second nature to me. I give the veg away, give them to neighbours, to people on the allotments. I grow an awful lot of potatoes! Once a week I am invited to go to lunch in Cumnor and I take a bag of potatoes. It's nice being in the open air, and if you're doing your own garden you never see anyone to have a chat to. There's always someone to chat to, you see others, check up on them. It's a big part of my life. I go down once a day.

NOA and the Ferry Centre

Groups formed round various nuclei have contributed greatly to the community. It is often strong, committed individuals who galvanise others to get things done. Vic Brown of Lucerne Road remembers his neighbour 'Jon' Murphy who was instrumental in founding the North Oxford Residents Association in 1966 (later simply the North Oxford Association, NOA) and getting the Ferry Centre and a swimming pool built.

Adelaide Murphy – Mrs Murphy – didn't like her Christian name, so she was always known as Jon. [She] had a social conscience, and she considered that this area lacked a centre of social activity, or communal activity. I think it was a project that she'd had something to do with in London, the Peckham Project, or something like that. It was built round a swimming bath, and she wanted something similar in North Oxford. She formed a Committee, and I – although I'm not a committee man at all – was, early on, a member.

The vicar Bill Fosdike was another of those rounded up by Mrs Murphy.

She had a very advanced social conscience indeed, somewhat overpowering really! She would also write everybody letters, long letters. Anyhow, she and Bridget Thompson, who's now the President of the place, got together a number of us – GPs, a bank manager, all in some sort of sense influential, or having a role in the community. Out of that meeting came the idea that we needed a place where people could meet. Then the Local Authority put money away for a Youth Centre, and gradually, it came up the list and was available. So it was possible, and we developed it, and NOA was given the management of it.

Mary Tregear's father Tom, living in Portland Road, was another who got involved: as she says, the building of the Ferry Centre in 1971, followed by the Ferry Pool in 1976, shows the benefits of having effective people living in the area.

We're a great committee place. My father was on the committee of NOA, and they used to meet in the Old Bakery. He was always interested in what was going on, and very enthusiastic about things happening. He always talked to people in their shops and that sort of thing, and he was a Quaker. He was a good committee man, so he was very keen on it. They gradually expanded themselves and worked hard and got it going, and really sort of physically built the place. Then there was a big drive to get the swimming pool going. There was a bank manager, and a Bodley Librarian – that was Ian Philip [28 Portland Road]. They were Oxford people, so they knew their way around. I think it helped having people up here who weren't necessarily members of the Council, or particularly politically involved, but who did, in fact, carry a little weight. They knew enough people – it seems always to work in Oxford, if you know people!

Mariele Kuhn was a foot soldier in this campaign.

I once had to canvass for a swimming pool, because there was no swimming pool in Summertown. So I went house to house and convinced people how important it is that we have a swimming pool.

Christine Butler was on the first Ferry Centre Committee, and was involved like many others as a helper in some of the many activities laid on there after it was built.

The lunch club was set up. I was more serving tea and driving old ladies around.

The whole process was good for community contacts, in Mary Tregear's opinion.

A lot of people got to know people. Strangely enough, I think the women got to know each other better, because it's not so easy being busy at home with a family, and only meeting like-aged children's parents. And the swimming pool has been enormous, because Cherwell [School] use it, and various people use it.

Other campaigning groups

Another active and very effective local resident was Helen Turner at 46 Hamilton Road. In the mid 1960s she was one of those who founded the Oxford Consumers Group, the first local group in the country. Jean Robinson of Lonsdale Road was also involved.

There was Helen Turner, who was married to a guy who worked at the History of Science Museum, and she went on to become a journalist in this field, and write books. It was a group of mostly women, mostly very intelligent women, who didn't have other things to do in Oxford, who didn't have proper jobs. It was a revolution in its time, and it was this changing pattern from being grateful for what you got, and being a passive consumer. So those were interesting times.

Helen Turner. (Gerard Turner)

Christine Butler, a neighbour in Hamilton Road, was also involved.

It was a very erudite committee. They were taking a keen interest in local conditions, so that they would do a local investigation or enquiry, and we produced little booklets, like a restaurant guide, and later a short walks from Oxford type of guide. Our restaurant guides were quite well thought of. Helen was a very vibrant person, and we used to meet quite often in her house.

Out of mounting concern for the physical environment of Oxford, and, pressingly, to campaign against proposals for a destructive inner ring road, the Oxford Civic Society was formed in 1969 by Helen Turner, her husband Gerard, and the architectural historian James Stevens Curl. This has grown to become an important organisation, with many members from these roads, working to preserve and enhance the amenities of the city. Helen Turner wrote influentially in the Oxford Times *and went on to become a key figure in the Oxford Preservation Trust, another organisation committed to the protection of Oxford.*

Prof. Bob Williams of Victoria Road, now retired, is chairman of the Sunnymead/ Cutteslowe Group, whose efforts to improve the environment of the area immediately north of these roads have recently won an Oxford Preservation Trust award.

We are seven people in all, four of us you would class as from the neighbourhood of these roads and, therefore, middle-class, and [the others] belong either to the estates, or one belongs in the flats on Water Eaton Road.

The group was formed around 1980 to reclaim what is now Sunnymead Park as a community area. The area had once been a fine sports field, connected with the well-known Cherwell Arms, but had deteriorated with the decline and end of the pub, and was overrun by motor-biking youths.

That meadow was used as a tip for the people in the estate, and it was really a right mess, the whole place. We started to raise small sums of money to improve the area, and at the same time we organised probably about 20 people to pile up the rubbish. It was partly a middle-class venture, and it was partly people from the estate who worked and cleared the place. Recently we've dug out the main ditch, which is called 'Cromwell's Ditch', the bit which is behind Water Eaton Road, and joins the Cherwell just behind the bottom corner of Victoria Road. That's a very famous ditch, of course, part of the fortifications that were set up by Cromwell himself, to protect his troops. I must say, the City, with some cajoling and pushing, have been exceptionally good about this development. We were always presenting to them the case that they had created an estate with no facilities whatsoever – they had a Community Centre, which was rather small, and nothing at all for the kids. They came up with schemes which were going to be put around Oxford, like street sports sites, and in the end, a skateboard site. Each time we saw this advertised I said, 'Right, put it here'.

Bob mentions another Victoria Road resident who was instrumental in shaping the Sustrans cycle route and getting the new bridge over the by-pass at Cutteslowe.

Geoffrey Nutt was an engineer – at least, he knew a bit about engineering – and he was a cyclist, and he'd gone to a meeting about the Sustrans cycle track which was supposed to come through Oxford. So Geoffrey said, 'Why not use the existing cycle track, which goes past the Frideswide School, and then come on up through our streets – King's Cross Road, Victoria Road, Water Eaton Road – and then make a bridge?' And Sustrans said yes. The bridge is a very great asset for us all, we can get into the park on the other side, and we can get down to the river.

The Hollands (right) outside their house in Portland Road with three of their children, all supporting different parties in the election of 2001. The area has been a stronghold of the Liberal Democrats for some years now. (Helen Holland)

Specific local planning issues can galvanise neighbours into formidable action groups. One such was the long-running battle against Owen Kernahan's plans for expansion of his garage in King's Cross Road. John Marsh, then a resident of Hamilton Road, became involved.

Oh, he had quite big ideas. There was some fairly lively people around, who were naturally terribly concerned. I had a friend [in Lonsdale Road], who was concerned about it, because he almost backs onto the Kernahan Garage, so I probably got to know of it through him, in the first instance. We just thought it was a monstrous thing he was trying to do, and became involved – and involved was the word! It went on for ages. Several years, I should think, all told.

Peter Thompson, whose account appears on p. 35f, has been an important figure in several planning battles over the site. John pays tribute to his skills.

He was absolutely excellent, and he'd got everything to his fingertips. He's a civil engineer, I believe, but he'd make a first class lawyer!

The recent proposals for a residents' parking scheme had the same effect of getting people together, as Philippa Berry mentions.

Hamilton Road were very instrumental in doing battle with the Council, on the parking scheme. Members of our road have worked extremely hard – Martin and Birthe Biddle – to try and make a more user-friendly car parking scheme.

Neighbourhood groups

Within the roads neighbourhood watch groups designed to keep an eye on security have existed at various periods, like that established in Hamilton Road. Birthe Kjølbye-Biddle and Ursula Gibbons inaugurated their group in one half of the road in 1982 with a successful Christmas party which established new links between neighbours. Bill Fosdike had a hand in developing Church Neighbour Groups.

> There'd be somebody appointed, or more than one person in long roads, who would keep an eye on the street, and visit when people came, or when they were leaving. They tried to be quiet friends to their neighbourhood, and also people that could keep the church administration in touch if somebody was ill.

There are all kinds of private groups meeting in the roads – a women's discussion group, a 'Friday group', book clubs, etc. Children have always created strong informal links between people, promoting neighbourhood groups and events, as Philippa Berry says, mentioning baby-sitting and carol-singing in Hamilton Road in the 1970s and 80s.

> We had a Babysitting Circle: we used to exchange curtain rings, all that kind of stuff. The Hamilton Road Carol Singers started when our children were small. We had the carols at 4 o'clock, and then we used to go to St Michael's Church for the Blessing of the Crib. So that was part of all our children's childhoods round here. That was the first Hamilton Road event really, and happened every Christmas Eve, with the Dimechs organising the music, and all the different children playing their instruments, as they were learning them.

Paloma Bevir recalls this warmly.

> To begin with, we sung in front of every single house but at some stage, it was thought that perhaps some people were not that keen to be serenaded! That was a good excuse to get all together in the street. And we had mince pies and a social gathering.

The Victoria Road Recycling Group, started in 1991, has been a particularly successful organisation, promoting connections between the inhabitants of the road. Jelly Williams describes its origins.

> The Victoria Road Group started as a recycling group, and a community effort and a community binding thing. On the other side of Victoria Road they were young families with youngish kids and they knew each other and they all had a sort of hippy alternative philosophy. Very very attractive. They were all in good jobs but there was something modern about them. And almost at the same time the Johnstons, who have now both died – he had been an ambassador, Sir Jack Johnston – they wanted to give a party for the oldest inhabitant of Victoria Road. We called them the Red Cross Ladies, the two sisters [the Woodwards, p. 39]. Anyway one of them had died and the other one was moving to the Red Cross Home in Osberton Road.

We continue the story from Sir Jack Johnston's interview.

> So we thought, 'Well, we must give her a good send off', and I did a little invitation, which we put in every door in the street, saying that we're having a party to say goodbye, would they come? Anyway, there was a very good turnout, and I wrote out, on a big sheet, a sort of mock 'Freedom of the Road', you know – 'We

by those present' etc., and as people came in, they signed it. Anyway, that was a huge success. And someone there said, 'This is a very good idea, why don't we have a street party every year?'

Jelly Williams again.

Jack Johnston very nicely made her an honorary citizen of Victoria Road, and it really was ... tears came to one. It was such a very very nice event. And at the same time this new hippy lot got involved in recycling events and they took over the street party. It sort of merged, because of the goodwill of everybody. They were all good citizens. And they are still going strong.

Margaret Woodward, displaying the Freedom of Victoria Road presented at a party in August 1990. (J. Johnston)

As Sam Clarke says, a core group of committed people has been important for establishing the recycling group.

The recycling group got started because Ali and myself and Nick and Jenny Lee and our neighbour Derek Wareham decided that we would like to try and see if there was a nucleus of people who were interested in this. Obviously the idea fell on fertile ground, because the group has been going from strength to strength since then. It has always been strongly social. The people who have been stalwarts have been the Lewises –Paul and Mary Lewis; Nick and Jenny Lee, while Jenny was alive, and Nick now; Jenny Goldrei was always there; and ourselves. That has been the core of the group. That has helped. Now it's feeling that its got much more a life of its own.

The garden party wasn't an activity of the group originally, it had a life of its own. Somehow we were encouraged to hold a garden party ourselves in our garden and it was a dreadful day. Every year since then there has been a garden party. We rotate it. It's something that the older people in the street find particularly easy. Jack used to also print the invitations for the garden party each year. We've built up a set of activities. The funds always look after themselves: the big chunks come from profits made at barn dances. Some of the older folk surprisingly slip us £10 or £20 and say 'I can't come to many events but I do like what you are doing'. It's really rather touching. That's their way of contributing.

Sally Bromley describes the Victoria Road Group's Green Balloon day.

We also have Green Balloon Day, which has now become a bit of a tradition, where you put things that you no longer need, but somebody else might get a bit more life out of. I remember walking along there the first time, with a coffee cup in my hand, and piece of cherry cake in my hand, and thinking to myself, 'My mother

Victoria Road Green Balloon Day, 2006. (Sam Clarke)

would kill me if she saw me walking out of the gate with a coffee cup and a piece of cake in my hand!' Even if you only meet people on that one day of the year, it's well worth doing, because it is keeping the community spirit. We've got a notice board on the road, where people can put things for sale.

Philippa Berry, along with Jackie Weaver, started a Hamilton Road Group in about 1996, in emulation of the Victoria Road Group.

We decided that it wouldn't be called 'recycling', because we didn't think we had enough green people in our roads, but we had party people, we thought. So we started what we eventually called the 'Hamilton Road Community Group'. We did a newsletter, and we had events. We had a Burns Night Party. And summer parties, one in this garden and one in the Weavers' garden, and we had a barn dance. And we had 'green balloon days', which, again, was copied from Victoria Road. And those were very successful: we had people with tables and chairs so we'd have coffee and tea and cake. You put a green balloon on your gate or your door, and everybody comes out on the day, wanders up and down the road and takes what they want. All sorts of things! There was a plumber who was working out on the edge of a property further down Hamilton Road, and he'd left his tools on the pavement. And somebody walked up and said, 'Oh, that's quite nice. I think I'll have those!' Fortunately, the plumber spotted this and got them back!

Like other voluntary organisations, the Hamilton Road Group depended on the energies of particular people, and succumbed to pressures on their time.

We had a wonderful core committee here in Hamilton Road, some staunch people who turned up, and who helped organise on every single occasion, but I think the nature of the road was changing. Jackie was busy, I was back working, and got really too busy, and it just got a bit too heavy, a bit too much.

Street parties

Philippa mentions another event that happened in Lucerne Road.

I used to work, as a volunteer, with the Abbeyfield House [residential home], on the Banbury Road on the corner of Portland. We used to have a summer party for the residents and all their friends and relations. Florence Paine, who lived in the Old Bakehouse, for years, her family have a river garden. They had a little bungalow with a kitchen, and they allowed us to use that. That was a nice regular summer event.

When an approach was made to use the river garden as part of the Millennium Street Festival in 2000 public liability insurance was a problem. 'Health and Safety' regulation is something that has made it much harder to mount community events in recent years. However there have been some memorable street parties in the roads. Clare and Monica Wagstaff of Hamilton Road remember celebrating the end of the war in a way which would not be allowed today!

At the end of the war – 1945, not 1946 – we had a big street party. It was at the end of the road here, there were tables put out, and a big bonfire. There was a hole in the road up there for ages, terrible hole it was, because of the bonfire.

In more recent memory there have been parties to celebrate the silver jubilee in 1977 and two royal weddings. Philippa Berry was involved with one for the wedding of Prince Charles and Lady Diana Spencer in July 1981.

Jenny Freeman, who lived in Hamilton Road then, and Roger, were the chief organisers. That street party was a sort of simple, happy occasion, with everybody just turning up rather casually, bringing a plate of food. But it was a lovely street party, the children were dancing in the street, and we had musicians. And then the [1986] one, which was Prince Andrew's wedding, we did have a torrential downpour, and I remember everyone just fled and took refuge! But it was at the end of the party.

While earlier street parties focussed on particular roads, the magnificent Seven Roads Millennium Festival in June 2000, supported by the Heritage Lottery Fund, drew together the wider neighbourhood, and was the origin of this book. The June weather was poor but did not spoil the event. Philippa was involved again.

1952 👑 1977
E II R
Victoria Road, Oxford,
celebrates
THE QUEEN'S
SILVER JUBILEE
at a Street Party in
Kings Cross Road (north end)
Tuesday June 7th 1977
from 5 to 7.30p.m.

Please wear a badge showing your house number
Fancy dress optional

Hand printed at 74 Victoria Road, Oxford

Above: Invitation printed at 74 Victoria Road by Conant Brodribb for the Victoria Road Jubilee party, 1977. (J. Williams)

Below: Tony and Pam Dale of 39 Portland Road at the Portland Road street party in 1981. (Lynn Ahmed)

201

[It was] a huge feat of organisation – mainly done by Ali Clarke, of Victoria Road – but she had a large committee who attended meetings at her house, and the bureaucracy had probably quadrupled in the intervening years. I was in charge of the café. That was actually quite informally arranged. I just said, 'Yes please, bring a plate of something', and trusted that it would all work out all right. I got urns from St Michael's Church, and various other churches. I borrowed little garden tables from everybody and tablecloths, and all the rest of it. All sorts of people turned up.

The beginning of the Seven Roads Millennium Festival street party in King's Cross Road, 2000. Ali Clarke, who led the organising, is behind the barrier. (Michael Hammand)

This party was very successful in bridging the generations.

I can remember seeing the older people sort of creeping out of their houses and standing around at the edges and really ... great smiles on their faces, to see the community, which they knew, getting on with enjoying itself. There were gladiator fights and drawings on the pavements, a pet show, lots of music, there was a sort of bandstand with a

Dancing in the evening at the Millennium street party. (Michael Hammand)

whole series of different musicians, all the way through from 12 noon, till midnight. I can remember [my son] Thomas, saying, oh well, he wasn't going to bother to turn up. But he and his friends absolutely loved it! And they were dancing away in the late evening, and really enjoying it very very much.

A new sense of community in these related roads was generated, as Sally Bromley says.

When we had that link-up for the Millennium, that brought another surge of interest. I think there is a great deal of interest among people in conserving and developing our community now.

11 The Neighbourhood and Neighbourliness

My observation would be that there are communities within communities here on this road, very much so, in this area.

Peter Clarke

This suburb of Oxford has seemed to its residents over the years a good place to live, friendly and convenient. While people protect their space and privacy it was abundantly clear from our survey and interviews that a high level of good neighbourliness under-pins a general feeling of satisfaction with living in these roads.

It has not always been love at first sight. Margaret Clarke, who has lived in Hamilton Road since 1962, recalls her first awareness of the road, at a time when she and her husband were living in the country, at Bladon.

Before we'd started thinking of moving, we came past the top of this road one day, and Leon said, 'Oh, that's the road where John Hays is living now'. I said, 'Oh, how dreadful! I couldn't bear to live in a road like that!' I don't know what it was that repelled me, but I thought it was the last place I wanted to live! I saw a long, dusty road, going down, and absolutely straight, and next to a main road. 'What an awful suburban ...' and never did I think we would end up here! But now, I don't really want to leave. I never thought I'd stay as long as this!

Defining the neighbourhood

Reflecting their historical development on land originally owned by one man, these seven roads do have a sense of coherence, defined on east and west by the physical barri-ers of the River Cherwell and the Banbury Road, and separated from areas north and south by more intangible issues related once to class, now more clearly to money. Hernes, Harpes and Islip Roads to the immediate north were developed a little earlier than our roads but with slightly lower-class housing. However it is the estates built in the 1930s north of there that shape this feeling of separation. Bob Williams lives at the end of Victoria Road on the edge of this other world.

The problem is that the roads that we live in – the Twining Estate roads – are all really middle-class housing, they're not upper-class by any means, but they cer-tainly aren't lower-class, if you like, working-class. If you just go down the road, to the end of Water Eaton Road, you come to the estate, and the estate was a com-pletely different set-up really, and there was a clear barrier, roughly where the pub was – the old Cherwell Arms [demolished for flats]. And immediately I sensed that the social division was very very considerable, between these two groups of peo-ple, and they actually hardly spoke to one another.

Peter Clarke agrees. He unusually had an allotment at Sunnymead in the 1980s.

Beyond Victoria Road, you were really in a kind of other world, that people didn't even speak about very much. That was definitely outside the boundaries. I got to know people because I worked on the allotments. And it was a very informative world, because they knew it all – Cowley Motor Works, what was going on down there, when they would be striking. When the strike would end, if there was a postal strike – you'd get it from there, because there was a postman there. It was like going to another world. The stories I heard, and the chat, it was all completely different. They were a bit condescending. They didn't feel inferior. They thought we were very impractical, a bit stupid, I suppose! You know, they'd help you out as well. They deplored the state of the nation a lot.

Lady Johnston, also living in Victoria Road, shared Bob Williams' sense of a division.

The people in Cutteslowe have a much harder time. It's extraordinary how differ-ent that bit of Oxford is. Even though [the Cutteslowe] Wall doesn't any longer exist, the mentality still exists, and there's a great difference between the people who live this side, the posh side, as it were, and that estate.

The notorious Cutteslowe Wall (p.27) was familiar to Gwynneth Twining.

We remember it being put up [1934], and being knocked down! [1959]

It was built by the developer of the private 'Urban' estate to prevent inhabitants from the adjacent 'slum clearance' council estate from passing through it, with the result that many workers had to come down our roads to gain access to the Banbury Road, as Monica Wagstaff of Hamilton Road remembers.

There used to be about four times a day a massive number of cyclists going up and down these roads from the Cutteslowe estate.

Sally Bromley grew up in Carlton Road in one of the houses of 'the Urban'.

The wall came down when I was about 10 or 11. I do remember some changes as I looked out of my door, because, obviously, there were an awful lot of strange stories about people who lived on the other side of the wall, you know, like coal in the bath, and chickens under the table, and things like this. I do remember seeing black fishnet tights with white stiletto heels, and a very high bouffant style, and a very short mini-skirt, and completely being gobsmacked by it!

There was also a sense of separation from the more upper-middle-class residential roads to the south of Summertown, home of the archetypal 'North Oxford female' – a feeling that our seven roads were 'town' not 'gown'. This persisted after academics started to move into the area. Celia Glyn and her husband, an economist, had enough money for a house in what estate agents call 'Central North Oxford', where most academics chose to live, when they were house-hunting in 1969.

The agent said 'There's one in Lonsdale Road, but you wouldn't want that.' I said 'Why not?' And since I'd been to the Flemmings I knew they were nice houses, so we looked at it. It was a much better layout than other houses we'd seen.

The Glyns bought the house and spent the spare money on alterations. As the houses here have become enlarged, and desirable for their location, our roads have been to some extent assimilated to the more upmarket areas to the south, as Peter Clarke suggests.

Summertown is a kind of part of North Oxford now, when it wasn't before. You definitely made the distinction. If people asked you where you lived, you'd say 'Summertown', you never said, 'North Oxford', whereas now, you'd probably get away with it. Although I see the new signs for parking make a distinction. If you go down to Belbroughton Road, you'll have an 'NO'. If you come here, you'll have an 'SN'. So they're reintroducing the divide!

Another way of looking at it is that 'Summertown' itself has more cachet than it once did, as it is commonly seen as Oxford's most desirable suburb.

A safe place

As a stable middle-class community this has been experienced as a generally safe neighbourhood. There was a local police presence in the District Station at 45 South Parade from the time of the expansion of Summertown in 1894 through to around 1956. Dorothy Bridge knew an ideal community policeman early in the 20th century.

We had a lovely policeman in Summertown, called Mr Steele. We regarded him as a friend.

Margaret Pickles, who came to Hamilton Road with her friend Hazel Leafe in 1961, records the concern of the local policeman on his beat.

When we first came here, a policeman came round and put a note in the door, 'Would you mind locking your back door, please?' We never locked it. Nobody did. He must have tried it one night.

Celia Glyn was similarly casual about security after she moved into Lonsdale Road in 1969.

It was a very friendly road. The front door was on the latch for years, people just used to wander in and shout 'Hello'. I didn't have a Yale on it for years.

Margaret's and Hazel's neighbours were very protective towards two young women on their own.

Cathy Berry, Holly Peebles (Kilpatrick) and a friendly policeman at the Hamilton Road street party in 1981. (Philippa Berry)

If anybody called, they'd say to us, 'Somebody came on a bike, and he had dark hair, and he was so-and-so, but we kept an eye on it', so you couldn't do anything without somebody knowing. But it was very helpful really, because you always felt that you were quite safe. They were mostly, the people down the road, were old. Evidently, they thought that we were going to have wild parties. Because we were youngsters, they thought that we're going to let the side down. But, of course, we never did! Every time we did anything at the front, they all offered us advice, and pieces of equipment, and told us 'Rome wasn't built in a day!' When we first came here we had some sand delivered, and a man down the road, said, 'Oh no, you can't put the sand on the pavement. It's only two girls, and they'll have it all to move. You will have to move it now, put it inside.' So they emptied it, and we couldn't get in at the front door!

Margaret Willis remembers this unofficial neighbourhood watch in Lonsdale Road in the 1950s and 60s.

Mr Hollingdale lived at about no. 59. He was a widower, and he liked to know what was going on, and so he was always in his front garden, leaning on a gardening implement! If you were going into somebody else's house, he would say, 'Don't go there, she's out!' In the end he was the first person I knew who was given a place in a Council Residential Home, and this was a great comfort to him, he knew he was going to be all right till the end of his days then.

Elsie Hill has lived in Portland Road for 40 years.

I still think of us as being incredibly privileged, in North Oxford, in that, relatively speaking, life here is very calm and very friendly, and though we have had burglaries in the past there's not a great deal of violence or vandalism.

Interviewed in 2001, John Herivel was more worried about security, though burglaries, which seem to happen in spates, have fallen away since then.

There have been so many burglaries. They've become much more common than they were. In the old days, I never remember hearing about them at all.

Leszek Kolakowksi in Hamilton Road is relaxed about the thefts they have suffered.

It's, as far as I can say, pretty safe. Once someone tried to break into our house, but unsuccessfully. Breaking the window in the kitchen. And once someone stole our lawn mower! The loss was very small, so we bought a new one. But those thiefs, as we should have expected, stole the new one as well! After a short time, I got a letter from, I don't remember what it was, a social service, because I was a victim of a crime: perhaps I would like to have psychological help!

There have been professional burglaries, and cars have been stolen, but most criminal activity is opportunistic and relatively minor. Also shrugged off as a part of modern life is the occasional disturbance and casual vandalism associated with young people, and generally laid at the door of those passing through the area from the less privileged north. Dr Bertram Mandelbrote has lived for many years in Lonsdale Road next to what is now the cycle path, the kind of alleyway that seems to attract bad behaviour: he registers it as 'a bit of a nuisance'.

The children were very destructive. We put up three sets of fences. They are constantly breaking bits of it down and writing obscene messages and things like that on it. And the police are quite hopeless from the point of view of doing anything. We've been in touch with the headmaster [of Cherwell School] and he said he can't really do very much about what they do outside of school. But they're not an enormous problem. We must have spent £1500 renewing the fence at various times.

Other stories can be collected – of unpleasant behaviour towards children playing at Sunnymead, or between those from private and state schools on the bike path. However the Schrigers from North America, who lived in Lonsdale Road for a sabbatical year in 2003–4, give a compensatorily positive view of our neighbourhood.

It's just a place where you feel very safe and very comfortable, and it's absolutely wonderful. It has all the small townish qualities – people are friendly, and you feel safe and all that – yet at the same time, because of, particularly in this area, who lives here – a lot of academics and things – it's as intellectually exciting as one could ask for, and that's an unusual combination. Here, the tendency is if you have the opportunity to do some pleasantness, to do it. We've been just very impressed by the general level of courtesy and kindness that we've seen here.

Communities within communities

Within this area the long roads tend to operate as separate entities, so that neighbourliness is linear. Residents of other roads may not have cause to go into them, unless as a back way to the shops. Those in the southerly roads especially might not often go north, as Verity Peto of Lonsdale Road acknowledges.

There was a dairy in Victoria Road, near the Banbury Road end of it. I think we even got our milk from it. But I wasn't highly aware of it, because I wasn't very adventurous when the children were small, and I don't think I ever walked to the end of Victoria Road!

Neighbours chatting on the wall outside Elizabeth Stewart's house, 22 Portland Road (she is second from right), as they wait for a bride to appear from the house opposite, August 1995. (Sally Owen)

Within the roads smaller communities are formed, with King's Cross Road making a natural barrier. This is marked in Lonsdale Road, where the houses beyond King's Cross Road are in a dead end, and perceived as a separate community. Monica Wagstaff says the same of Hamilton Road.

It was extraordinary – we knew most people this side of the crossroads, and very few people on the far side. It's a real barrier.

Paloma Bevir also sees Hamilton Road in three distinct parts.

The street is long enough to be divided for meeting purposes, in three chunks. One is from Banbury Road to roughly no. 30. From no. 30 to King's Cross and from King's Cross to the very end, because most people living at the end of Hamilton Road would never walk [down it] to go to the shops, they would always cut across.

Portland Road is shorter than the others, ending at King's Cross Road, but is typical in breaking into a 'top', 'middle' and 'bottom'. Ruth Bader Gilbert moved from one end to the other in 1979 and speaks of it as a different community.

The ones I knew down that end, I didn't have much contact with when I came up here. We've got to know several neighbours up here, who I'm in contact with.

Her husband Philip however saw the difference more sharply.

I noticed the change, moving from one end of the street to the other. When we lived at the other end of the street, we got to know some of the neighbours quite well. Up here, there are people, I don't even know their names. I suppose they think they've got their own lives to lead and they just don't mix.

Hawkswell Gardens represents a later 20th-century suburban concept, the 'close'. This has made the group of houses very separate and self-contained. Peter Clarke lived round the corner in Lonsdale Road for many years but claims never to have been in Hawkswell Gardens before he moved there in 2004.

Friendly relations where houses are generally so close together naturally begin with immediately adjacent properties – with the exception that people can share a boundary with houses in the next road and have no idea who their neighbours at the bottom of the garden are. People tend to know more neighbours on their own side of the road. Peter reflects on this, talking of Lonsdale Road.

The thing I've always observed – and I can understand it sociologically and psychologically – whichever side you want to take, the right side never speak to the left, not in my time. By and large, there was no communication across the road.

Jean Robinson was one of those living on the other side of Lonsdale Road.

It just so happened that it was at a time when a whole lot of people of similar age [moved in], with kids of similar ages, and similar backgrounds. And we were all on the same side of the road, so that the kids ran up and down into each other's houses, became great friends. Oddly enough, we virtually knew no one on the other side of the street!

Peter tells the extraordinary story of how he actually met the person living on the opposite side of the road.

I met him in Africa. I was sitting in the Senior Staff Club in the University of Ibadan, having a drink with a Nigerian colleague, and this fair-haired guy walked up, and said, 'Do you mind if I join you?' And we said 'No'. After a while, I said, 'And where are you from?' He said, 'England'. I said, 'Oh, whereabouts? He said, 'Well, in the south, in Oxford.' I said, 'Oh, whereabouts?' He said, 'Lonsdale Road'. I said, 'What number?' I said, 'Oh, well, I'm across the road from you.' That's how I met him!

He also reflects on how some people prefer to keep lines drawn, speaking of another neighbour across the road. He met her at a party.

We chatted away, but after the party, I never [spoke to] her again! It's just one of those things you don't do. I mean, I've always wanted to, but you can't. Because I suppose people mark out a fence, and say, 'Well, if I get involved with all of those people, I'll never stop saying hello!' She obviously thinks this kind of general, ordinary, everyday nodding is not worth it. She may have a point, I don't know. To me, it makes the world go round. It's not a trivial thing.

He wonders if the fact that the houses on the south side are bigger than those on the north has something to do with it, as with the section of Lonsdale Road beyond King's Cross Road.

That is a separate unit – I never thought of it as part of Lonsdale Road, really. But whether this is something sociological – boundary maintenance, marking off, different style of house, bigger houses, some of them detached – all of this may be part of the story. My own feeling is that people will separate out over nothing, if we give them half a chance.

Margaret Willis, who now lives right down at the end of Lonsdale Road where there are several larger detached houses set back in gardens, having earlier lived among the more cheek-by-jowl Edwardian semi-detached houses in the main part of the road, confirms a difference mainly due to type of house and location, related to income.

Left: Margaret Willis at the door of her house in the 'isolated' part of Lonsdale Road, 2006. (P. Kinchin)
Right: Her children, Richard, James, Mary and William Helsby, near 55 Lonsdale Road, c.1962. (Margaret Willis)

The households, themselves, are more separate. We don't, on the whole, mix a great deal. It's isolated. Living further down there [at no.55], people drop in much more, and certainly, when all our children were little, we used to leave a pram in the front garden while we went off to shop. It was very good, exchangewise, then. Living up here, of course, is quite different. Well, nobody passes by, and we're all on perfectly good terms, but I wouldn't say it was a great mix like further down the road. When we lived there, we all knew each other and helped each other out. As you come further up here, they get a bit more prosperous!

Making connections

Back in 1954 when Margaret moved into 55 Lonsdale Road as Margaret Helsby, the previous owners of the house introduced them to neighbours.

The night before they left, among the packing cases they gave a little party, and they asked the people they thought we'd get on with. And that was Cicely Davies next door. She was wonderful. And Sonia and Michael Argyle, who lived at no. 30. And they became close friends of ours. We all knew each other forever after that. Michael Argyle, in fact, was the godfather of my daughter.

Pam Robinson was effectively selected by the previous owners of 24 Hamilton Road for potential to fit in.

We looked all round, and she said, 'Oh, we want you to buy the house. We like you!' So we went round to our friend in Victoria Road, and sort of talked it over, and we decided, yes, we'd buy the house. So we went back and told them, and they were so pleased, because they thought we'd fit in with the neighbours. So she then insisted on introducing us to everyone in the neighbourhood!

A gathering of neighbours from both sides of Lonsdale Road at a party on the occasion of the Queen's Jubilee in 2002. (Roy Foster)

Philip Allen spoke warmly of when he and Carolyn lived in Hamilton Road in 1985–96.

It was special, Hamilton Road. Nowhere – and we have lived all over, Europe, Ireland – have we received such a warm welcome.

Definite efforts to make contact, most easily done when new residents arrive, do really make a difference. The Schrigers, from the USA, were welcomed to Lonsdale Road in this way.

The people immediately around us were quite friendly and open, they came over and introduced themselves, the people across the way. Our immediate neighbours introduced themselves, and, it's first very respectful, we didn't know exactly what relations were between neighbours. But over the year, we've really got to know our immediate neighbours, the Petos, quite well, and they're very gracious, and let my daughter use their piano for practice. By the end, the doors were open, and people were moving back and forth quite often! We got to know a fair number of people on the block.

A first contact does need to be made or one can live for years without acknowledgement from people who are seen regularly. Peter Thompson, on the corner of King's Cross Road and Lonsdale Road, describes this clearly, and shows the importance of front gardens as 'defended space' promoting interactions.

The people that live around here, display absolutely the archetypal English characteristics of being fairly reserved about first making contact. We have remarked how you can walk down the street here, and people who you know by sight, but you've never spoken to, will walk down the street, and they won't look you in the eye. I have an interest in vintage cars, and I tend to work on them in or outside my garage, and sometimes, particularly in the summer, it's actually quite difficult to do anything because of the number of people that come past and want to talk to you about it! And secondly, Sonja is very much into her garden, and almost whenever she's working in the garden, people talk over the fence to her. Possibly through those initiations, we've got to know a lot of the people, especially at the top end of Lonsdale Road – the dead-end section. I wouldn't say they're unfriendly. In fact, they're very friendly, and they're very concerned, and very supportive. But they are pretty reserved at making an initial introduction.

Sonja Drexler chatting from her garden to Perilla Kinchin, 2006. (Philippa Berry)

John Lynch, a retired Irish builder who lives on King's Cross Road, also feels that it can be hard to make the initial breakthrough with people round here. In his case a dog made an astonishing difference.

When my dear wife died they said 'Get a little dog'. I got a little dog and I went out and I walked up the road, and by the time I got to the end of the road fourteen people stopped to talk about the dog, people who wouldn't have talked to me otherwise!

Betty Marshall, returning to Victoria Road in 1985, did not find Oxford very friendly after Kenya – though thinks it is different now.

In Oxford, people do have a name for being rather unfriendly. It takes a long time to get to know anybody. In Kenya you just made friends with people. You didn't necessarily want them as bosom friends, but you helped each other out. They didn't shut themselves behind their doors and their curtains and their windows, retreat from you the moment you say, 'Hello, how are you?' Now it's a very friendly road. We've got a little group that if somebody new comes into the street, we make a point of welcoming them. It does pay off, but you have to work at it.

The Faulkners, long-term residents of Victoria Road, are remembered by Sam Clarke for Sid's way of interacting with his neighbours.

We've just lost Sid and Peggy Faulkner. Sid was a fireman, he was a very entertaining and engaging person, and they used to make their own wine, you'll see the vine just in front of their house. And Sid would sit outside his house in the evenings drinking a glass of his own wine and would welcome anybody who walked past and invite them to join him. The wine was disgusting, I always found, but the idea of doing it was great! They were a great couple.

It's clear that particular people can have an effect on changing the atmosphere of their immediate neighbourhood. Peter Clarke mentions Max Peberdy who used to grow dahlias in the front garden: being out there fussing over them gave an opportunity for talking to people.

Very cheerful kind of a man. Chatty. Opened the road up. The road was a bit kind of closed.

Expectations were confounded when Cathie Ashley came to 12 Portland Road in 1976.

When we were moving from Bristol to Oxford we were told 'Oxford? No one will speak to you!', but in fact Portland Road was wonderful. Elizabeth Stewart and James were the great integrators of the street at that point. Within a day they knocked at the door. They were very welcoming.

Dorothea Pelham paid tribute to Cathie as an 'integrator' in her turn.

Cathie Ashley came in '76, and that really made the difference. She was lovely. She just had open house. She's one of these people who just cooks all the time, and always inviting people in. You could just go in any time of day, and she's always sitting there with other people, neighbours, chatting and stuff. They had three very nice children. She was brilliant! Just what we all wanted. Other people, well, they do it in other ways. There's some very nice people across the street now, just living in a slightly different way. You feel you can turn to them, definitely, for help, and I hope they can turn to me. I feel this is a very nice friendly street. Definitely.

In roads where people walk up and down you can certainly have a sense of connection with people without knowing them, as Peter Clarke remembers of someone further down Lonsdale Road.

You know them in the sense that you miss them if they're not there, and they probably miss you. He didn't appear for ages. And I said to somebody, I was walking by the house, 'Well, where is the owner?' 'Oh, he's dead.' He had a tumour, and died of this tumour. And I missed him, because he wasn't shuffling around any more.

Margaret Clarke, who arrived in Hamilton Road in 1962, mentions the importance of walking up and down the road for getting to know people.

Having three children, you bonded with people. I don't know half the people down there [now], because they get in their cars and they go, and I don't know what they look like, whereas then, people walked up and down the road, and I walked up and down the road, obviously, with the children, and I reckoned I knew, at least by name, everybody in the road, up as far as King's Cross.

The easiest bonds are formed between families bringing up children, as Mariele Kuhn neatly puts it.

When you have a pram and babies, you get to know people, you look into others' prams!

Children from Portland, Hamilton, Victoria, and King's Cross Roads: Hallowe'en 1984. (Lynn Ahmed)

She remembers the particular sociability of wartime.

We all queued at Oliver & Gurden's. Stood in a long queue. People were engraving their initials on the bricks. You got to know each other that way. In many ways, people got together more, because one was interested what happened to husbands who were away on work or at war, and I think it created a kind of community.

Children were the origin of strong neighbourly ties in Hamilton Road, as Philippa Berry says.

Hamilton Road really was a community from the very beginning, because of the children and us parents all getting to know each other. Of course, the children are all grown up now, and flying away.

Busyness is often given as a reason for not having more neighbourly contact. An obvious change in the lives of women is reflected by Yvonne Hands' memories of the late 1950s and 60s.

We all met, and ... well, we didn't work, and I don't think we knew what to do with ourselves half the time. We had endless coffee mornings and things, and I seemed to have endless dinner parties, and endless tea parties.

Women's working in particular has obviously cut down the time available for socialising, as Elsie Hill says of Portland Road.

It was always a relaxed and friendly road, but since we worked about a twelve-hour day on Günther's publishing business, we were sociable in quite a casual way, and had occasional musical parties and things like that, but I never had time to do much neighbourly mixing.

Bill Fosdike, rector of St Michael's from 1964 to 1989, sees a change rather than a diminishing of neighbourly feeling.

I think neighbourliness has changed in its expression. For one thing, people are involved in much wider groups, so neighbourliness isn't necessarily the immediate next door. Also, the number of families where both work has increased, so there aren't the people around during the day, in the way that there used to be. But I don't think there's less neighbourliness, in sort of energy. Of course, if somebody's around all the time, you know that Mrs Jones down the road is ill, whereas this way, if both husband and wife are out they probably only occasionally think, 'I haven't seen Mrs Jones recently.' Ties have changed. I think neighbourliness has changed, rather than decreased.

Local community spirit is strong in Peter Clarke's opinion, speaking of Lonsdale Road.

I don't think it's lessened in any way. I don't think people have become more individualistic and less sort of community minded. But it takes you time to get into a road and discover what people are all about. There are quite a lot of people on the road who are very positive and helpful and understanding. I don't think it's an over-gossipy road, not in my experience. People talk, but it's not negative stuff. It's a good road. Most people, if they can, within reason, will give a hand to someone else that needs it. Years ago, when my car broke down, it was a very very cold winter, and right up on the left-hand side, in no.10, I remember seeing this chap with a jump lead, out the front, and I just went up and knocked on the door, and 'Oh yeah, I'll come down'. When people say, 'There's no community spirit left any more', I think, 'Well, that's not quite true, in my experience!'

Jelly Williams, living in Victoria Road since 1963, describes a positive resolve to be friendly.

> We were very lucky with our neighbours. If a new person came round the corner we met up and were friendly. I did feel it was ... not particularly interesting, but just very nice people. How very very friendly people were and unsnobby. 'We are neighbours in the same area and we will be friends', that is what it was.

She mentions a comfortable relationship with their elderly next-door neighbour.

> She was a charming old lady and she didn't have a television and we had one by then, and she always came to watch *Panorama* with us. It was a very nice friendship.

For very many people in the roads good neighbourly relations become real friendships.

Tolerance of neighbours

Living at close quarters demands an ability to ignore neighbours to a certain extent. John Marsh remembers the Butlers.

> He wasn't a shouting man, but he had a good carrying voice. You always knew when 'Uncle Bert', we called him, was about! Of course, we could hear the house quite a lot, because the kitchen area is opposite theirs, so you couldn't help but overhear when they were on song! But they were very nice people.

Again there is an interesting perspective from the Schrigers, accustomed to a different model of suburbia in the USA, more spacious but correspondingly more isolated.

> It was interesting sharing a wall – we didn't know quite how much of the noise of our household was transmitted to the people on the other side! They claimed very little, but they may just be being polite! It took a little bit of adjustment, sitting in the front room where you walk down the street and people would have their windows open late at night, watching the telly, and just leave the whole world to look in, like a fishbowl. We weren't quite used to that, so we tended to pull the shades. By the end, we were 'OK, we can live our lives in public just as well as anybody else!' In the States, there's a tendency to be more private, even to the point, now, where everyone is gating their driveway, so it's like your own little mini fortress. That's the mentality now, and it takes them a while to let down their guard. I found it [here] to be much more of a neighbourhood, where people knew each other, and talked to each other, and had each other for a drink, or for tea. There's a real sense of community here, more than we have in Los Angeles.

Much of this he put down to the American habit of driving everywhere, and the absence of pavements. As we saw, walking up and down the roads and stopping to chat is indeed an important part of making and maintaining neighbourly connections.

There have of course always been neighbours from hell, though surprisingly few were mentioned in interviews. Miss Steward's neighbour in Portland Road was remembered by her friend Dorothea Pelham.

> First they had three huge dogs that barked incessantly, and if you went out in the garden, this Great Dane would sort of throw itself against the fence, it was growling and barking. And she had a pedestal up the garden, and she used to call the

pigeons through this thing, and from everywhere, all round the city, vast numbers of pigeons came! And this woman was a totally desperate woman. She was a singer, and she'd go out and sing in the garden. And Miss Steward used to pray to God that she would somehow be relieved of this singing noise. And eventually she said, 'God had given her [neighbour] a television set', so she went into the house and watched the television!

This is the person from whom the Gilberts bought their house.

All the neighbours hated [these pigeons]! She presented us with a 7-pound bag of peanuts, and said, 'You will carry on feeding the babies!' And then we got deputations from all the neighbours. So we stopped feeding them, and, of course, they found somewhere else to go, much to everyone's delight.

Noisy neighbours are a problem when houses are so close together: John Herivel remembers earlier inhabitants of Lonsdale Road.

Fantastic people! They nearly drove the Clarkes mad. I don't know whether they were married, but they were a couple, and they were always fighting.

John Marsh, living in Hamilton Road, had a bad time with the house across the road at a period when many houses in this area were let out, something which does diminish neighbourly ties.

Students' houses aren't necessarily the same as ordinary working folk. And there were always people coming home in the small hours, some of them rather noisily. And then, of course, there were parties, and for several years, we couldn't guarantee to get a number of nights' sleep. It was really rather worrying, because (a) that was bothering you, and (b) you're thinking, 'Well, the value of the house is plummeting. No one will want to buy this place!' It culminated in a late night visit, from the police, who sealed off Hamilton Road, they were looking for drugs. We watched what was going on. They had police cars top and bottom!

Defective burglar alarms have become a trial in more recent decades. Monica Wagstaff recalls a generally quieter era.

Today there's this awful noise problem, from music mainly. We didn't have that volume, we only had radios, and even if you turned them right up, you couldn't get anything like the volume you have today. And do you know, occasionally on the radio you would hear from the announcer, 'It's a lovely sunny day, and no doubt a lot of you have got your windows open: could you check on your volume and turn your radios down?' You never hear anything like that today! People expect it to be that much noisier.

Some people are less considerate than others, and some have a lower noise threshold than others. Persistently noisy neighbours can cause a lot of distress, though if underlying relations are friendly people will put up with a lot, as Jocelyn Morris implies. The family had come from Australia where children were accustomed to playing outside, and lived in the dead-end part of Lucerne Road which was safe for street play.

The Murphys actually were very kind to the children, every Christmas they always had crackers for all the children. And I'm sure it was hard for them having five very noisy children playing outside. Vic Brown, I think they used to annoy him a bit, the kids in the street, but he was always pretty good about it.

Verity Peto says something similar.

> We've lived, all the time, next door to completely delightful neighbours who always say, 'Noise? What noise?' if we go round and apologise a bit belatedly for loud children's parties!

But she speaks of other less obvious pressures from neighbours.

> Living in a long row of semi-detached houses, whose sitting room window faces on to the street, does bring unexpected problems! I've had a neighbour pop in several times, to tell me that my children are sitting too close to the television and damaging their eyesight! Not just that, I was stopped in the street one day by a neighbour who'd heard the news that our cat had had yet another litter of kittens, and stopped me, with a pained expression, to tell me how irresponsible we were being about letting our cat over-populate the country with kittens. I don't think that's quite right, actually, because we always managed to find homes for our kittens, through the children's school friends. The one time when somebody let us down we decided to advertise in the *Oxford Times* and got over 50 responses. And I did have several people completely in tears, telling me how desperately difficult it was to find kittens. I think this is all part of responsible North Oxford middle-class society, people always neuter their cats, and we didn't!

Holly Kilpatrick agrees that while the neighbourhood is relaxed and tolerant in matters relating to appearance, child-rearing is subject to pressures.

> Nobody is the slightest bit bothered about whether you ever dig your garden, or sweep your step, or clean your house – that's all very relaxed round here, and when I think of some areas I've lived, it's very nice. But the expectations of how one should raise a child, and what should be done with and for the child – I think maybe there have been subtle pressures around that.

Help from neighbours

Dorothea Pelham remembered unexpected help when she had a fire in Portland Road not long after her husband had left.

> I had a fire. And it was very frightening, and all the street lights were blinking, and there were sort of balls of fire coming out of the fuse box. Then all these neighbours rallied round. It was quite incredible! A lady across the street, who'd never spoken to me, came here with her bucket and started mopping, because the whole house was black inside. At that point, I suddenly thought, 'These are really nice people around here.' And I'm still friends with that lady.

Practical help and care from neighbours has often played a crucial role in the lives of the elderly or disabled. The Gilberts' first house in Portland Road was bought by Mary Sternberg, who became chair-bound after a stroke, as Ruth describes.

> The neighbours were around, and they enabled her to live in her own home for about seven years, by people popping in. She had to have Social Services but, nevertheless, practically every day there would be somebody there.

Her husband Philip however contrasted this aspect of the neighbourhood unfavourably with the close Jewish community in which he grew up.

I used to visit her every Sunday afternoon to have a chat and a cup of tea, and some of her immediate neighbours never went near her to ask how she was. I find that disgusting. That would never have happened in the East End of London.

John Herivel did a lot to support his elderly neighbour Arthur Manders (p.76).

His best man lived in Stratfield [Road], just over the way, and I remember asking him once, 'Do you ever see him?' And the answer was no. The man never came, and he never went. It strikes me that's typically a man, they won't make the first move in certain things, and they wait for other people to come. So there weren't very many visitors to his house. I went regularly to play chess with him. And it was very lucky, because we were both about the same strength, and we enjoyed that enormously. I had a game of chess with him a week before he died, and then he was getting a bit feeble, and so I allowed him to win!

I don't think he would have been as lonely as many people, because he had an active mind, and he read the paper, and he wrote things. But there was one problem. He wouldn't have any help in the house. Therefore, it looked as if, if the place was going to be cleaned, we would have to do it. Kathy [Clarke] was very good, she used to iron his shirts for him. I helped him with messages from time to

Arthur Mander, aged c.92. (Kathy Clarke)

time. And I often went in for an evening, and had a glass of whisky with him. He'd have a certain amount of whisky, he'd put hot water in, he dropped a sugar lump in, and then he had a certain sort of biscuit, Rich Tea biscuit, that we had with it. So we had many a jolly evening with the whisky and the Rich Tea biscuit, in front of the miserable little fire. I remember the day he died, going up to his bedroom. I rang the doctor, and eventually he went off in an ambulance. I'd never been in his room before. The sheets were black with dirt! And the dust was really about an inch thick! Which shows you that people can live in the most fantastic conditions.

Kathy Clarke cared for him too.

He was a great old chap. He would come and have meals with us, which he loved, and he had lots of stories about the war. He was very correct. He always wore his three piece suit and his white shirts, which I used to wash for him. I only used to get one shirt a week – you can imagine the colour, bless his heart. Eventually when he got older he would give me his underwear and hankies. But he kept up till he was nearly 90: he would only give me a shirt a week and he would do the rest himself. He used to iron with an old iron that he used to heat on a gas cooker. The house was always freezing.

John Marsh speaks of how his wife and another neighbour looked after Mr Butler, who was bereft when his wife died.

> He was considerably older than her, and she died in her early seventies, quite suddenly. And he, poor chap, he went to pieces completely. Looking back, I think it was probably depression. He didn't do anything. He didn't go to bed, he just slept on the sofa. He didn't prepare meals. Doris and Mrs Cooper, between them, used to give him a midday meal. But he got so down that he didn't even wash the plates. He just sort of ate the food and pushed it on the side. And the snag was, if you went to see him, he was always cheerful, asking after the children and so on. But I have a feeling, now, that once you left, he just sat. He had some relatives – I think there was a little bit of feeling, in the family, that she had married down – whatever, they were singularly unhelpful to the poor old boy. Eventually Doris said, 'It's getting too much for Mrs Cooper and me, we can't keep up this sort of thing', and she got him into Cutteslowe Court for a holiday. It went very well, and he got a permanent place there. And he changed completely. He was back to his old self. They said, 'He's one of our best residents. He's always helpful, always cheerful'. Just like he used to be.

Distances and privacy

Feeling rooted-in is a function of how long you have lived in the neighbourhood, but sometimes those who have been here a long time find the people they knew have gone, and the neighbourliness they once experienced is hard to maintain. Elizabeth Johnston touched on this.

> We came to Victoria Road when Jack retired [in 1978], and we've been here ever since. We've never lived in one house for such a long time! We've been very lucky, with lovely people all round us. Now there are different people in the road, and it's harder to get to know people, but the ones we do know are very kind, and because I'm now disabled, they do a lot to help.

It is hard to tell whether younger people are really more wrapped up in their own lives now, or whether it is simply that bridging generations is much harder than forming connections with people at a comparable stage of life, as Elsie Hill says.

> I've seen this generation that came here as young marrieds, move into being middle-aged marrieds, with their children growing up and going to university. I think I have noticed that the very young now – by which I mean the under-35s – are not as friendly as the older generation were. This is just my feeling, that people don't hail you in the street as much as they used to. I think they're just so busy, and I probably look as old as I am, and I go around with my little trolley, and they probably think I'm slightly ga-ga! I don't know!

Philip Gilbert did feel a general change for the worse in society in general.

> I think, now, people are harder, they haven't got so much time for you, they're acquisitive, and they're rude. And a lot of them just don't care, period. I think there was more caring and feeling in our country during the war years and just after, than what there is now.

King's Cross Road coming into its own as the connecting street of the seven roads at the Millennium Festival street party, 2000. (Lynn Ahmed)

Rolling change is a natural part of a mixed neighbourhood, as old people give way to younger families, who in turn grow older. Sally Bromley has lived in Victoria Road since 1984.

This is such a happy road. Obviously there have been some changes to friends and neighbours around here. The road, at the time, was relatively quiet, because there was still a large number of quite elderly people living here – so there weren't that many cars. Today, it's a very different story, because a lot of the houses have now moved on, they've moved out of the hands of the older people, and younger people are moving in with young families, so it's a very vibrant road.

Hilary Lloyd has lived in Hawkswell Gardens since the early 1990s.

It's very quiet and very enclosed. If the residents were families with young children there would be a lot of activity outside – apparently it was like that when the families moved in but the feel now is a very quiet cul-de-sac. There aren't that many of the houses that have changed hands, only two houses in 13 or 14 years. There's going to be a spate in due course. Most of the neighbours are older. We are friendly but we are not popping into each others' houses.

Geoffrey Paine of Lucerne Road is one who values a good measure of privacy in the context of a generally pleasant neighbourhood.

To a large extent, people keep themselves to themselves. I mean, if I see people I know, I always say hello. It's about right, because I think you can get too close to people. It's nice to have people there in emergencies, on the other hand you don't want them popping in, perhaps, every two minutes. Well, it suits us, any rate. Normally, if people say [a neighbourhood] isn't friendly enough, the fault is with them. Having lived here all my life, I know an awful lot of people, and life, in the end, is about people.

Many indeed are content with good relations with their immediate neighbours, without

wanting a connection with the wider communities of the roads. A few people did not want to have anything to do with this project when we sent round our survey, regarding it as intrusive, though the great majority were interested, and willing to contribute information and opinions. Active promotion of community comes and goes: Philippa Berry was a facilitator of the Hamilton Road group (p.200), which is at present in abeyance.

A Hamilton Road Group garden party, 1997. (Bojana Kozul)

I can remember talking to one newcomer, and he was just completely adamant that he didn't want anything to do with it. You get that sort of person in every road, I'm sure, but it sort of puts you off. But there are some new younger people with children who are interested in community events and we may start the group again in due course.

Many would echo Ruth Bader Gilbert's appreciation of a balance of friendliness and non-intrusiveness.

They're very nice people along Portland Road. They're friendly, but not in your pocket.

The survey we carried out and our interviews all returned a clear feeling that good neighbours are the thing most valued about living here. The late Dr Harle, who lived in Hawkswell Farmhouse, Portland Road, is typical.

We do know most of the people in the road, and we're blessed with extremely nice neighbours, which is a very important thing. And we have been very happy here.

A good place to live

Altogether we can say that this has been a settled area in which people have generally very much liked living. Mariele Kuhn has lived in Victoria Road since 1938.

It is a nice community here. I must say that. And we are not snobbish! Quite a number of them are linked to the University, but it hasn't disturbed the neighbourhood in the slightest.

Beryl Phillips was glad to return to the roads in 1968 after living in Headington for some years.

I loved Summertown, I always wanted to come back here. I think it's the best part of Oxford.

Peter Clarke thought about moving but couldn't do it.

When I was separated, I searched Oxford for a place, and I couldn't find anywhere more convenient, that I liked more. This was within striking distance of both rivers, nice walks, everything, so why move? I do like it. I do find it easy to live here.

Peter Thompson lists the advantages he sees.

This location was ideal from the point of view of schools for the children, of general cultural facilities in the town, the fact that you can get to pretty well anywhere in the town, readily, on a bicycle, you don't need to use a car. Living here is very pleasant, and very simple. And on top of that, the neighbours are very interesting, we've got a lot of friends, and we get on with them very well.

The Thompsons moved briefly to a farmhouse outside Oxford but were glad to return to suburban living.

The hassles of living 14 miles outside town, and Sonja having to ferry Joe to school, and sit in traffic jams to get here and so on, were just becoming intolerable, basically. And what with the motorway noise that you could hear, continuously, in the distance, the agricultural traffic which went on 24 hours a day during the summer, the clay pigeon shooting that happened every weekend, it was really a lot more peaceful living in suburbia!

Jean Robinson has been here since the late 1960s and her assessment too is positive.

I have mixed feelings about Oxford, but Summertown, and Lonsdale Road, was a good place for the kids to grow up in. They were surrounded by families whose values were pretty similar, so there was this reinforcement going on, and you knew that they were safe with these people. It wasn't a society where they got this idea that money and possessions were important, and having the latest this, that or the other. I guess it was a kind of continuation of shabby gentility of the middle classes. To be so near all the facilities, so near the centre of town, so near the richness of the libraries, and to have somewhere quiet and spacious, and without a lot of social pressures – there aren't that many places where we could have that. It's been pretty good really, considering all the changes that have taken place in society during this time. It's been pretty good.

Appendix 1: House Dates and Builders

Specific dates given are those of planning applications: houses would normally be built soon afterwards, though in more recent decades there is a greater interval between application and completion. The names are those of applicants – in earlier days normally the builder, later often the owner and/or the architect. Residents' title deeds will clarify the date when the plot was first sold and details of subsequent transfers of the house. (Deeds are no longer needed for legal purposes and are well worth retrieving from solicitors etc., as they give fascinating information.)

Lonsdale Road

SOUTH

2–10 (terrace)	2/4/1902	N. Capel
12&14	1/10/1902	N. Capel
16–26 (terrace)	1903	N. Capel
28&30	2/3/1904	J. Wooldridge
32&34	2/3/1904	J. Wooldridge
36&38	2/3/1904	J .Wooldridge
40&42	5/7/1905	N. Capel
44&46	5/7/1905	N. Capel
48&50	5/7/1905	N. Capel
52&54	5/9/1906	N. Capel
56&58	5/9/1906	N. Capel
60&62	5/9/1906	N. Capel
68&70	5/4/1903	Simms & Son
72&74	4/2/1903	Organ Bros

King's Cross Road here

76	4/3/1908	Hutchins & Son
78,80,82,82a	9/4/1975	Pearson/Boseat
84	1936	For Mrs E. Twining
86	4/7/1923	Wooldridge & Simpson
88	3/9/1924	N. Capel
90	1/8/1923	N. Capel
92	6/12/1926	A. Simmons
94	4/4/1927	A. Simmons
96	2/5/1976	Pearson/Boseat
104	6/5/1958	For Wm Oliver
104a	12/4/1978	

NORTH

St Michael & All Angels Church	2/12/1908	Wooldridge & Simpson
37 Vicarage	3/12/1924	Kingerlee
39	29/10/1925	G. Simmons
41& 43	4/8/1925	G. Simmons
45&47	6/4/1925	G. Simmons
49&51	3/12/1924	G. Simmons
53&55	6/6/1906	N. Capel
57&59	7/1/1906	N. Capel
61&63	6/9/1905	N. Capel
65&67	5/4/1905	N. Capel
69&71	2/3/1903	N. Capel
73&75	2/3/1903	N. Capel
77&79	4/2/1903	N. Capel
81&83	5/10/1904	N. Capel

King's Cross Road here

85&87	6/2/1907	N. Capel
89	1/10/1924	N. Capel
91&93	7/1/1925	N. Capel
95	29/10/1924	N. Capel
97	2/7/1924	N. Capel
99	6/12/1924	N. Capel
101	4/7/1927	Knowles
103	2/3/1925	Hinkins & Frewin
105 Field End	6/6/1923	Benfield & Loxley
105a, 105b	12/4/1978	
107 Ways End	3/8/1926	Hinkins & Frewin

Portland Road

SOUTH

2	6/8/1924	E. Organ
4	7/12/1921	Capel & Son
6	7/3/1923	N. Capel
8	2/8/1922	N. Capel
10	6/10/1909	N. Capel

NORTH

Summertown Church Hall	1/10/1924	
1	7/1/1981	
3	1/7/1908	N. Capel
5&7	2/9/1908	N. Capel, Mountain arch█

12&14	2/6/1909	N. Capel		9&11	7/4/1909	N. Capel
16	4/5/1910	N. Capel		13	31/10/1908	N. Capel
18	6/7/1910	N. Capel		15	1/7/1908	N. Capel
20&22	1910			17	4/3/1908	N. Capel
24	6/7/1910	N. Capel		19	4/12/1907	N. Capel
26	26/9/1932	D. Mealing		21	4/3/1908	N. Capel
28	4/5/1910	N. Capel		25&27	30/10/1907	N. Capel
30	6/10/1909	N. Capel		29	30/10/1907	N. Capel
32	27/10/1964	L. Norwood		31	3/7/1907	N. Capel
34 Hawkswell Farmhouse	early 19th century?			33&35	3/7/1907	H. Capel
				37&39	31/10/1906	N. Capel
36&38	c.1911			41&43	6/3/1907	H. Capel
40&42	1911			45–51 (terrace)	6/6/1906	H. Capel
44	5/10/1910	N. Capel		53&55	27/3/1933	D. Mealing

Hamilton Road

SOUTH				NORTH		
342 Banbury	c.1982			5	6/4/1904	Simms & Son
344	1938	D. Mealing		7&9	12/10/1931	H. Collier
2a	c.1982			11&13	5/7/1905	C. Turner
2	11/7/1967	J. Jones/Reynolds&Part.		15&17	3/1/1923	E. Harris
4	4/4/1923	Kingerlee		19	3/6/1914	E. Wallis
6&8	4/5/1910	G. Money		21	3/5/1926	D. Fisher
10	4/5/1910	Stroudley		23	15/11/1996	Watkins/D. Riach
12	26/10/1954	R.E. Smith		25	4/3/1924	Barrett & Son
14&16	31/10/1912	J. Pricket/Newport		27	10/3/1930	Saunders
20&22	3/3/1909	T. Basson		redesign	1/3/2000	Useful Loft Co.
24	4/6/1924	Harris & White		31&33	4/6/1913	J. Pricket
26&28	6/2/1924	H. Capel		35	23/6/2001	Rocklead/A. King
30	5/10/1904	W. Gray		37&39	1/3/1926	G. Simmons
32	6/6/1988	D. Winstone/Assoc Design		41	23/4/1996	R. Morgan/D. Riach
34&36	2/6/1909	G. Money		43&45	3/7/1907	G. Ashley
38&40	5/7/1926	G. Simmons		49	4/4/1927	Bennett & Son
42	6/11/1974	G.L. Turner		51&53	6/4/1910	G. Parsons
44&46	7/3/1906	F. Capel		55&57	7/5/1924	Knowles & Son
50&52	1/7/1908	G. Money		61	3/5/1922	Wooldridge & Simpson
54	8/8/1979	D.J. Joseph/B. Hook				
56&58	1/7/1908	G. Gardner				
60&62	3/7/1907	G. Money				
64	1936					
66	7/5/1924	W. Gray				

King's Cross Road here   *King's Cross Road here*

68	6/8/1924	Barrett & Son		63&65	1/6/1925	Hinkins & Frewin
70	6/9/1926	Bradbury Bros		67&69	2/7/1924	Hinkins & Frewin
72&74	4/6/1928	F. Watts		71&73	4/6/1924	Hinkins & Frewin
80	1937			75 Westfield	1908	
86&88	5/6/1910	G. Gardner archt		77	4/10/1926	Hunt & Church
92&94	6/5/1908	T. Basson		79	c.1969	D Riach archt
94b	5/1/1921	Knowles & Son		83	7/9/1925	Hinkins & Frewin
94a	4/5/1969			89&91	c.1934	?D.Mealing
96 White House	1/2/1911	F. Capel		93	3/12/1928	Hunt & Church
now 96,98,100				95	3/5/1926	P Randall

Victoria Road

SOUTH

364 Banbury	4/7/1923	Kingerlee & Son
2a&2b	6/2/1996	Todd/A. King
2&4	1/1/1908	G. Pipkin
10	1938	
12&14	5/7/1926	W. Gray
16&18	5/4/1922	Hinkins & Frewin
22	1/6/1925	P. Chick
26&28	5/4/1926	F. Watts
32&34	29/10/1924	Symm & Co.
36	4/6/1924	W. Herbert
40&42	3/8/1926	Hunt & Church
44	20/12/2001	Lewis/C. Franks
46	c.1910	?G. Money
48	2/4/1928	D. Mealing
50&52	5/10/1925	J.Watts
56&58	3/10/1921	Billing & Co.
60&62	3/5/1926	P. Chick
64	10/9/1948	A.E. Harvey
66	7/10/1914	Bennett & Son

King's Cross Road here

68&70	5/7/1911	G. Money
72	5/8/1914	G. Pipkin
74	1/3/1926	F. White
80&82	1/2/1911	J. Laitt
84	4/7/1973	T. Hodson archt
86	7/9/1925	H. Hunt
88	4/1/1905	G. Grant
(88–100 terrace)		
90	3/5/1905	G. Grant
92	6/6/1906	G. Grant
94	3/3/1909	G. Grant
96	7/9/1910	G. Grant
98	5/4/1911	G. Grant
100	5/7/1911	G. Grant
102&102a	5/5/1964	T.K. Noble
104 Rylestone	2/5/1928	R. Hedges
106	23/4/1968	D.J. Joseph

NORTH

368 Banbury	2/10/1907	G. Pipkin
1&3	c.1931	
5&7	4/3/1929	H. Capel
9&11	1939	Knowles & Son
13	1939	Knowles & Son
15&17	1939	Knowles & Son
19&21	1939	Knowles & Son
25&27	2/3/1910	Organ Bros
31&33	2000	Rocklead
35&37	24/10/1932	Knowles & Son
39	24/10/1932	Knowles & Son
39&41	24/10/1932	Knowles & Son
43	6/4/1925	P. Chick
45&47	7/1/1925	P. Chick
49&51	7/5/1924	W. Gray
53	6/12/1922	Coppock
53&55	2002	Rocklead
on site of 53		
57	2/5/1923	Hutchins & Son
59	2/3/1925	Bennett & Son
61&63	2/2/1925	P. Chick
65	23/1/1933	Calcutt & Hunt
67	14/11/1932	Calcutt & Hunt
69&71	4/8/1925	H. Hunt
73	5/4/1926	G. Pipkin
75	23/10/1925	Hutchins & Son
75&75a	2/11/1998	Rocklead/A. King
on site of 75		
77	3/8/1910	W. Gray
79	c.1980?	
85	14/7/1972	Malin & Co.
87&89	29/10/1924	H. Hunt
89a	14/9/1971	Angell/G. Banks
91	4/7/1927	H. Cope
97	7/4/1920	H. Collier
99	6/3/1973	Ede/Oxford Architects
103	7/6/1926	H. Collier
101&103	23/7/1997	Rocklead/A. King
on site of 103		
105	3/5/1926	Pye Bros
107&109	5/4/1926	H. Hunt
111	21/11/1979	
113	6/4/1925	F. Bell
115	25/11/1929	N. Harrison
115&117	19/5/2000	Rocklead/A. King
& 2 houses in Water Eaton Road built on site of 115		

King's Cross Road

WEST				EAST		
King's Cross Garage				1&3	c.1934	?D. Mealing
store	2/11/1921	H. Capel		3a	29/3/1984	
garage	7/3/1923	H. Capel		3b	26/4/1984	
motorshed	11/7/1923	R. Alden		5&7	c.1934	?D. Mealing
garage building	3/8/1965	O. Kernahan		7a	20/6/2003	Ahmed
series of applications	1975–7	O. Kernahan		9	c.1936	
rebuilt as 14–34	2003–5	Thomas & Co.				

2 King's House 10/1/2003

Lucerne Road

WEST				EAST		
2	5/4/1926	P. Chick		1	1/4/1908	Simms & Son
4	7/1/1925	P. Chick		1a	28/10/1958	L. Preston
6	1980	D. Josephs		3	23/3/1931	F.H. White
8 Chagford	2/8/1927	H. Cope		9 chalet	25/5/1975	
8A	21/6/1960			11	15/2/1970	
14	?1938			17	28/7/1964	
				19 St Cyres	1928	
				21	26/7/1985, finished 1989	Wadsworth
				23 Bishop's Mill	15/2/1955	

Hawkswell Gardens

Built by Knowles & Son, architect Peter Reynolds/Guy Knowles, mostly between approx. 1960 and 1963; no. 18 c.1964; no.20 c.1965; flats in 1968–9.

NORTH	SOUTH
1	2
3	4
5	6
7	8
9	10
11	12
15	14
17–39 Hawkswell House (12 flats)	16
	18
	20

Appendix 2: Summertown Shops

The information in these lists is drawn from Kelly's Oxford directories for 1936 and for 1976, the year in which these invaluable volumes sadly ceased publication.

Banbury Road 1936

WEST

201	Star Imperial Laundry
201–3	Lloyd's Bank
203a	Hill, Miss J.N., hairdresser

Oakthorpe Road here

205	Alden, Reg.T. & Son, butchers
205a	Paternoster Dairy
207	Bird, E.E., stationer
209	Morris, Chas, fruiterer
211	Barclay's Bank
213	Barrett, P.H., ladies' hairdresser
	Bateman, M., ladies' tailor
215	Goundrey, John, ironmonger
217	Eliz. Swann, ladies' outfitters, lingerie
219	Marshall & Co., confectioners
221	Bond, E.E., cycle agent
223	Burton Dairies Ltd
225	Cooper & Boffin, bakers & confectioners
227	Sidney Smith, bootmaker
229	private house
231	private house
233	Winstone, W.E., boot & shoe retailer
235	King, F.F.C., wireless engineer
237	Wallington, Chas, fruiterer
239	Argyle, Dan & Sons, fishmonger
239a	Butler, A. & Co., corn merchants
241	Pulker, E.W., tobacconist
243	Hitchman, E.H. & Son, tailors
245	Turrill, Jas, fishmonger
247	Oxford Co-op & Industrial Society, grocers
249	Westminster Bank
251	Swift & Presswell, dyers & cleaners
253	private house
255	Macwilliam, John, chemist
257–9	King Bros, house furnishers
261	Charles, ladies' hairdresser
261a	Hutt, Thos, hairdresser

Banbury Road 1976

WEST

193	Lodge Bros, watchmakers, jewellers
197	Lotus House, restaurant
201–3	Lloyd's Bank
203a	Wool Shop

Oakthorpe Road here

205	Martin, newsagents
205a	Brooke, I.R. & Co., estate agent
207	Denton's, florists
209	Alden, R., butchers
211	Barclay's Bank
213	–
215	La Dolce Vita, restaurant
217	Jackson, E. & Sons, outfitters & drapers
219	NSS Newsagents
221	Gough Bros, wine & spirit merchants
223	Burton, W.E., dairyman
225	Westlake, W.K., chemists;
	A4 Printers; Impact Advertising;
	Frandon's hairdressers
227	Andrea & Achille, ladies' hairdressers
229	Trustee Savings Bank
231	Shergold's, ironmongers
233	Jack Venn, footwear specialists
235	Coventry Economic Building Society
237	Fresh Gro, fruiterers
239	–
239a	–
241	Dewhurst, J.H., butchers
243	Rising's, toys, sports, radio, TV & electrical appl.
245	Shepherd & Woodward, outfitters
247	–
249	National Westminster Bank
251	Bollom's, dyers & cleaners
253	Autoparts, motor car accessories
255	Brooks, E.J. & Son, chartered surveyors
255a	Linnell & Murphy, solicitors
257–9	Durham's, greengrocers
261	Cowan's, turf accountant

263	Hartwell's, automobile engineers	263–5	*Suffolk House*
265	private house		

263   Hartwell's, automobile engineers
265   private house

263–5   *Suffolk House*
    1–4   Charrington & Co., brewers
    5   Pik-N-Save, supermarket
    6   Wholefoods, healthfood store
    7–9   Great Wall, Chinese restaurant
    8   Paolo of Florence, ladies' hairdresser
    10 Launderettes Launderama
    11 UK Provident Institution
    12 Cunningham Hart & Co., loss adjuster
    15,18,21   John, Booksellers

South Parade here

267–73   houses

South Parade here

267   Prama House
    1   Patrick, Stephanie, ladies' hairdresser
    2   Cotton Elmer Ltd, sports outfitters
    3   Rumbelows Ltd, television
    4–5   Midland Bank
    6–7   Westlake, W.K., chemists
    8   Fine Fare, supermarket

273a   Howard & Son, butchers

273a   Coulling, F.C., butcher

Church Street here

279a   Capel, N. & Son, builder
279   Capel, Noah

Rogers Street here

279a   Capel Barrington Ltd, builders
279   Dental Surgeons

Grove Street here

283   King's Arms Public House, Geo. Salter
285   King's Arms Motor Garage, Geo.W. Salter
291   Jones, P.J. & Sons, motor body builders

Grove Street here

283   King's Arms Public House
285–91   Jones, P.H., vehicle body builders

Albert Street here

311–15   Pulker, Ernest, garage

Hobson Road here

311–21   Bristol Street Motors

EAST
194   Bellamy, C.J.V., pharmaceutical chemist
198   Midland Bank Ltd
200   Giddens, Mrs Kate, confectioner
202   Dorothy Ann, gown specialist, outsizes speciality
204   Simmonds, Joseph, greengrocer
206   Pitcher, Fred, cycle maker
212   Pether, Percival, builder & decorator
214   Preston & Son, tailors

218   Dunlop, Geo., coal & coke merchants
220   Trinder, Miss G.M., gen. stores & P.O.
    houses
240   Hall, Wm, butcher

EAST
194   Denton's Cycles
198   Hills, C.W., confectioner & P.O.
200–2   Clows Garden Centre

214   Curtain Shop
216   Summertown Antiques
218   Bush, D.T. & M.D., confectioners

Diamond Place
226   RAC
228–40   Budgens Grocers; Straw Hat Bakery

Ewart Place

242–50   Organ's Garage

242–54   *Barclay House*
Barclay, J.D. Ltd, Rolls Royce, Bentley distributors
BBC Radio Oxford

Summerfield Road here

Summerfield Road here

258   Vallis, beer merchant

Mayfield Road here

280   North Oxford Garage
292   Webb, painter
294   Twining Bros, grocer
296   Congregational Church

364   Paternoster Dairy (Alfred Stanley),
        & at College Farm, Yarnton

256   *Mayfield House*
        Chicken Barbecue, café
        Lyster Hair Styling, ladies' hairdresser
        Henry's TV sales & service
        Oxford Electrical Rentals Ltd, TV rentals
        Drake, M.E., Ltd, carpet dealers
        Mayfield Flooring
        Spink insurance & mortgage brokers
        Rhodes Ltd, opticians
258   Dewdrop Inn
260–2   Windsor Fish Saloon

        Oxfam House
264   Wendy Cook, travel agent
266   Radio Rentals Ltd
268   Discount Co., shoe retailers
270   Miranda, ladies' outfitters
272   Landau Restaurant
274   Oxfam House HQ
        Speedwell dyers & cleaners

Mayfield Road here

276   Casuelle ladies' outfitters
        Rediffusion, TV rentals
        Rainbow decor, paint merchants

278–90 North Oxford Garage
294   Moore's wine & spirit merchants
296   United Reformed Church

364   Paternoster Dairy, A.M. Stanley & Son

South Parade 1936

SOUTH

45	Oxford Police, District Station
42	Paine, Fredk, boot repairer
40	Le Conte, Chas, hairdresser
39	Smart, Hy & Sons, fruiterers

Stratfield Road here

38	Taylor, Egbert, furniture dealer
37	Edwards, Edwin, butcher
36	Burbank, J.A.R., chemist
35	Goodey, H.J., provision merchant
34	Edmonds, Walter & Son, dairy

NORTH

1&2	Paine, G.W. & Sons, bakers
3	(Miss Salter)
4	Oxford Co-op & Industrial Society
5	Bruce, J.H., plumber
	Bruce, A.W., carpenter/funeral director
6	Horn, C.E., wireless engineers
8	Walker, Geo., plumber
9	Wright, Jas, draper

George Street here

13–14	Howes, Geo., grocer & P.O.
15	Chapman, Mrs Eliz., confectioner
17–19	Beckinsale, Wm, florist, seedsman, garden requisites

South Parade 1976

SOUTH

Suffolk House

	Phipps & Wynn, builder
	Joule Heating Engineers
40–1	Town & Gown Travel
39	Bonner's, fruiterers

Stratfield Road here

38	Lord & Chapman, auctioneers
37	Edwards, E. & Son, butchers
36	John Hathaway-Bates, interior design consultants
35	Preston, M., antique & modern furniture
34	Anatique, antique dealers

NORTH

1	Nixey, F.T., bakers
	Taylor, A.R., canvas goods manufrs
2	(Mrs F.E. Paine)
3	Summertown Pet Stores
4	Oxford & District Co-operative Society
5	Peter Reynolds & Soanes & Hey, architects
6	Horn's of Oxford, radio & TV engineers
8	Paintpot, paint merchants
9	Cowling, C., decorators' merchants; Michael Drake, furnishers & carpet retailers
12	Michael Drake, furnishers & carpet retailers

Middle Way here

13–14	Erlund, Hugh, china & glass dealers; Watkins, K. & C., hardware stores & P.O.
15–16	Wright, confectioners
	County Libraries
	Child Health clinic

Index

Italicised page numbers refer to illustrations.